Shrinking the Federal Government

Shrinking the Federal Government

The Effect of Cutbacks on Five Federal Agencies

Irene S. Rubin
Northern Illinois University

Longman
New York & London

Shrinking the Federal Government: The Effect of Cutbacks
on five Federal Agencies

Longman Inc., 95 Church St., White Plains, N.Y. 10601
Associated companies, branches, and representatives
throughout the world.

Developmental Editor: Irving E. Rockwood
Editorial and Design Supervisor: Barbara Lombardo
Production Supervisor: Karen Lumley

Library of Congress Cataloging in Publication Data

Rubin, Irene.
   Shrinking the federal government.

   Bibliography: p.
   Includes index.
   1. United States—Appropriations and expenditures.
I. Title.
HJ2052.R83   1985   353'.07   84-27820
ISBN 0-582-28473-2 (pbk.)

Manufactured in the United States of America
Printing: 9 8 7 6 5 4 3 2 1   Year: 93 92 91 90 89 88 87 86 85

Contents

v

Foreword

A perceptive, in-depth analysis of efforts to reduce the size and scope of government is both timely and timeless. Since the success of several popular efforts in the mid-1970s to limit government spending, cuts in the number of government employees and activities has been an issue of current concern. This contemporary issue highlights longstanding theoretical and practical questions about organizational dynamics and public accountability of government agencies. Irene Rubin has made an invaluable contribution to the discussion of retrenchment and, likewise, to our understanding of public bureaucracies.

Concerns about the appropriate size and scope of government and efforts to cut public sector costs are not likely to be passing issues. The success of specific efforts has provided visibility to concerns that have been and will be an important part of political dialogue. Whether people object generally to levels of taxation or specifically to certain programs, a prescription for cuts will be made.

Irene Rubin uses rich case studies of five agencies to examine government retrenchment. She goes beyond numerical analyses of dollars and positions to a discussion of the organizational and human dynamics generated by budget reduction efforts. Her lessons are clearly relevant to other federal agencies. They are also suggestive of patterns in other jurisdictions.

Students of government and those in government will learn from—although perhaps not enjoy—the pages that follow.

Dennis L. Dresang
University of Wisconsin-Madison

Acknowledgments

Many of my informants in the bureaucracy made an explicit request to remain anonymous, a wish which I have requested. I would like to thank all my informants, named and unnamed, for the time and information they gave me, especially since the stories they told were often painful to them. I am particularly grateful to the administrators of the Health Planning Program for allowing me to observe their decision making over many months.

Most of this study was financed out of pocket, but I was assisted by several small grants, which I would like to acknowledge with thanks. The Bureau of Health Planning financed a small study of adaptations of local health planning agencies; Northern Illinois University awarded me a summer grant to work on the book; and the Political Science Department at Northern Illinois University made a contribution toward travel back to Washington for follow-up studies.

I was assisted by a number of people and agencies who opened their files and shared their data. I am particularly grateful to Ray Sanders, who trusted me enough to share materials he had collected for his Ph.D. dissertation. Several groups of researchers at the General Accounting Office shared their data with me. The Task Force on Government Employees made its data on "Reductions in Force" available to me, and Congressman Anderson's office shared with me files on the reorganization at UMTA.

Finally, I accumulated additional debts when reviewers critiqued drafts of the manuscript for me. I would particularly like to thank Jeffrey Straussman, Charles Levine, Richard Bingham, and Allen Schick. I wish I could blame them for any errors or omissions remaining, but since they haven't volunteered to take the blame, I suppose I have to take it myself.

Irene S. Rubin

Shrinking the Federal Government

1

President Reagan's Cutback Program

OVERVIEW

Though we sometimes think of the federal government as growing continuously, in fact, it has tended to grow in spurts, level off, and then grow again.[1] The most recent round of government growth began in the 1960s with the creation of new programs that would increase the security and health of the poor and the elderly. These programs were expanded in the early 1970s,[2] but by the middle of the 1970s, a faltering economy was unable to keep up with the new expenses without increasing the burden of taxation and the size of the deficit. Partly because of lagging productivity and large deficits, the rate of inflation increased, threatening the economy and eroding take-home pay.

By the late 1970s, economic and fiscal problems triggered efforts to bring deficits under control by cutting back expenditures. The Carter administration tried to slow down the rate of expenditures and reduce the size of the deficit, but the effort to cut back the federal government became more dramatic with the election of President Reagan in 1980.

President Reagan ran for office on a platform calling for increased military expenses, decreased nonmilitary expenses, reduced regulation, and reduced taxes. Describing his program for cutbacks, he declared, "My administration seeks to limit the size, intrusiveness, and cost of Federal activities as much as possible, and to achieve the needed increase in defense capabilities in the most cost effective manner possible."[3] The goal

1

of the Reagan administration was not to shrink the whole federal government but to curtail the rate of growth. Because expansion of the military was part of his plan, curtailing growth overall meant deeply cutting back the nonmilitary portion of the budget.

The president successfully implemented large parts of his cutback program in the first two years of his administration. His successes were both dramatic and puzzling, raising a series of questions for political scientists and public administrators.

First, why would a politician, such as the president, want to lead a cutback movement? Where did the cutback program come from, and what was the nature of its political support? Was it part of a right-wing movement, led by a small but hardy band of Republicans, to shrink the size of the public sector, or did it have widespread public support?

Second, how was the president able to implement the program in the face of potential opposition from grant recipients, clients, federal employees, and Congress? Don't interest groups from "iron triangles" (relationships with both agencies and Congress) to protect programs and prevent cuts? Don't bureaucrats form policy independent of the president? Won't they fight the demise or the reduction in their programs? Won't Congress disagree with the president over which programs to cut and by how much? And if Congress does disagree, won't congressional preferences dominate? Have we traditionally overestimated the power of interest groups, bureaucrats, and Congress to protect their programs, or did the president find a way around them?

Third, what has been the effect on federal agencies of the cutback process? Are they better managed with less money? Have they stabilized at a new, lower level of funding, with less fat in their budgets? Have new personnel systems encouraged employees to work harder and for longer hours or less pay? Or has the quality of management deteriorated, with poorer morale, lower productivity, rotating leadership, and poor decision making? Are we getting more service for each tax dollar after budget cuts than before?

This book outlines the economic and political factors which contributed to President Reagan's cutback program, describes the politics of the cutback process, and surveys the impact of the process on federal agencies.

The first chapter deals generally with President Reagan's election, the nature of the president's cutback program, and the extent to which the program was implemented. The second chapter describes the politics of cutting back the government, including obstacles to the accomplishment of the president's goals, strategies used to overcome or bypass them, and the success (or failure) of these strategies. Chapters 3 through 7 present case studies of agencies that were cut back and illustrate the impact of cutback processes on the agencies. Chapter 8 discusses what we have learned from the case studies about the politics and impact of cutbacks.

PRESIDENT REAGAN'S ELECTION: THE BASIS OF SUPPORT

The idea of a politician running for office on a platform of cutting back the budget is paradoxical. If budget cuts translate into service and benefit cuts, then aren't citizens voting for a candidate who is promising to take things away from them? The apparent contradiction vanishes, however, on closer examination of the president's platform. What he promised was improved economic conditions, lower interest rates, and, most important, lower taxes. Given the economic conditions prior to his election, this package of promises was most attractive.

In the years just preceding the 1980 election, government grew faster than the economy, and thus tax bills grew faster than workers' salaries. The result was reduced take-home pay. When take-home pay shrinks because of the government's bite, people are likely to protest high taxes. "The most obvious problem is the growing resistance to taxation. This has been manifested most obviously in the U.S. in the form of Proposition 13 and the numerous tax limitation proposals which have followed. At the federal level, ideas such as the Roth Kemp tax cut plan . . . [which President Reagan adopted in a modified form] . . . indicate some interest at all levels of government in reducing or controlling the size of tax obligations for citizens."[4]

The idea that the size of government should be stabilized or reduced has been widespread since the middle of 1970s, according to citizen surveys commissioned by the Advisory Commission on Intergovernmental Relations. In 1982, 42 percent of the national sample favored stabilizing services and taxes at current levels, while 36 percent advocated cutting government back. Only 8 percent favored increasing the size of government and the level of taxes.[5]

The widespread sentiment for stabilizing or cutting back government expenditure was expressed through elections. Proposition 13, a citizens' initiative to limit property taxes in California, was passed in 1978 in a statewide election. It became symbolic of the link between citizen concern with the size of the tax bite and political action. By the time Proposition 13 was passed, thirteen other states had a tax or spending limitation on the ballot, and other measures were proposed later. Some of them were defeated at the polls, but politicians across the country interpreted these restrictive measures as evidence of a popular political will. One of their responses was to encourage tax reform, thereby heading off popular referenda and public demands before they reached such a restrictive stage. In addition, the politicians themselves took the opportunity to lead tax limitation movements and to argue for reduced services and tax levels.

The new fiscal environment was so potent that even some liberal politicians espoused fiscally conservative doctrines. This new breed of politician, which appeared both at the local and the national level,[6] was often populist as well, appealing directly to citizens rather than going through political parties or interest groups.

In short, by 1980 there was evidence of widespread public support for halting the growth of the public sector, which was being translated into action at the polls. Politicians often responded by leading cutback movements and making preemptive cutbacks before citizens could demand them. Thus when President Reagan, a conservative, advocated traditional conservative policies of cutting back the size and power of the federal government and curtailing its redistributional policies, he tapped into a broad base of support. Like the fiscally conservative liberals, he too often appealed directly to this base in a populist manner.

THE PRESIDENT'S PROGRAM

The president reflected in his program many of the popular concerns that underlay the tax protest movement. For example, in his speech on 5 February 1981 he argued, "All of you who are working know that even with cost of living pay raises, you can't keep up with inflation. In our progressive tax system as you increase the number of dollars you earn, you find yourself moved up into higher tax brackets, paying a higher tax rate just for trying to hold your own. The result? Your standard of living is going down."[7]

The president repeated his argument in his February 18 speech in 1981. "One worker in a midwest city put it to me this way: He said, 'I am bringing home more dollars than I ever believed I would possibly earn, but I seem to be getting worse off.' And he is. Not only have hourly earnings of the American worker after adjusting for inflation, declined 5% over the past five years, Federal personal taxes for the average family have increased 67%."[8]

To resolve the problems of the economy, the president proposed a four-point plan: reduce program spending, especially in nondefense areas; reduce taxation; reduce regulation; and control inflation through monetary policy. Though the president emphasized the need to reduce the size of the deficit, he argued that a tax increase was not the appropriate tool; Americans were already overtaxed, and the heavy taxation reduced individual incentives to work. Tax policies and heavy regulation, he argued, prevented investment in new equipment, holding productivity down. The result was reduced ability to compete in world markets.[9]

Each element in his program was presented with a view to explicit political appeal. The president proposed to take government off the backs of the people and of industry through deregulation. This proposal appealed to recipients to federal grants, such as cities, and to businesses subject to federal regulation, such as oil companies. The tax reduction that the president advocated also had wide political appeal to individuals and businesses. Moreover, the president not only promised to bring inflation and interest rates under control but also tried his program to the American dream of home ownership, which would again be possible once interest rates were lowered.[10]

The direct appeal to so many different groups led to an apparent contradiction in the program: a substantial tax cut on the one hand and a reduction in the size of the deficit (to help control inflation) on the other. The contradiction was resolved by arguing that "supply-side economics" would help close the revenue expenditure gap.

Supply-side economics was an untried theory which assumed that as the size of the government was reduced, the private sector would boom; the resurgence of the private sector would in turn make taxes more productive and reduce the deficit. An important part of this theory called for tax cuts to the relatively well-to-do so that they would invest in the expansion of the economy. The theory is called supply-side economics to emphasize the supply of capital for growth and to differentiate it from demand-driven models of the economy, which urge tax cuts to moderate- and lower-income people to stimulate demand for products.

To summarize, from a programmatic point of view, the president's vow to reduce the size, intrusiveness, and cost of the nonmilitary portions of the federal government entailed three basic strategies: 1) a tax reduction, 2) a cutback in programs and reduction in the number of federal employees, and 3) a reduction of regulation.

In accomplishing these primary tasks, he needed also to achieve two related goals. First, he needed to turn over programs to the state governments in order to reduce the cost and size of the federal government and decrease federal regulation. Second, he needed to improve the overall quality of the management of federal agencies. In particular, he needed to demonstrate that he could cut back funds for agencies while maintaining necessary services, simply by reducing waste, fraud, and abuse and improving productivity.

IMPLEMENTATION OF THE PRESIDENT'S PROGRAM

Although the president's program for shrinking the federal government ran into some difficulties, a remarkably large part of it was implemented. In the remainder of this chapter, we shall describe the extent to which each of the five goals of the president's program was accomplish.

Tax Reduction

The first goal, to reduce taxes, was fully implemented. The Economic Recovery Tax Act was enacted into law on August 13, 1981. President Reagan lobbied extensively for his tax reduction bill in Congress. He not only invited congressmen to meet with and be photographed with him at

Camp David, but also offered incentives to individual congressmen to vote in favor of the bill. In addition to lobbying with individuals, the president made a televised appeal to the public two days before the House vote, which prompted citizens to lobby on behalf of the measure. Individual representatives, "such as Dan Glickman, D. Kansas, whose office received 1500 calls, were swamped."[11] The lobbying effort was effective.

The new law provided tax reductions for citizens and businesses as well as a minor readjustment in Social Security. The cuts averaged 1 percent for 1981, because they were in effect for only three months of the year, 10 percent in 1982, 19 percent in 1983, and 23 percent in 1984. To encourage investment, taxes on income from investments and capital gains were reduced, and businesses received an accelerated depreciation allowance for equipment.

Program Cutbacks

The second major goal in President Reagan's agenda was to cut back programs. This necessitated both budget cuts and a reduction in personnel.

Budget Cuts

The president wanted to make an immediate impact on the budget, and he took office in January 1981 under a budget drawn up by his Democratic predecessor, President Carter, which would last until the end of September 1981. Thus Reagan's first goal was to modify President Carter's budget through impoundment proceedings (requesting permission from Congress not to spend all the money Carter had budgeted for fiscal year 1981).

The president began these proceedings on a number of programs of which he disapproved. For fiscal year 1981, he requested $16.5 billion in *rescissions* (permanent legislative withdrawals of the appropriation) and $9.5 billion of *deferrals* (temporary delays in committing funds or in actual outlays.) President Reagan proposed 166 separate rescissions and 131 separate deferrals.[12]

The president met with substantial success in shaping the budget to his preference through the use of impoundment from January to September 1981. Congress generally approved these proposals, acting favorably on $11,715,000,000 of his $16.5 billion in rescissions and allowing all but $361 million of his $9.5 billion of deferrals. This is a very large reduction for the middle of a fiscal year. The total of President Reagan's rescissions and deferrals in 1981 far exceeded the dollar level of impoundment of the Nixon year ($18 billion), which had so irritated Congress that it was moved in 1974 to revise the whole congressional budget process.[13]

While the president was reshaping fiscal year 1981 along budgetary and programmatical lines, he was also preparing the 1982 budget proposal, which he submitted to Congress in March 1981. Congress gave him almost exactly what he asked for in July, in the omnibus reconciliation. The reconciliation is a process of agreement among congressional committees to limit themselves to certain specified spending levels. This agreement is supposed to determine the spending levels in the appropriations bills, which are passed just before the new fiscal year. The omnibus reconciliation cut about $35 billion from the 1982 budget.[14]

The reconciliation was completed by July 31, but Congress had not yet passed the appropriation bills when the president on 24 September 1981 asked it to come up with a second cut for the 1982 budget. This second request was for an additional 12 percent across-the-boad cut in administrative costs for nonmilitary agencies and would therefore particularly affect staffing levels.

Congress balked at a second major cut coming so soon after the reconciliation. Instead of passing the appropriations bills, it passed a continuing resolution to keep the government from closing down at the beginning of the fiscal year. The continuing resolution gives agencies permission to continue spending at a specified level without an appropriation. The most common choices are to continue spending at last year's rate, at the level passed by either the House or the Senate if one of them has passed the appropriation, or at the level recommended in the president's proposed budget. In this case, the continuing resolution was funded at a level considerably above the president's revised September request. It extended from 1 October to 20 November 1981.

Instead of vetoing the continuing resolution because it provided for greater expenditures than his September budget recommendation, the president chose to defer those expenses which exceeded his recommendation until the November 20 deadline, or until Congress voted on the appropriations, whichever came first. The president argued that he did not want Congress to be unable to vote on a budget agreeing with his recommendations because it had locked itself into too high a rate of expenditure during the first two months of the fiscal year. He therefore controlled the rate of expenditure as if his budget had passed. In essence, he substituted his proposed budget for the congressionally mandated level in the continuing resolution by deferring the difference. Technically, Congress could have overturned the president's request for deferral, but it did not do so.

In November, when the continuing resolution was about to expire, Congress feared that if it voted appropriations higher than the president requested, he would veto them. It therefore passed a second temporary continuing resolution instead of the normal annual appropriations bills. This resolution, like the first one, did not contain the additional 12 percent cut requested by the president. Moreover, Congress built into the proposed resolution floors as well as ceilings on expenditures, to prevent the president from withholding the funding as he had with the October 1 to November 20 continuing resolution. However, the president vetoed this resolution, complaining that it gave him barely a 4 percent cut instead of the 12 percent he had requested.

After the president's veto, Congress was forced to try again because the government was temporarily without the authority to spend money. This time it passed a continuing resolution that would extend the first one for an additional three weeks. The purpose of the three-week extension was to give Congress some time to develop a compromise acceptable to the president.

In December of 1981, Congress passed a third continuing resolution, this one to last from December through 31 March 1982. The new resolution included pay raises for top federal employees and approved about $4 billion in cuts. It gave the President only about half the cuts he had asked for in September, but these were enough to prevent a veto. However, for many domestic programs the outcome was still only an additional 4 percent cut rather than the 12 percent cut requested.

The third continuing resolution approved pay raises but did not provide extra funds for them; thus if the agencies could not prevail upon Congress to pass supplemental appropriations, they would have to cut their own budgets further to provide funds for the increase. The actual size of the cuts made by Congress was thus ambiguous, since it was not clear whether it would provide supplemental funding.

On 31 March 1982, when the continuing resolution expired, Congress passed a fourth one covering those agencies whose appropriation bills had not yet passed. The fourth resolution embodied all the provisions of the third.

The president did not accept the compromise worked out by Congress. Although he did not veto the third continuing resolution and hence force the closing of the government, he shifted from trying to get Congress to pass his budget cuts to trying to get the budget appropriation rescinded for a large number of programs. On 8 February 1982 he proposed twenty-two program rescissions, amounting to over $10.5 billion. Congress was unwilling to rescind the proposed amount that it had just passed, and in April the rescission proposal lapsed. The Office of Management and Budget had to release the funds and allow them to be spent.

The budget process for the 1983 budget was parallel to that for 1982 in that the president's proposed budget called for deep cuts, the first budget resolution called for deep cuts and contained reconciliation language, and Congress was initially unable to pass a budget but passed several continuing resolutions instead. What was different was the increased feeling in Congress that the president could be defied on budget matters and that congressional priorities could be expressed in the budget. In particular, there was increased sentiment for cutting military as well as social programs and for eliminating or reducing the tax cuts, because they exacerbate the deficits.

By the time the 1984 budget request was submitted to Congress, the president had reduced his intense pressure on Congress to produce cuts. Not only did he ask for fewer cuts but he offered increases in some areas of interest to Congress and promised not to use the rescission and deferral mechanism for program cuts. Although he continued to press for the termination of some programs, the 1984 budget was markedly different from its predecessors. Even with these presidential concessions, Congress was still determined to put its own stamp on the budget. In 1984 the House proposed an alternative to the president's budget.

To summarize, the president achieved billions of dollars in budget reductions, mostly in exactly the areas he wished. Initially cooperative, Congress gradually became increasingly balky, passing continuing resolutions instead of budget appropriation bills in an effort to prevent a presidential veto. Congress reacted to the president's use of deferrals by trying to build into a continuing resolution language guaranteeing floors as well as ceilings on spending. Moreover, it did not give the president all he asked for in cuts, despite both the threat of and the use of presidential vetoes, and it gradually became more adamant about imposing its priorities for cutback.

Personnel Reductions

As with budget reductions, the president did not wait for the 1982 budget to have an impact on personnel levels. He took action to reduce the number of personnel as soon as he took office. In fact, his first official act took place on 20 January 1981, when he announced a total hiring freeze. The freeze lasted about seven weeks and was retroactive to his election.

In March 1981, when the freeze was withdrawn, position ceilings were reduced for the remainder of the fiscal year. Position ceilings limit the number of full-time permanent staff members in each agency. The March reduction meant that agencies had only six months to get down to the new ceilings. That action effectively continued what had been a government-wide freeze on an agency-by-agency basis, because agencies generally left positions vacant in an effort to get down to ceiling levels. Between January and September 1981, the Office of Personnel Management, which keeps records on the number of people employed by the federal government, reported a reduction in federal employment of 43,454.[15]

At the end of July 1981, the Omnibus Reconciliation Act of 1981 was passed, which cut back many programs' budgets and eliminated other programs entirely. Many agencies found that they could not afford to keep even the number of staff members allowed by the new lower ceilings. Consequently, many agencies began to plan for hiring freezes, furloughs (unpaid, mandatory vacations) and layoffs (reductions in force).

In September 1981, when the president asked for a 12 percent additional budget reduction for 1982, he also asked for a reduction of 75,000 positions. This reduction was to be accomplished over a three-year period. According to the OMB plan for staffing reductions, employment in nondefense agencies was actually to be reduced by 81,800, because 9300 full-time equivalent staff had to be added to the Veterans Administration after the target of 75,000 was announced.[16]

The plan assumed a drop in staffing levels from 1981 to 1982 of about twenty-eight thousand civilian positions, but year-end estimates of civilian full-time equivalent staffing levels indicate that they actually increased somewhat. Part of the problem was that the civilian positions in the military increased by twenty thousand despite OMB's assumption that they would not increase.[17] This increase swamped the moderate reductions (down about four thousand positions) in nondefense areas. Moreover, the number of full-time permanent staff members grew markedly, while the number of other than full-time positions sharply decreased by thirty-two thousand.[18]

Data from the Office of Personnel Management confirm the impression that after an initial dip from 1980 to 1981, civilian staffing levels stabilized and began to increase. Overall civilian employment increased from 2,729,324 in November 1981 to 2,735,108 in April 1983; the full-time permanent staff increased from a low of 2,330,662 in November 1981 to 2,346,128 in April 1983.[19] These figures suggest the administration probably will not meet its goal of reducing overall civilian employment.

That is not to argue that some agencies or areas were not markedly reduced in staffing levels. What is particularly significant is that while overall full-time permanent staffing increased over the period, staffing in Washington decreased consistently, reflecting decentralization of programs and perhaps a disproportionate tendency to lay off staff in headquarters rather than in the field.

OMB's staff reduction plan suffered from a number of problems that hampered its execution. First, it assumed congressional approval of a number of administration proposals, such as the dismantling of the Department of Energy and the Department of Education, that were never accepted by Congress. Second, department and agency heads negotiated with OMB concerning the staffing levels, and powerful agencies reversed their reductions. Third, a highly publicized GAO study found that the administration's estimates on how much money would be saved from personnel reductions had been greatly inflated. The study was embarrassing (it claimed that OMB had no record of how it had come up with its estimates and could not explain any discrepancies) and cast doubt on the wisdom of personnel cuts as a method of budget cutting.[20]

To summarize, the administration was "committed to reducing Federal civilian employment,"[21] but its success in reducing staffing levels was mixed. An initial freeze and ceiling reduction did effectively reduce staffing levels from January 1981 to September 1981, but although levels in Washington were successfully reduced, the September personnel reduction target of an addition 75,000 positions was hard to achieve.

There were at least three reasons why the administration had a difficult time achieving the new personnel reduction target. First, increases in the number of civilian positions in the military drowned out decreases elsewhere. Second, Congress did not go along with some presidential initiatives, such as dissolving some cabinet-level departments. And third, OMB wasn't strong enough to impose its planned cuts on all departments and agencies.

Deregulation

The third major program goal of the president was to reduce the level of regulation. The word "regulation" (and hence "deregulation") is used in two different ways in Washington. On the one hand, it refers to the rules promulgated by agencies as they attempt to implement legislation. These rules govern such matters as how to apply for a grant, how grantees should draw down money from federal accounts, and how they should keep records of their expenditures. On the other hand, regulation refers to the government's role in telling state and local governments and private organizations how to conduct their own business. Typical of this second kind of regulation are rules from the Environmental Protection Agency that tell cities they may not dump untreated waste in rivers and streams.

The president argued that the cost of compliance with both types of regulation was enormous and that excessive regulation reduced productivity in the private sector, weakening the competitiveness of U.S. products abroad. Moreover, some regulations, such as the Davis Bacon Act (which requires that workers on federally funded projects be paid prevailing wages), increase the cost of public-sector projects.

Between 22 January and 18 February 1981, the president began a flurry of activities with a view to controlling the amount of regulation and required paper work. In some areas, he sought to decontrol or deregulate by suspending rules and changing laws. In other cases, his choice was to terminate regulatory agencies or to render them less effective or less zealous.

Suspending Rules and Changing Laws

On 22 January 1981 the Task Force on Regulatory Relief was announced. It was chaired by the vice-president and hence was dubbed the Bush Committee.[22] The job of the task force was to review major regulatory proposals by executive branch agencies, assess regulations already on the books, oversee legislative proposals of the agencies, and make recommendations to the president on how to reform regulation.

On 29 January the president requested a postponement for sixty days of regulations in process until they could be reviewed. The purpose was in part to weed out the "midnight" regulations of the Carter administration, those designed in its last days but not yet effective.

During February a number of regulations were withdrawn or delayed, some indefinitely. The secretary of education withdrew proposed and highly controversial requirements for bilingual education. The secretary of transportation announced a one-year delay in regulations requiring passive restraints (such as air bags) in automobiles. The Environmental Protection Agency asked the District of Columbia Court of Appeals to remand to it a rule setting noise emission standards for garbage trucks. The Occupational Safety and Health Administration (OSHA) withdrew for reconsideration a rule that chemicals be labeled in the workplace. New rules under the Fair Labor Standards Act dealing with the determination of eligibility of executives for overtime pay were postponed indefinitely. An extension of the Davis-Bacon rule requiring that different categories of employees on federally funded projects receive the prevailing wage rates was postponed.

The Office of Management and Budget withdrew a policy memorandum concerning the prevention of federal support for excessive hospital expansion. The secretary of energy announced an indefinite delay in rules requiring more energy-efficient measures for energy conservation, including compressed work weeks, vehicle-use stickers, and odd-even-day motor fuel purchases. OMB withdrew the Department of Energy's clearance, under the Federal Reports Act, for the collection of industrial data on energy consumption.[23]

The president also made some changes in the process of creating regulations, thereby giving OMB a greater voice in evaluating new rules. Proposals for new regulations now had to be approved by OMB before they could be announced in the *Federal Register* as under consideration.[24] He also tied information collection restrictions more closely to regulatory reform, on the assumption that since intelligent regulations require data collection, without such collection, regulation would be hampered or eliminated.

While the Bush Commission examined regulations and OMB monitored requests to collect information and to issue regulations, the administration focused on necessary legislative changes as well. Many of these were embodied in the Omnibus Reconciliation Act of 1981. For example, the Department of Housing and Urban Development's Community Development Program was rewritten in such as way as to simplify application procedures. New block grants generally reduced the ability of agencies in Washington to issue regulations.

There was an enormous amount of activity in the area of withdrawing rules and changing laws, but it did not produce as many gains as might have been expected. "The current administration took office with the announced intent of reducing regulation, but it has not been easy for it to find reverse gear on the regulatory machine. Relatively few repeal efforts have been carried through to completion, and of those, several have not survived the courts."[25]

Estimates of the effectiveness of OMB's control over regulations are often based on the number of pages of regulations published in the *Federal Register*. The estimate by the end of 1981 (after intense efforts to deregulate and a sixty-day moritorium on rules) was that the production of new rules was running at about 90 percent of 1980 level.[26]

Another way of looking at the effectiveness of the deregulatory effort is to look at the number of regulations examined and the number acted on. The Bush Commission received twenty-five hundred suggestions on "burdensome, unnecessary and counterproductive" regulations. During 1981, the commission examined one hundred regulations, and proposed modifications on thirty-eight. Of those, twenty-five affected state and local governments, of which six were reviewed and acted on. In its first nine months, the commission achieved major changes in nineteen regulations, many of which aroused opposition.[27]

Although the number of rules changes was limited, action occurred on some very important regulations. The Department of Transportation modified the requirement for equipping buses for the handicapped by allowing a local option on how to service the handicapped; some changes were made in how prevailing wages would be calculated under the Davis-Bacon requirement; and the A95 review process (a regional planning function to coordinate the impact of federal grants on neighboring local governments) was dismantled.[28]

The effect of the president's changes in regulations was often obliterated by the courts, however. The air bag (passive constraint) rule that was withdrawn by the administration was reinstated by the District of Columbia Circuit Court; the D.C. Circuit Court also found that the Department of Labor did not have authority to reinterpret Davis-Bacon. The Civil Aeronautics Board had rescinded the smoking rules on airplanes in 1981, but in 1983 the courts reversed the rescission. And a 1981 Treasury Department repeal of a rule requiring alcoholic beverages to either list ingredients or tell consumers how to get such a list was overturned. In two of those cases, the court ruled that the government's explanation for repeal of the rules was inadequate.[29]

Terminating or Weakening Regulatory Agencies

The Reagan administration was probably more successful in its efforts to weaken regulation by terminating or weakening regulatory agencies. Soon after taking office, the president was able to terminate the Wage-Price Standards program of the Council on Wages and Price Stability with an executive order, because the unit was in the president's office. The staff was to be reduced from 170 to 35.[30] In most cases, however, the president did not have the discretion to terminate regulatory programs, and Congress did not oblige by terminating them for him. Hence his main approach was to weaken the agencies or reduce their enforcement capacity.

One technique the administration used was to reduce the budget and staffing levels in regulatory agencies. "Since 1980, the staff and real budgetary levels of federal regulatory agencies have dropped significantly, around 11%. (Most of that drop, 8.6% took place in fiscal year 1982.) Since then, the trend has been much more modest, but still down."[31]

Because almost all domestic agencies were cut in 1982, a reduction of 11 percent does not indicate a particular targeting of regulatory agencies. What is more significant is that if Congress would not go along with the president's proposals to cut a regulatory agency's budget, the administration cut personnel levels anyway. "Staffing figures in some cases diverge from those for budgets. The Anti-Trust Division of the Department of Justice has had a relatively stable budget since 1982, but is nonetheless decreasing its full time positions from 829 to 704 in 1984. The Mine Safety and Health Administration's Staff similarly dropped from 3763 to 3184 over the same two year period, and the Federal Maritime Commission from 308 to 252."[32]

The Reagan administration's approach to reducing the enforcement of regulations was illustrated in the president's plan for the Department of Energy. One section of the Department was involved in monitoring the conformity of fuel companies to fuel price regulations. It reportedly had caught a number of violators and was in the process of prosecuting them with the help of the Justice Department. The administration wanted to disband the entire department, allocating some of the pieces to other departments, but there was no support in Congress for this proposal.

The administration then proposed sharp budget cuts and personnel reductions in the enforcement branches of the Department of Energy. The Subcommittee on Investigations and Oversight of the House Committee on Energy and Commerce held hearings on the administration's attempt to reduce enforcement.[33] The committee chairman, John Dingell, accused the administration: "In the face of this [regulatory] activity, the Reagan administration is cutting the heart out of the Energy Department's enforcement budget, effectively granting amnesty to these price gougers and potential criminals. . . . Now under the guise of balancing the budget, the administration has proposed reducing the Department's enforcement spending by over $40 million. This will reduce the current level of about 1300 auditors, attorneys, clerical and administrative personnel to about 300 people in fiscal year 1982. . . . The practical effect of this reduction will be the virtual elimination of the enforcement sections as an effective force."[34] Later in the hearing, testimony from agency administrators indicated that budget cuts and personnel reductions would force the agency not to pursue a number of pending cases, in which about $6 billion was involved.[35]

In addition to attacking the Department of Energy, the administration attacked the enforcement capacity of the Environmental Protection Agency. The EPA suffered three reorganizations of the enforcement office within a very short time, and the scope of authority of the head of that office was reduced. All his decisions had to be funneled through the general counsel. Staffing levels in the enforcement sections were greatly reduced, and the agency's budget was markedly cut back. The EPA's budget was reduced 16 percent in 1981 and 1982. For 1983, Ann Gorsuch, the agency administrator at that time, proposed an additional 18 percent cut, which OMB raised to a proposed 36 percent cutback. Though the final cut was more moderate, the requested figures illustrate the administration's strategy. The turmoil, the budget and personnel cuts, and the policies of the agency administrator all contributed to a reduction in enforcement. The number of cases referred to the central office from the regional offices for enforcement dropped from 313 in 1980 to 66 in 1981.[36]

To summarize, the Reagan administration's effort to deregulate involved a revamping of the procedures by which rules are made, a delay of some rules and rescission of others, and an attempt to weaken enforcement through budget cuts, personnel cuts, and reorganizations in the enforcement sections of regulatory agencies. Some of the rules changes have survived, but others have been overturned by the courts, and though the changes made have been significant, they have not been numerous. Perhaps more important has been the moderation of the enforcement efforts of the regulatory agencies.[37]

Decentralization and The New Federalism

Part of the president's program was to reduce the size of government by shifting functions and programs to state and local governments. In particular, the president wanted to return welfare functions to the states. He also sought to cut back aid from the federal government to state and local governments and to attach fewer restrictions to grants which were to be continued, allowing recipients more flexibility in how program funds could be spent.

The president's most dramatic success in this area occurred as part of the 1981 omnibus reconciliation. The president had proposed that eighty-four categorical grants (grants for a single specific purpose) be grouped into six block grants. The block grants would contain a number of related special-purpose grants, and the recipient would have the choice of how to allocate the funds among the special purposes allowed.

Though the categoricals had often been granted by the federal government directly to agencies or cities, most of the new block grants were given to state governments to administer. The change from categoricals to block grants was thus intended to increase the discretion of state officials.

Congress did not approve all the proposed block grants, but in 1981 it consolidated fifty-seven categorical programs and nine new block grants. In 1982 it passed two more major block grants.[38] Although a substantial proportion of the proposed block grants became law, some of the other new federalism proposals were not implemented.

One of the president's major new federalism proposals was a swap of programs between the state governments and the federal government. A number of major programs had been shared by the federal government and the states; the president now proposed that the state governments take over complete control of some programs while the federal government take over others. In his 1982 State of the Union message, President Reagan proposed that the federal government assume all responsibility for Medicaid and the states take all responsibility for Aid to Families with Dependent Children (a major welfare program) and food stamps.[39] Another portion of the plan was to turn over some federal revenue sources along with the programs.

Neither the program swap nor the shift in federal revenues to the states ever occurred. The president wanted the states to take over all welfare programs,[40] but the governors quickly calculated that the takeover would cost them more money than the president proposed to give them. Negotiations ground to a halt.

Even the removal of many of the strings attached to grants turned out to be less than liberating for grant recipients. For one thing, the block grants to the states were turned over with greatly reduced budgets, leaving the governors with only the discretion to allocate cutbacks. Even so, the governors appreciated the increased choice of how to spend funds, but they claimed that the reduction in rules and paperwork was not significant.

"The consensus among state officials seems to be that while they like the greater program flexibility of many of the block grants, the full 'benefits' of deregulation have been less than expected in the procedural area. Federal agencies have reduced program requirements in some areas, giving states more policy flexibility, but they still require extensive and detailed paperwork and reports for audits and financial reviews. The states aren't sure just what to expect in the way of audits from federal agencies."[41]

To summarize, the New Federalism initiative, which implied a return of federal functions to state and local governments, along with greater discretion to run such programs, began with the creation of a number of new block grants but then gradually petered out. The determination of the administration to reduce the amount of money attached to block grants counteracted the effect of increased discretion at the state level, and the fear of audits kept grant recipients busy filling out forms despite the simplification of application procedures.

Improved Management

The last of the president's goals was to improve management. The emphasis was on reducing waste, fraud, and abuse and improving productivity.

In March 1981 he announced a government-wide commitment to reduce waste, fraud, and abuse and formed a council (the President's

Council on Integrity and Efficiency) to make recommendations on how to manage money better. This council was composed of the inspector generals of the departments and independent agencies, six other appointees, and the deputy director of the Office of Management and Budget.[42] Although this council was intended to bolster the inspector general system, the president may have weakened the system rather than strengthened it.

When President Reagan first came to office, he fired all the inspector generals who had been appointed by President Carter so that he could put his own appointees in their places.[43] The inspector generals were intended to be independent auditors who resided in each of the major agencies to examine management practices and improve control systems. They were to report any abuses they found to the secretaries of the agencies and to Congress. The dual reporting system was intended as a guarantee of independence. The inspector generals were not intended to report directly to the president or be loyal to his programs. President Reagan's action immediately suggested that he did not intend to have independent auditors examining his secretaries. In the tumult that ensued, the president rehired several of the laid-off inspectors, but the question of their independence remained.[44]

The president claimed that the inspector generals found many problems and "saved or put to better use" almost $17 billion over two years.[45] The General Accounting Office (known as the GAO), which is the investigative arm of Congress, argued that "an overall assessment of the effectiveness of the Inspector General system cannot be made." The reason was that the data issued by the President's Council on Integrity and Efficiency "suffer from serious problems of validity and comparability of quantitative data."[46]

The GAO criticized the savings figures, while the Office of Management and Budget defended them.[47] Consequently, it is difficult to evaluate how much money the inspector generals saved, and it is fairly certain that their credibility will continue to be questioned because of their political appointments.

The president claimed that in 1981 and 1982 the administration had made improvements in cash flow management, collection of debts owed to the federal government, and procurement systems. He did not attach any dollar figures to these efforts, however, making it impossible to estimate how well they were carried out.[48]

During the first year and a half of the administration, the management side of the Office of Management and Budget, which had never been large, "withered to a tiny fragment."[49] By the fall of 1982, however, the President had increased his visible efforts to improve management. There were three presidential initiatives to improve management. One of them, called "Reform 88," was presumably a long-term effort to improve management, but its purposes and results remain vague.[50] The second initiative was "The President's Private Sector Survey on Cost Control," which was commonly called the "Grace Survey," after its leader, J. Peter Grace. This was a huge effort, bringing in business leaders and having them search for ways to make government more efficient. The third initiative was to create a Cabinet Council on Management and Administration. Although the composition of this council suggests that it will be effective, the nature of its recommendations and the impact of the council are not known.[51]

To summarize, improving management was not initially a high priority of the Reagan administration. For the first year and a half very little was done in this area. However, as the initial impetus of the rest of the cutback program wore down, interest in improved management increased. Part of this improvement was intended to come from the agencies themselves as they sought to cope with reduced budgets and constant workloads, but part was intended to come from the administration. The administration's initiatives included a survey of government by private businessmen to find ways to control costs and a cabinet-level council on management.

CHAPTER SUMMARY

President Reagan was swept into office by a mass movement. Citizens were concerned about economic conditions and especially about the increased size of the tax bite when their incomes were declining and their purchasing power was shrinking.

The president's cutback program, reflecting popular concerns, had five parts: tax reduction, program cutback, deregulation, decentralization of control to the state governments, and improved management.

Implementation of this program was much greater in some areas than in others. The president's tax reduction proposal was implemented. Most of his requests for program cutbacks were passed by Congress during the first year of his administration, but the president never got all he asked for, and Congress became increasingly balky. There was a wave of deregulatory activity when President Reagan first took office, but some of it was too hasty and was overturned by the courts. The program of decentralizing responsibility to the states was only partly successful; a number of new block grants were passed and given to the states to administer, but the swap of functions envisioned by the president, to be accompanied by a shift of resources, never occurred. The goal of improved management received less attention from the administration than the other areas of the cutback program. During the first three years, relatively little was accomplished in this area, although more may be accomplished later.

In this chapter we have described what the president accomplished. However, the full impact of his achievements cannot be felt without an understanding of how the program was implemented, what the obstacles to success were, and how the president did or did not manage to get around them. The next chapter, which describes the process of implementing the cutback program, should help explain why the president accomplished more in some areas than in others.

NOTES

1. Herbert Kaufman, *Are Government Organizations Immortal?* (Washington: Brookings Institution, 1976), pp. 66–68.
2. Martha Derthick, *Uncontrollable Spending for Social Service Grants* (Washington: Brookings Institution, 1975).
3. Office of Management & Budget, *The Budget in Brief*, 1984, Government Printing Office, p. 11.
4. The material in this paragraph is from Richard Rose and Guy Peters, "The Growth of Government and the Political Consequences of Economic Overload" in *Managing Fiscal Stress: The Crisis in the Public Sector*, ed. Charles Levine (Chatham, N.J.: Chatham House, 1980), pp. 33–70; and Guy Peters, "Fiscal Strains on the Welfare State" in *Fiscal Stress and Public Policy*, ed. Charles Levine and Irene Rubin (Beverly Hills: Sage Publications, 1980), pp. 23–48. The quotation is from Guy Peters, in Levine and Rubin, *Fiscal Stress*, p. 32.
5. Advisory Commission on Intergovernmental Relations, *Changing Public Attitudes on Government and Taxes* (Washington: Government Printing Office, 1983), p. 17.
6. Terry Clark and Lorna Ferguson, "Political Leadership and Urban Fiscal Policy" in *Urban Policy Analysis*, ed. Terry Clark, Urban Affairs Annual Reviews, vol. 21 (Beverly Hills: Sage, 1981), p. 91; and W. Schneider and G. Schell, "The New Democrats," *Public Opinion*, November/December 1978, pp. 7–13.
7. Martha Gottron, ed., *Budgeting for America* (Washington: Congressional Quarterly, 1982), p. 200.
8. *Ibid.*, p. 201.
9. President Reagan's Speech to the Nation, 5 February 1981, in Gottron, *Budgeting for America*, p. 200
10. *Ibid.*, p. 199.
11. Gottron, *Budgeting for America*, p. 192.
12. There are three sources for this information. Rescission and deferral requests are required by law to be submitted by the president to Congress. In addition to the individual requests, the Office of Management and Budget issues periodic cumulative reports. The General Accounting Office, which is the official watchdog of rescissions and deferrals, also issues reports.
13. Allen Schick, *Congress and Money* (Washington: Urban Institute, 1980). See especially p. 45.
14. Gottron, *Budgeting for America*, p. 70.
15. General Accounting Office, *Recent Government Wide Hiring Freezes Prove Ineffective in Managing Federal Employment* (FPCD-82-21) (Washington: Government Printing Office, 10 March 1982), p. 10.
16. Office of Management and Budget, "Civilian Employment in the Executive Branch," *The United States Budget 1983* Special Analysis "I." Government Printing Office. February, 1982.
17. General Accounting Office, *Savings from 1981 and 1982 Personnel Ceiling Reductions* (FPCD-82-23) (Washington: Government Printing Office, 15 January 1982), p. 2.
18. *U.S. Budget 1983*, Special Analysis "I," p. 8.

19. Office of Personnel Management, *Federal Civilian Workforce Statistics*, Table 8, "Statistical Summary of Federal Civilian Employment." This series is published monthly. I charted the figures for each month, and reported selected months from that chart.

20. General Accounting Office, *Savings from 1981 and 1982 Personnel Ceiling Reductions* (FPCD-82-23) (Washington: Government Printing Office, 1982), p. 1.

21. *U.S. Budget 1983*, Special Analysis "I," p. 3.

22. Other members were the secretary of the treasury, the attorney general, the secretary of commerce, the secretary of labor, the director of OMB, the assistant to the president for policy development and the chairman of the Council of Economic Advisors.

23. The information in the preceding paragraphs on the president's actions is taken from a White House press release, "America's New Beginning: A Program for Economic Recovery," 18 February 1981.

24. John William Ellwood, ed., *Reductions in U.S. Domestic Spending: How They Affect State and Local Governments* (New Brunswick, N.J.: Transaction Books, 1982), p. 119.

25. James V. DeLong, "Repealing Regulation," *Regulation*, May/June 1983, p. 26.

26. Catherine Lovell, "Federal Deregulation and State and Local Governments," in *Reductions in U.S. Domestic Spending*, ed. Ellwood, p. 120. Lovell cites as the source of this information David Walker, Albert Richter, and Cynthia Colella, "The First 10 Months: Grant in Aid, Regulatory and Other Changes," *Intergovernmental Perspective* 8, no. 1 (Winter 1982), p. 15.

27. Lovell, "Federal Deregulation" in Ellwood, *Reductions in U.S. Domestic Spending*, p. 122.

28. *Ibid.*, p. 125.

29. James V. DeLong, "Repealing Rules," *Regulation*, May/June 1983, pp. 26–30.

30. White House Press Release, 18 February 1981.

31. "Perspectives on Current Developments: Regulations and the 1984 Budget," *Regulation*, March/April 1983, p. 8.

32. *Ibid.*, p. 10.

33. The hearings were entitled: "DOE Enforcement: RIFs and Budget Reductions." House Subcommittee on Investigations and Oversight of the Committee on Energy and Commerce.

34. *DOE Enforcement: RIFs and Budget Reductions: Hearings*, 97th Cong., 1st sess., 1981, p. 1

35. *Ibid.*, pp. 564–65.

36. "EPA Promises More Enforcement," *Chicago Tribune*, 21 May 1982; "Environmental Aide Loses Some Enforcement Powers," *New York Times*, 4 April 1982; "Ecology Unit Cut Reportedly Urged by Budget Office," *New York Times*, 19 November 1981.

37. Lovell agrees with this conclusion. See her article, "Effects of Regulatory Changes on States and Localities," in *The Consequences of Cuts*, ed. Richard Nathan, Fred Doolittle and Associates (Princeton: Princeton Urban and Regional Research Center, 1983), p. 187.

38. *The Budget in Brief*, 1984, p. 12. Other authors count differently, and argue that only fifty-four categoricals were made into seven block grants in 1981. Nathan, Doolittle and Associates, *The Consequences of Cuts*, p. 4.

39. Nathan, Doolittle and Associates, *The Consequences of Cuts*, p. 3.

40. Gottron, *Budgeting for America*, p. 108.

41. Nathan, Doolittle and Associates, *The Consequences of Cuts*, p. 174.

42. Chester Newland, "A Midterm Appraisal—The Reagan Presidency:

Limited Government and Political Administration," *Public Administration Review* 43, no. 1 (January/February 1983): 14.

43. *Ibid.*

44. *Ibid.*

45. *The Budget in Brief*, 1984, p. 11.

46. John D. Young, "Reflections on the Root Causes of Fraud Abuse and Waste in Federal Social Programs," *Public Administration Review* 43, no. 4 (July/ August 1983): 366.

47. Newland, "A Midterm Appraisal," p. 14; General Accounting Office, *Validity and Comparability of Quantitative Data Presented by the President's Council on Integrity and on Inspector General's (IG's) Activities* (AFMD-82-78) (Washington: Government Printing Office, 1982).

48. *The Budget in Brief*, 1984, p. 12.

49. Newland, "A Midterm Appraisal," p. 14.

50. *Ibid.*

51. *Ibid.*, p. 19.

2

The Politics of Cutback

WHY STUDY THE CUTBACK PROCESS?

The *process* of shrinking the federal government is important for several reasons. It helps explain the successes and limits of President Reagan's program and it provides an example of how bureaucratic politics works. For political scientists, the cutback process provides a new vantage point from which to look at some traditional concerns. For practicing administrators, especially those who have been caught up in cutback, it provides a context that helps explain their individual experiences.

THE CUTBACK PROCESS AND THE LIMITS OF IMPLEMENTATION

There are a number of reasons why we would expect it to be difficult, if not impossible, for the president to cut back the federal government, yet we know he was successful in some areas. There were a number of potential obstacles to the implementation of the president's program. The seriousness of the obstacles and the success of the president's strategy for eliminating or bypassing them framed the limits of implementation of his program.

These barriers included potential opposition from federal agencies threatened by cutback, from Congress, jealous of its perogatives, and from interest groups fearful of losing benefits from federal programs and from personnel groups fearful of losing their jobs. To make the picture more complex, the whole cutback process set up an obstacle to improved management.

The strategies and tactics devised by the president and his staff to deal with these obstructions included more careful selection of appointees loyal to the president and his program, internal reorganizations, use and threatened use of the veto power, rescissions and deferrals, revisions of regulations, reductions in personnel ceilings, and reductions in force. Many of these strategies evoked opposition from agencies, members of Congress, interest groups, and personnel groups.

THE CUTBACK PERSPECTIVE ON BUREAUCRATIC POLITICS

The series of actions and reactions involved in the cutback process provides an ideal opportunity to observe bureaucratic politics at the peak of its activity. The cutback process provides a situation in which nearly all the key actors—the president, the federal agencies, Congress, and the interest groups—are visible and interacting with one another, with clearly stated motivations. Because the cutback situation is so extreme, it delineates the limits of power and the limits of management more clearly than more routine situations.

There are four general issues of bureaucratic politics that are particularly useful to look at from the perspective of cutback: 1) whether elected officials can control federal agencies, 2) whether the president dominates Congress, 3) whether interest groups determine political outcomes, and 4) whether it is possible to improve the management of federal agencies.

The general question of whether elected officials can control bureaucracy is addressed here is terms of whether the president has enough control over the bureaucracy to successfully order agencies to terminate or cut back their own programs. Since programs and agencies are likely to fight their own demise even if they fight the president on no other issues, if the president can successfully order agencies to terminate programs or to destroy their own capacity to manage or implement programs, then he can certainly control the bureaucracy.

The second question involves the balance of power of the president and Congress. When viewed from the perspective of cutback, the question becomes does the president have or can he get enough power to force Congress to cut the budget? Or can he cut back programs without congressional consent? If he can cut back or destroy programs that Congress wants to protect, then the balance of power has certainly shifted to the president.

The third question, when viewed from the perspective of retrenchment, is whether organized interest groups determine who will be cut back and who will not. An interest group that does not determine the outcome when its programs are threatened with serious cutback or termination is not very powerful.

The fourth question is whether it is possible to simultaneously shrink the federal government and improve the quality of management. Managing the federal government is difficult in the best of times, and cutback introduces a series of additional difficulties. If the administration can improve management during a period of cutback, then the federal government is decidedly manageable.

In this chapter, we will explore the processes of shrinking the federal government in terms of these four questions. We will describe the obstacles to implementation of the president's policies and evaluate the seriousness of each potential obstacle. Then we will lay out the president's strategy for combating or evading each obstacle. Finally, we will evaluate the success of each of these presidential strategies.

The presentation of these processes is separated into four sections, one for each major obstacle, but the presentations are intended to be interdependent, because the strategies used to handle one obstacle affected the way other obstacles could be handled. Most important, the strategies for handling opposition from agencies, Congress, and interest groups generally made management problems worse.

DOES THE PRESIDENT CONTROL
EXECUTIVE BRANCH AGENCIES?

The Statement of the Problem

Agencies pose a potential threat to implementation of the president's policies because ultimately the agencies are the ones who have to implement the policies. When that policy is to cut back or terminate a program or eliminate the agency itself, the agency is in a bind. It cannot survive and maintain its funding levels while carrying out the president's policy. If agencies opt to oppose that policy, they may be able to reverse cutback and termination proposals or otherwise thwart the implementation process.

The Seriousness of the Problem

Before determining whether the president has enough control over executive branch agencies to implement his cutback programs, we need to know how serious the problem is. Are agencies really likely to try to fight a termination or cutback proposal? Would they have the resources to do so if they wanted to? How would they go about it? What is the nature of the problem with the President's control over the agencies?

Herbert Kaufman, veteran observer of the federal bureaucracy, argues that agencies will resist cutback and termination. He argues that agencies "are not helpless passive pawns in the game of politics as it affects their lives; they are active, energetic, persistent participants. The motives of their leaders and members to preserve the organization to which they belong are very strong." Kaufman concludes, "Most organization members will therefore join the battle for agency survival."[1] Aaron Wildavsky, a long-time observer of federal budget processes, argues that not only will agencies usually fight against termination, but they will resist cutbacks as well.[2]

Assuming that agencies want to survive, there are several strategies they can adopt. They can try to rouse their potential allies to fight for them, alerting them to the imminent danger of program cutback or termination. For example, they can inform congressional backers of the program and rouse their client groups to argue on their behalf. They can document and dramatize the consequences of program termination, or they can focus on demonstrating both the continuing need for the program and its successes in achieving its goals in the past. One way or another, agency administrators need to demonstrate the indispensability of their program. (Sometimes this happens inadvertently, as when a mine disaster precedes a proposed cut in the mine safety inspection program.) If agencies are able to carry out these strategies, they will increase the political cost of program termination.

Even though there is a general belief that organizations try to survive, it has not been demonstrated that they have the power to carry out a successful opposition campaign. Some agencies have so little interest group and congressional support that there is no support group to rouse. Others have an exceedingly difficult time demonstrating the past successes of the program. Many agencies have so little autonomy that they cannot form any successful strategy to reverse threatened termination of programs. Bureau chiefs are hemmed in by constraints from many different institutional actors.[3]

However, even when agencies have little independent power and cannot reverse cuts, they can make implementation of program termination and cutback difficult. Agencies can sometimes cut across the board, instead of cutting a particular program; they can try to save programs whose federal funding has been terminated by teaching grant recipients how to survive without federal funds; they can simply avoid planning for termination, increasing the cost and confusion in closeout management.

The potential of agencies to resist the president's policies thus varies from reversing the proposed cuts or program terminations to thwarting the intent of the cuts or making them less cost effective. Clearly, close control by the president over agency response to threatened cutback would be useful to prevent some of the more negative responses.

Traditionally, the president has not had such control. His major source of control over agencies has been through political appointments to head departments and independent agencies. Often these appointments have been based not on loyalty to the president or his program but on representation according to geography, gender, or race.[4] When secretaries are chosen for reasons other than loyalty to the president, there is little reason to assume they will adhere to his program if it means attacking their own agencies.

Not only does the president typically not control his appointees but it is not clear that his appointees themselves have control over the agencies. The politically appointed leadership at the top of the agencies is often more absorbed in external relations—such as those with Capitol Hill—than in controlling agencies' management. In addition, the appointed heads of agencies come and go, developing very little program knowledge, while the bureaucrats who know their programs stay for years.

Sometimes cabinet members have been chosen for program knowledgability. Such knowledge should enhance their control of their agencies, but at the same time it is likely to encourage them to become program advocates rather than presidential loyalists. It has often been argued by White House staff members that secretaries "go native" and quickly become advocates of their agencies' point of view.[5] Once that happens, the secretaries oppose cutbacks proposed by the president.

To summarize, the literature generally assumes that agencies will try to fight budget cuts and resist termination. Because agencies are assumed to want to stay alive and maintain or enhance budget levels, they are assumed to be in opposition to any president who wishes to terminate programs and cut back budgets. The secretary is seen as often siding with the agency in its desire to maintain programs, and even when the secretary sides with a president trying to cut back, he or she is seen as not having very great control over the department.

The President's Strategy

In the face of possible opposition from agencies to his plans and a history of lack of presidental control over the agencies, President Reagan and his staff formulated a three-part strategy to enhance this control. The first part involved the implementation of former President Nixon's unused plan for taking control of the federal agencies. This plan, which has since been named the "administrative presidency,"[6] had several parts, but the dominant theme was to appoint to all key positions people loyal to the president who shared his ideology. The second part of President Reagan's strategy was to sort out upper-level career officials—that is, non-appointed officials—into those who supported his policies and those who were more loyal to their programs. Those in the latter category were more likely to be put "on the shelf"—that is, taken out of policy-making positions. Those more ideologically sympathetic carried out the program and personnel cutbacks. The third part of the strategy was to strengthen the control of the Office of Management and Budget over the agencies through enhanced control of regulations and information collection and integration of both of these means of control.

The Administrative Presidency

The administrative presidency idea assumes a recalcitrant bureaucracy and outlines a strategy in which the president (not the White House staff) takes control. The idea comes from the experience of Richard Nixon, who in his first term in office relied heavily on White House staff members who were loyal to him. When these staff members tried to take control of agencies, they ran into intense opposition. For his second term, the president outlined a new strategy to take control of the bureaucracy and cut it back.[7] This strategy had four components:

1. Appoint to cabinet and subcabinet positions loyalists to the president who had no independent standing and could be removed easily if they did not follow directions or "went native." "Within their new agency homes, it was expected that Nixon's new team would also redeploy career program managers, selecting the most cooperative, sympathetic, and talented officials for top posts."[8]
2. Budget impoundment and reductions. Whole programs were to be stopped by impoundments.
3. Reorganization. Anything that did not seem to require congressional approval was to be reorganized internally to give trusted officials leverage to act. Reporting relationships would be changed, and some programs would be reorganized out of existence. "The reorganization approach was not limited to the Executive Office and the Cabinet: within their respective agencies, Nixon's new appointees were expected to take advantage of opportunities to rearrange their agencies in ways that would enable them to obtain stronger managerial control."[9]
4. Regulation writing. Rules would be issued curtailing eligibility for entitlement programs, for example, or programs would be decentralized to eliminate offending regulations.

The Nixon plan for an administrative presidency in his second term foundered after the Watergate episode, which involved an illegal break-in of Democratic Campaign Headquarters by the Committee to Re-elect the President (CREEP). Because Nixon was forced to resign, the plan for an administrative presidency was never implemented. Nevertheless, it remained as a blueprint for control over the bureaucracy by a president with similar policies.

President Reagan followed the blueprint in a number of ways as he cut back the federal government. He appointed not only secretaries but also undersecretaries who were loyal to his program. This group then looked for other Reagan policy supporters within the agency and put them in positions of increased power.[10] As advised, the president relied heavily on impoundments to achieve his policy ends. He rewrote regulations and decentralized program administration to bypass existing regulations.

Policy Versus Program Loyalists

The administration paid particular to upper-level bureaucrats who had made a career in the civil service and had achieved policy-making positions. These career officials do not come and go, leaving for other types of jobs. The policy positions they occupy are the rewards of a lifetime of work. The sanction of being ignored is severe for them. They do not rise through the bureaucracy without being very sensitive to both congressional and presidential pressures on the agency from outside. Whether the pressures are for policy expansion or budgetary contraction, the bureaucrats will try to conform.

Though the image left over from the Nixon administration was that most career officials oppose cutbacks and the rest of the conservative agenda, many of these key officials are more responsive to the president's policies than to the programs they administer. The Reagan administration tried to take advantage of this responsiveness while controlling or defusing those career bureaucrats who appeared to be more loyal to programs than to the president's policy. Many of the program loyalists were in fact "put on the shelf." For example, the offices they supervised were stripped of functions, or they were sent on assignment to a U.S. trust territory or given an office in an empty suite with nothing to do.

There was also an effort to reduce the number of middle-level managers through reductions in force. Most of the effort was not in firing people but in demoting a group of people out of policy-making positions. To follow through on this strategy, in 1983 a White House spokesman announced a program to eliminate forty thousand middle-level jobs by abolishing them when they became vacant.[11] In part, downgrading employees and reducing the number of positions for middle managers was part of a management improvement scheme to reduce the span of control of senior appointed officials. But it was also part of a scheme to create a loyal cadre at the top of each agency that had sole responsibility for policy making.

Strengthening the Office of Management and Budget

The third strategy to help take increased control over the agencies was to strengthen the control functions of the Office of Management and Budget.

This portion of the strategy was not part of the earlier Nixon's plan; when Nixon had tried it, it had created so much opposition that it resulted in an increase in congressional control over the OMB. President Reagan's plan was more modest: he simply continued the plans of the Carter administration to control the amount of regulation and to implement the paperwork control legislation, but he added to the amount of control that OMB exercised over these functions, and put the two kinds of control together.

Agencies had to submit all proposed regulations to OMB for approval, and had to obtain OMB approval before the proposed regulations could be published in the *Federal Register* for congressional and public comment. OMB reportedly examined the proposed regulations not only for financial impact but also for policy agreement with the president.

The Success of the President's Strategy

The president's strategy to take over the bureaucracy was remarkably successful. Although some agencies fought the cuts and program terminations, most did not. The president's appointees generally remained loyal to him, while civil servants bemoaned their failure to win over their political appointees. The appointees, and the career staff they selected to support them, defended the administration's cuts to a puzzled and occasionally frustrated Congress.

Members of Congress had a difficult time getting administrators to document the damage that was being done by personnel and budget cuts or even to tell them when a Reduction in Force was pending. The following excerpt from a congressional hearing illustrates the frustration some Congressmen were feeling.

Mr. Hoyer: [a Congressman from Maryland] What I am getting at, Mr. Kincannon, is that one of the problems some of us see in the budget process in 1981 is that the consequences of the adoption of the budget were unknown to most people . . . what I am trying to discover, therefore, was there any basis upon which the Congress or the administration could expect the RIF's that subsequently occurred to have occurred, as a result of communication from your agency?[12]

In short, Congressman Hoyer wanted to know why the agency had not told Congress that the cuts would require reductions in force.

Though the president's strategy to take increased control of the agencies was certainly successful, it was not without costs. Individual officials got caught between the president and Congress, agencies were internally polarized, and there was occasional sniping from inside the bureaucracy.

Political appointees were loyal to the president, even in the face of hostile questioning by members of Congress. But some of the upper-level career officials who tried to follow the president's instructions were torn if Congress did not go along. Sensitive to pressures from both sides, they had to find a way to carry out the law made by Congress while trying to obey the president's orders.

Agencies, like individuals, were sometimes split internally. Policy decisions were taken away from many program-oriented career officials and given to a politically loyal cadre at the top, who made the cutback and reorganization decisions and often ordered reductions in force. Consequently, this policy-making group earned the dislike or distrust of many of the career officials, especially those who were more loyal to their programs than to the president's policy directives.

This increased polarization inside the agencies sometimes encouraged officials who were not part of the decision-making elite to anonymously complain to the inspectors general and the press about misuse of funds by the political appointees. These complaints did not affect policy decisions, but they did sometimes bring down particular officials and embarrass the administration, which was trying to collect credit for a campaign against waste, fraud, and abuse.

To summarize, opposition from agencies to their own cutback and termination is a natural obstacle to implementation of the president's program, and lack of firm executive control over agencies could have made it more severe. But the administration was able to take effective control of the agencies. Part of the reason was that there are bureaucrats in top policy positions who are very sensitive to presidential policy. In addition, there was a blueprint for taking control over the bureaucracy which President Reagan followed. There was some reaction to the president's increased control, but it was usually not sufficient to thwart implementation of his policy.

CAN THE PRESIDENT CONTROL CONGRESS?

The Statement of the Problem

The reason Congress poses a potential threat to the implementation of the President's cutback policy is that Congress basically controls both appropriations (which determine how much money will be spent on a program in a given period) and program authorizations (which control eligibility for federal funding and/or total spending ceilings for each program). In recent years, Congress has been unwilling to cut the budget on its own initiative, yet it has also been reluctant to give up its perogatives to control budget levels. Thus if Congress does not go along with presidential initiatives to cut back budgets and rewrite legislation, a real stalemate can occur.

The Seriousness of the Problem

How serious this potential problem is depends on two factors, First, does Congress have reason to disagree with the president? If not, the problem is only theoretical and not politically serious. Second, does the president have enough formal and informal power over Congress to make or persuade Congress to go along? If so, the greater the president's power, the less important the problem.

Reasons for Congress to Disagree with the President's Policy

President Reagan came to office on a wave of popular support for his programs. It is reasonable to expect that Congress, which is an elective body, would also reflect the same voter sentiments and that there would be little disagreement between the President and Congress over enacting cutback proposals, tax breaks, and reduced regulations. Popular support for the president's cutback plan was seen as so strong that members of Congress were reportedly afraid to voice opposition to the plan, let alone go on record as voting against it. If that was indeed the case, why need we be concerned about possible opposition from Congress and how that opposition might have structured the cutback process?

Though most members of Congress could agree that deficits were too high and that some program cutback was called for, there was no overall agreement on what should be cut. There was disagreement on the president's plan to increase spending on the military while cutting back social services and on the wisdom of providing a tax cut while trying to pare back the size of the deficits. The president could not count on party loyalty to support him in the House because of its Democratic majority.

Congress had reasons other than party ideology to oppose some presidential proposals. For example, members of Congress often feel a loyalty to programs that they have introduced, voted for, and helped to implement over the years. That loyalty is likely to spark opposition to program cuts, especially if they are cuts that reduce the ability of the program to achieve its legislatively mandated goals. Congress will also defend programs that have broad popular support, especially if members are receiving a lot of pressure from constituents concerning the program.

Some of the programs that members of Congress feel loyalty to are ones that reflect their own beliefs or the interests of their constituents. Others are "pork barrel" programs, which allocate jobs and projects to their congressional districts and thus help them gain reelection. Members of Congress, both Democrat and Republican, can be expected to fight fiercely to maintain these programs.

In short, Congress had a number of reasons to oppose various portions of the president's plans, but the opposition was important only to the degree that the president lacked the ability to force or persuade Congress to do what he wanted.

The President's Influence over Congress

The president, through the Office of Management and Budget, submits a complex budget proposal to Congress. Congressional committees can accept or reject the president's assumptions and targets and can change his recommended budget levels on a program-by-program basis. If the president does not like the budget as finally passed by Congress, he can veto the appropriations bills. Because Congress usually cannot muster enough votes to overturn a veto, the threat of a veto can keep it from passing too large a budget.

The president does not have a "line-item" veto—that is, he cannot disapprove a single item of the budget and approve the rest; he was to approve or disapprove in total each appropriations bill that passes Congress. To reduce the president's use of the veto, Congress often creates a situation that makes it difficult to veto the whole bill. That means either putting into the appropriations bills money for projects that the president wants or not passing a budget at all. Instead of passing a budget, Congress sometimes passes continuing resolutions, which keep the government running without formal appropriations. If the president vetoes a continuing resolution, the government shuts down for lack of money.

In addition to exerting his formal powers over the Congress, the president may also use his informal power to persuade Congress to go along with him. Certainly President Reagan's informal control over Congress was enormous following his 1980 election victory. However, this kind of informal power can come and go with the popularity of the president. The congressional elections of 1982, though not overwhelming in their rejection of the president, provided some Democratic gains, enough to show that opponents to the president could still get elected. After 1982, the president lost much of his informal support in Congress, and it became more difficult to cut back programs.

The president has considerable influence over the budget, but he cannot selectively reduce a program's funding if Congress raises the appropriation above what he requests. Rescissions and deferrals are more effective techniques for cutting back the level of congressional appropriations for particular programs, but requests for these have to be submitted to and approved by Congress. If Congress is committed to higher funding levels on a particular program, presumably it will reject the president's requests for deferrals and rescissions. In that case, he has little formal recourse but to keep vetoing money bills or continuing resolutions and risk closing down the government for lack of funds.

President Reagan had to rely on congressional supporters to introduce his specific cuts in Congress, and then he had to use his informal support in

Congress to get his version of cuts passed. As the president's informal support in Congress declined, his ability to dictate cuts also decreased.

The President's Strategy

Given the motivation of Congress to defy the president in his choice of agencies to cut and the limited presidential power to coerce Congress on budget reduction issues, President Reagan devised a strategy that pressed Congress for cuts while using whatever powers he could, independent of Congress.

Pressuring Congress

The president used a number of tactics to pressure Congress, including packaging the cuts in such a way that Congress found it difficult to break into the package to change the parts inside, pacing events at such a speed that Congress had little chance to evaluate what was being cut or with what effect, submitting proposals for rescissions and deferrals, and vetoing and threatening to veto congressional appropriations and continuing resolutions. To understand the success of this strategy requires a fairly detailed knowledge of how the congressional budget process—particularly the "reconciliation process"—works.

Since 1974, responsibility for the budget process in Congress has been divided among four committees or groups of committees. There are revenue committees that decide on tax proposals, authorizing committees that design programs and put ceilings on program costs, appropriations committees that decide how much should be spent on programs each year, and budget committees in both the House and the Senate whose responsibility it is to coordinate the work of the other three groups. More specifically, the budget committee's job is to coordinate the efforts of the revenue and spending committees so that the budget is balanced. To do this, the budget committees set spending and revenue targets. These proposed spending and taxing targets are called "budget resolutions" and must be passed by each house. In fact, Congress collectively passes not one, but two budget resolutions each year, one at the beginning of the budget process, when the economic forecasts are unclear, and a second one in the fall, just before the beginning of the new fiscal year. The budget resolutions guide and limit both the tax proposals and the spending bills that fund the federal government.[13]

The question that occurs in the administration of this system is whether the budget committees have enough power over the other committees to bring about budget cuts. There is no apparent friction in the system as long as the budget committees set targets in accordance with the known spending and taxing desires of the other committees, but real difficulty can arise if the budget committees set targets cuts that the other committees do not want to observe.

There was a provision in the 1974 Congressional Budget and Impoundment Control Act (which specifies the congressional budget process) that gives the budget committees some leverage in imposing spending and taxing targets on the other committees. That feature was "reconciliation," which denotes the process of getting two sets of figures to agree with each other. In this case, it means getting the other three sets of committees to agree with the budget committee's targets.

In a reconciliation, the budget committees give instructions to the other committees to stay within certain spending and taxing limits. The committees are free to figure out how to cut or change programs or alter taxes to stay within the targets. Once the taxing, authorizing, and appropriating committees have figured out how they want to comply with the instructions, they make proposals to the budget committees. The budget committees put these proposals together to create an "omnibus reconciliation" and present the measures to the floor of each house for a vote. If it passes both houses (and both houses can agree on one measure), the omnibus reconciliation then informs the spending and taxing bills. President Reagan used this reconciliation procedure to get his budget cuts through Congress.[14]

When the president submitted his proposed budget to Congress in March 1981, congressional committees of each house soon had their proposals for the first budget resolution. The president was satisfied with the Senate's proposed resolution but reportedly found the House Budget Committee's proposal too high. When the House committee reported the resolution to the floor of the House, two committee members, Phil Gramm and Delbert Latta, introduced the president's preferred resolution as an amendment, and the House chose the Gramm-Latta version.[15]

The budget resolution contained reconciliation instructions. With some difficulty, the committees carried out their instructions and presented the results to the budget committee. That committee combined the proposals into an omnibus reconciliation and reported the measure to the floor of the House for a vote. The reconciliation provided even deeper program cuts than the president had requested, but they were not of the exact composition he had asked for. Congressmen Gramm and Latta again introduced a substitute measure, and again the House passed the amended version.

The president's strategy to induce Congress to cut the budget in accordance with his priorities involved the substitution of the Gramm-Latta amendment for the committee version of the 1981 omnibus reconciliation. Since an omnibus reconciliation has to be voted on as one measure rather than several separable proposals, the president, by substituting his own version, forced Congress to vote his package up or down without reacting separately to the pieces inside. Had they considered the proposals separately the representatives probably would have rejected some of them. But given the president's popularity at the time the measure was being passed, most were reluctant to vote down the whole package.

A second advantage of the Gramm-Latta amendment (from the president's perspective) was that it was written and passed so quickly that many representatives did not know what they had voted to cut. The normal deliberative processes of Congress were bypassed.[16] It is unlikely that the amendment would have been passed with such speed if the president had been less popular at that time.

Another part of the president's strategy was to push for program rescissions and deferrals. At first these proposals were accepted by Congress, but later they were rejected. When that began to occur, the president initially persisted in requesting rescissions and deferrals. On the one hand, he changed the package of programs for which he proposed rescissions and deferrals, hoping to persuade Congress to go along by withdrawing the proposals he believed it would not approve. On the other hand, he used some unintended flexibility in the law to achieve unilateral cuts and delays in spending.

There were two ways that the president used the rescission and deferral requests in spite of congressional opposition. First, even if Congress eventually denied his request, he could normally withhold funds from the agencies while the impoundments were pending, often for a lengthy period. Congress was supposed to act on rescissions within forty-five days in which Congress is in session, but it often failed to act within that time. In 1982, many agencies were denied the use of millions of dollars from 8 February to 23 April, a period of two and half months, while Congress considered the measure. Second, if the president submitted the request for deferral or rescission toward the end of the fiscal year, Congress often did not have time to examine and act on the proposal; thus it became a de facto deferral.

By 1983, to make peace with Congress, the president gave in and promised to keep his rescission and deferral requests to a minimum in the 1984 budget request.

In addition to the reconciliation and rescissions and deferrals, the president used the power and threat of the veto to try to keep Congress in line. Especially after he had used reconciliation and it was clear that Congress did not want to use it again, the president threatened to veto any budget that was too high and did in fact veto one continuing resolution, closing down the government for a day.

Using Powers Independent of Congress

Besides putting direct pressure on Congress to produce cuts, the president did what he could without congressional concurrence. Since he had greater autonomy over staffing levels than over the budget, he focused on reducing these; and since he had wide autonomy over internal reorganizations of the departments and independent agencies, he also used that power extensively.

Staffing Levels. The president can control staffing levels in several ways. First, he can declare a general hiring freeze and not allow agencies to fill vacancies as they occur. Second, he can reduce personnel ceilings, which are allocated to each agency based on its workload. Third, he can use the reduction-in-force procedure to lay off employees. President Reagan used all three of these techniques.

The president declared a hiring freeze as soon as he took office. It was across the board, affecting all agencies, and it was based on attrition. Whatever agencies had vacancies were forced to absorb the personnel reductions. This technique was clearly not cost effective, since revenue producers were cut back at the same time as revenue spenders. The president dropped the freeze within a few months of taking office in favor of reduced personnel ceilings allocated to the agencies.[17]

Personnel ceilings are allocated to agencies as a way of preventing them from hiring too many people. Ceilings are a managerial control device to link staffing levels to program size and managerial complexity. If agency budgets are cut back or programs simplified, reducing the work level, then personnel ceilings should be reduced accordingly.

Personnel ceilings reductions were not considered an acceptable reason to lay off staff under the reduction-in-force regulations in effect until the fall of 1983.[18] A real budget reduction for a lack of work could provoke both a ceiling reduction and a reduction in force, but budget and program changes had to be passed by Congress. The personnel ceilings were supposed to implement those congressional changes.

The Office of Management and Budget sets the personnel ceilings, allocating positions to each agency in accordance with the administration's budget *request* and *proposed* changes in legislation and management. If the proposed changes are not passed by Congress, the personnel ceiling allocations should be revised accordingly. The procedure normally provokes no controversy except when the administration tries to use personnel ceilings as a tool to defy congressional intent rather than to implement control of staffing levels implicit in congressional mandates.

Nevertheless, it is clear that the administration did use personnel ceilings as a way of reducing staffing independent of congressional intent. Personnal ceilings were sometimes reduced independent of budget reductions. For example, the president announced on several occasions targets for the reduction in the level of staffing over a several-year period. These targets, such as seventy-five thousand civilian positions over two years, were then allocated to the departments and independent agencies as personnel ceilings.[19]

Since personnel ceilings independent of budget cuts and reduced workloads were not supposed to provoke reductions in force, the implementation of the ceiling reductions was tricky. In part, they were to be accomplished by freezes on hiring inside the agencies. Indirect evidence suggests that reductions in force *were* used to carry out reductions in personnel ceilings. There is no possible budgetary saving (in a given fiscal year) from a reduction in force that takes place toward the end of that year, but there is a reason to carry out a reduction in force at the end of the year if the goal is to come under personnel ceilings. There were a number of reductions in force planned in May or June, for the end of the fiscal year. (Some of these late reductions in force are documented in the case studies presented later in this book.)

The third technique for reducing staffing levels (besides freezes and ceilings) was the reduction in force. This technique was intended explicitly to reduce staffing levels, but it was to be used under circumscribed conditions. It was designed to allow staffing reductions if budgets were cut or programs reorganized, or if the amount of work was reduced. This procedure was controversial because the administration could use it to reduce the work force below the level necessary to carry out congressionally mandated programs, thereby producing friction between Congress and the president.

As with reduced personnel ceilings, it is quite clear that reductions in force were used as a way of getting around congressional opposition to program cuts. They were often planned before the congressional level of funding was known. As mentioned earlier, the president reduced the staffing levels in several regulatory agencies, while budget levels remained stable. There were also extensive personnel reductions in the Department of Education, of nearly one-third from 1980 to 1983, while budgets remained fairly stable despite the efforts of the administration to cut the budget severely.[20]

Reorganizations.   In addition to personnel ceilings and related personnel policies, the administration also relied heavily on reorganizations. These were sometimes used as a way of taking control over agencies and making them more responsive to the president's policy guidance. Some of the reorganizations reflected both decentralization (reducing the central office functions) and efforts to reduce the influence of interest groups on a particular program. Thus they were an important element in the president's effort to carry out his broader objectives.

Congress has the power to accept or reject major reorganizations, such as the creation or dissolution of departments, and it used that power to block the administration's proposals to eliminate the Departments of Education and Energy. But it had delegated broad power over internal structure to the secretaries.[21] The functions of subordinate offices, employees, and agencies were transferred to the secretaries, who were authorized to redelegate those functions at will. They could freely transfer records, property, personnel, and funds within their departments. Thus the administration had broad control over reorganization and used that power extensively.

To summarize, the president's strategy in dealing with Congress was twofold. First, he pressed Congress for cuts by packaging cutback proposals, pushing proposals quickly, doggedly proposing rescissions and deferrals, and constantly using (or threatening to use) the veto power. He used his persuasive powers to lobby individual members of Congress. The second part of his strategy was to bypass Congress, relying on hiring freezes, personnel ceiling reductions, reductions in force, and reorganizations.

The Success of the President's Strategy

With respect to the budget, the president first tried rescissions and deferrals, which Congress initially approved. Later, however, when the president requested rescissions and deferrals in the middle of 1982, Congress refused the bulk of them. It went along with the president's cuts in the omnibus reconciliation of 1981 but thereafter never gave him all the cuts he asked for.

Congress controlled the power of the purse, and its refusal to cut program levels in accordance with the president's desires was binding, but when the president chose to focus on nonbudgetary cutback issues, then he had more power and Congress had less. Despite some congressional attempts to fight back, the president was generally able to do what he wished in the area of personnel and reorganization. It is worth noting, however, that these were not areas in which major amounts of money could be saved.

Because of the possibility that the administration was trying to destroy the agencies or reduce their ability to carry out congressionally mandated tasks, several members of Congress and congressional committees tried to stop or control the reorganizations and reductions in force occurring in the agencies. Individual members of Congress and congressional committees responded to personnel reductions and reorganizations in a number of ways, most of them rather ineffective. Some committees asked for information about the causes, effects, and costs of these measures, and others tried to take some control over staffing levels and reorganizations.

Information Gathering

Members of Congress had several techniques for collecting information about what was happening to the agencies. They often wrote to the agency heads, asking for documents and reports. Sometimes they held hearings on reductions in force and reorganizations in particular agencies, and occasionally they sent in their own staff to do a study or commissioned the General Accounting Office to investigate an agency or a presidential tactic.

Most (but not all) of the interest in investigating the administration of cutback came from two congressional groups, the House Committee on Post Office and Civil Service and a task force of congressmen interested in how the reduction-in-force legislation was being enforced. This latter group was composed primarily of members of Congress who had a large voting constituency of civil servants in their districts. Headed by Congressman Barnes of Maryland (where many civil servants live), they were the elected representatives of the civil servants.

The members of Congress who sought information on reductions in force and reorganizations were seeking instances of violation of the law that they could use to stop the administration from cutting back personnel—instances in which either the agencies were no longer able to carry out congressionally mandated tasks or the President had overstepped his bounds and usurped congressional autonomy. If in the process they found other kinds of irregularities that they could use, so much the better.

The fact-finding techniques harassed the agency heads but did not have much effect on the administration's tactics. Agency heads answered letters and questions in hearings in ways that were impossible to refute without total access to decisions and calculations that had been made months earlier. Even the General Accounting Office, which sent teams of researchers to the sites of several agencies to study the cutback process, generally returned the administration a clean bill of health. Nothing obviously illegal was happening. (The GAO did report possible illegalities at the Department of Housing and Urban Development, but events later proved that suspicion wrong.)[22]

The General Accounting Office did manage to embarrass the administration and give Congress some small victories. For example, the GAO found that the president's freeze on personnel hiring was inefficient because it was across the board, and illegal because it violated staffing levels which had been written into the law for veterans hospitals and clinics. Later, when the president tried to defer the savings from the reduction in personnel in the veterans hospitals and clinics, Congress denied the deferral. The General Accounting Office also embarrassed the administration by pointing out that the Office of Management and Budget had grossly overestimated the financial savings to be achieved by reductions in staffing levels, particularly because of the expense of reductions in force.[23]

Direct Efforts to Block or Control the Administration

Several committees tried more direct ways to control reorganizations and reductions in force. The House Committee on Public Works, which is the authorizing committee for the Urban Mass Transportation Administration, required the agency to inform it of any pending reorganizations. The agency conformed with the requirement but in a way that precluded any input from Congress. Committee members were frustrated by being excluded but had no way to punish the agency.

The appropriations committees for the Department of Housing and Urban Development in both houses of Congress tried a different tactic. They wrote into the appropriation for the department that the money could not be spent on reorganizations until 1 January 1983 *without prior committee approval*.[24] The department was careful to observe the restriction, but it carried out a reduction in force, claiming that no reorganizations was involved and that the "prior committee approval" clause was illegal anyway.[25] The courts later proved the department correct.

The House Public Works Committee tried still a third tactic. It sent committee staff out to explore agency management and look for violations of the law and other potential scandals. By holding well-publicized hearings on these violations when they found them, committee members could both bring down individual agency administrators who were destroying their agencies and embarrass the administration. This committee contributed to the forced resignation of Anne Gorsuch Burford, director of the Environmental Protection Agency, and brought down Carlos Campbell, the head of the Economic Development Administration. However, forcing the resignation of the agency heads was a limited tool and did not guarantee that the next appointee would be more responsive to congressional desires. Presumably, however, these firings would send a message to other administrators that they were not responsible only to the president.

Congressional committees that felt the administration was destroying agencies through the cutback process generally had little recourse. Their major sanction over agencies was to cut back budgets, and that sanction was rendered meaningless, since they wanted to maintain the program and the administration wanted to cut it back.

To summarize, potential opposition from Congress presented a formidable obstacle to the president as he carried out his program, but this hindrance was much more severe in budgetary than in administrative matters. The president's election success helped influence Congress in budgetary matters for roughly the first eight months of his administration, but after that, it began to respond to presidential pressures with countermeasures. Many of these were unsuccessful, but Congress exerted increasing resistance to cuts, and the president gradually yielded to this pressure. Congressional countermeasures to the president's personnel reductions and reorganizations were more sporadic and less effective. In this area, the president was able to do pretty much as he chose, despite occasional harassment from Congress and its investigatory branch, the General Accounting Office.

DO INTEREST GROUPS DETERMINE POLITICAL OUTCOMES?

The Statement of the Problem

Interest groups are organizations that represent individuals or agencies who have common interests and have agreed to pursue those interests by pressuring government. Some governmental agencies have a number of different interest groups, including clients, grant recipients, professional societies, community organizations, business groups, associations of state officials, and labor unions. Sometimes their own employees join groups to lobby for increased job security or better pay. Those who stand to benefit by government programs often lobby Congress to create such programs, and later they are likely to stand by the programs if they are threatened with termination. Organizations of employees will presumably try to protect their jobs and resist cutbacks in personnel levels.

As Herb Kaufman put it, "whether an agency provides services for its clients or regulates them, its clientele can frequently be counted on to come to its assistance when it is trouble. At the very least, even if its clients are critical of the agency they may oppose efforts to terminate it.... Automatically, therefore, a beleaguered agency will ordinarily be joined in its struggles by its clients."[26]

Clients are not the only organized interest group to take a stand on retrenchment and termination issues. Kaufman notes, "Another set of external allies is the professional or trade association with which the dominant occupational group to be found in almost every bureau is identified. Doctors, lawyers, engineers ... and many other specialists are particularly influential in one agency or another.... When "their" respective agencies are menaced, they mobilize to defend them."[27]

Unlike the agencies and Congress, interest groups have no formal status or power. They generally gain influence by lobbying Congress. When dealing with Congress, they normally choose the committees that authorize and fund the agencies and programs of concern to them. They provide these committees information; sometimes they even draw up model legislation and ask congresspersons to introduce the bill as their own. They inform committee members when proposed legislation affects their group adversely and can usually mount extensive letter writing and telephone campaigns. Sometimes they help candidates get elected to office, making contributions to campaign funds.

Interest groups also gain influence by developing close ties with agency officials in programs they are interested in. These officials tell them about pending program changes and perhaps discuss proposed regulations with them. The agencies can expect their interest groups to argue for them in Congress if their budgets or programs are threatened.

The Seriousness of the Problem

The ability of interest groups to successfully defend their programs differs considerably from program to program. Not all interest groups have connections with both Congress and the agencies, and those without this dual connections are less able to fight cuts. Not all interest groups are strong, well organized, and easily roused to support programs, but many of those supporting programs targeted by the administration for cutback or termination were powerful and provided strong opposition to the president.

The *Congressional Quarterly Weekly*, a journal that watches the political activity on Capitol Hill, concluded in the middle of July 1981, that "self styled fiscal conservatives, watched over by a determined President and playing by novel budget rules" had made Capitol Hill treacherous terrain for formerly untouchable programs.[28] That meant that many programs protected by powerful interest groups could no longer take congressional support for granted. The article went on to say, however, that broad constituency support still offered an effective shield against cuts.

If an interest group represented a broad constituency, or if a group of interest groups could form a coalition and give the impression that they represented a broad constituency, both the president and Congress were likely to be impressed. Under these circumstances, interest group opposition was indeed a formidable obstacle to cutback.

Internal groups, such as organized employees, posed a much smaller threat. The unions showed themselves to be relatively powerless to stop reductions in force in the agencies. Although they played an important information and gadfly role inside the agencies and may also have been instrumental in keeping the cutback process honest, they did not have the power to oppose the administration. Even when they sought allies on Capitol Hill, they were not very effective in stopping reductions in force. While successful interest groups attracted the attention and support of major congressional committees, the unions attracted only particular members of Congress who were sympathetic to labor or to the civil service.

The interests of the employees collectively should also have been represented by the civil service in the area of job security. It has been the responsibility of two agencies, the Office of Personnel Management and the Merit Systems Protection Board, to oversee the implementation of the civil regulations and ensure that civil servants are not fired for political reasons. The elaborate reduction-in-force regulations were designed with that end in mind. But the regulations did not prevent actual reductions, and the Office of Personnel Management and the Merit Systems Protection Board did not act as defenders of the employees.

To summarize, interest groups were certainly not uniformly powerful. Some agencies had no interest groups or weak interest group support, and employees presented no major problems to cutbacks. But the problem was acute in some agencies which the president was determined to cut back, and which were defended by powerful, easily activated interest groups.

The President's Strategy

The administration's strategy for dealing with interest groups was divided into two parts. The first contained tactics for *getting around* interest group opposition to budget cuts; the second embodied ways of gradually *reducing the influence* of the groups.

Getting around Interest Groups

There are some suggestions in the literature on how to get around interest group opposition if you are going to terminate a program. One author suggests, for example, cutting programs or terminating them quickly, giving interest groups no time to organize and rally. He also suggests wrapping narrow issues of appeal to interest groups into broader packages so that others may be attracted to the proposal. He advises program terminators to try to attract a clientele for the program's termination, a counter–interest group. Finally, he suggests that officials who want to cut back programs should take advantage of broad ideological sweeps.[29]

President Reagan adopted many of these techniques. He certainly took advantage of a broad ideological sweep, as described in Chapter 1. He moved very quickly, so quickly that not only did interest groups not have time to mobilize, but many members of Congress reportedly did not know what they had cut when they voted for the Gramm-Latta amendment in 1981. The president successfully wrapped up termination of programs in broader ideological issues, such as reduced inflation, lower taxes, and reduced regulation, thus creating a counter–interest group for cutback.

The omnibus reconciliation of 1981 was successful precisely because it bypassed interest groups. The reconciliation process itself was helpful because it wrapped up a number of proposed cuts into one package that had to be voted up or down. The voice of an individual interest group, could it have figured out what was happening in time to protest, would have been swallowed up in the whole package. Moreover, because the Gramm-Latta amendments bypassed the work of the committees, who had established long-term understandings with particular interest groups, they also bypassed the interest groups.

Weakening Interest Groups

Simultaneously with trying to bypass interest groups, the administration engaged in a series of tactics to try to weaken them. For example, it tried to undermine their connections with agencies. In most cases, the president chose appointees who were willing to cut back or terminate the agency programs and therefore had no desire to try to rouse interest groups to fight for them. In one extreme case, James Watt, who was President Reagan's Secretary of the Interior, forbade any agency contact with interest groups. There was also a government-wide pressure to reduce leaks of all sorts.[30]

The president also adopted some other tactics to help him deal with interest groups. He proposed both reorganizations and reauthorizations that would weaken interest group control. For example, when the Urban Mass Transportation program was reauthorized in 1982, the new law made it more difficult to sort out how much money was being authorized for various functions. It was thus more difficult for interest groups to argue that the administration was killing programs. Without a clear program termination, it is more difficult to mobilize interest groups to protect the program.

As categorical grants were changed into block grants which gave state and local governments more discretion over spending, the funding for these grants was systematically reduced. To any interest group protesting the reduction in funding, the administration argued that if a program had high priority, the local government could put more money into that program. This argument shifted the blame to state and local governments. This tactic seems to have been particularly successful in the social services area, where a number of block grants were adopted.

The whole decentralization thrust of the New Federalism also had the effect of weakening interest-group pressures on the federal budget. It is relatively easy to maintain one lobbyist in Washington D.C. and maintain a visible presence, but it is much more difficult to maintain lobbyists in fifty states.

The administration also attempted to weaken interest groups by pitting one group against another. One such instance occurred in the proposed block grant for education of students with special needs. Because the proposed grant included both disadvantaged and handicapped students, it would not only reduce the number of grants, each with a separate interest group supporting it, but also pit two important interest groups against each other as they competed for limited funds in the same grant pool.[31]

The Success of the President's Strategy

The more powerful and better-organized interest groups responded to the administration's pressures with determination to fight back. They fought the administration on funding levels for the 1983 and 1984 budget and won, restoring funding or stabilizing it in the face of administration pressures for program termination.

In the example cited above, concerning a proposed education block grant, interest groups reportedly blocked the grant. The "proposal was greeted with what one department official described as a 'firestorm of protest,' in part because advocates saw it as an effort to pit interest groups against one another."[32]

Despite administration attempts to discourage contact with interest groups, the groups generally maintained contacts with the agencies, although not necessarily with top-level officials. There were officials in many agencies who disagreed with what was happening to their programs and were willing to provide information to the interest groups. Reductions in force reinforced the information flow as many program loyalists found themselves unemployed and then found new jobs in the interest groups, where they could continue to fight for their programs.

The interest-group strategy focused on funding levels, on key allocational decisions (such as the level of targeting funds for the poor), and on maintaining or attacking regulations that served their interests. They were not concerned with maintaining the level of staffing in the agencies or preventing continuing reorganizations.

If the major interest groups composed of those outside the agency who benefited from its programs had no interest in maintaining staffing levels or protecting employees' jobs, the unions and other representatives of federal employees certainly had such an interest. Many agencies were unionized, although the number of professionals represented in the unions varied from local to local. The union locals usually had a branch in each department as well as representatives in each program and supported the whole operation with a central staff in Washington. Individual union members set up relationships with sympathetic members of Congress, and the national union office helped provide technical and legal assistance.

The level of activity of each union local depended a great deal on the recent history of the agency and the inherited distrust of the agency's administration. In some agencies, where there was a history of cooperation with unions, it took some time for the unions to develop a more militant stance. In other agencies, political abuses of the civil service system were still in the minds of some employees and fed into a militant and well organized union, which was ready to act to defend employees. The personality of the head of the union local also affected the activity levels.

The unions' main achievement was to encourage employees to file grievances concerning reductions in force and furloughs (forced, unpaid leaves). Although individuals could file such grievances on their own, the unions encouraged the filing and helped employees fill out forms and figure out grounds for appeals. They also helped the employees through hearings. In doing so, the unions certainly both annoyed the agencies' managers and increased the cost of reductions in force and furloughs. In general, however, organized employees were not very successful in protecting employees.

Since Congress was unable to exert much influence over the administration in the area of personnel, and employee organizations were not very effective in protecting employees from administration policies aimed against them, the administration had broad latitude in the area of personnel management.

CAN THE MANAGEMENT OF FEDERAL AGENCIES BE IMPROVED?

The Statement of the Problem

Poor management was not just a problem like a weak economy that the Reagan administration could blame on its predecessors and try to fix; it was a preexisting problem made worse by the implementation of the president's cutback program. The quality of management was affected by both the achievement of the other goals in the president's program and the tools available to do the job.

Managing any large and complex organization well is difficult, and the federal government is larger and more complex than most. These normal difficulties have been exacerbated in recent years by understaffing and reorganizations. "Despite much political rhetoric to the contrary, the total number of federal employees has remained constant for a decade and a half in the face of a virtual doubling of the number and scope of federal programs and a quadrupling of federal expenditures...."[33] The result has been a lack of adequate supervision of programs and, at times, virtual ignorance of what is going on in the field. In addition to understaffing, many federal agencies have been plagued by constant reorganizations, which result in a different form of mismanagement. "Reorganizations do produce significant employee demoralization and cynicism while bringing the work of the agency or unit to a near halt, sometimes for months."[34] The problems of both understaffing and reorganizations are made worse by cutback, which reduces staffing levels further and stimulates a new round of reorganizations.

Not only does cutback make preexisting problems worse, but it creates managerial problems of its own, regardless of how good or bad management was before. It introduces a new level of uncertainty; eliminates the incentives to keep good workers; encourages good managers to leave, creating a leadership that has little knowledge of the organization or its potential; and tends to create poor morale and lower productivity.[35] These problems are made worse when the issue is threat of termination rather than threat of budget cutback. When termination seems likely, morale tends to dissolve, everyone is threatened by the likelihood of unemployment, and there is little incentive to improve the quality of management.

The Seriousness of the Problem

Managing budget and program cutback is intrinsically difficult and likely to disrupt programs and reduce productivity. However, during the Reagan administration, these problems were made more severe by the other goals of the administration, three of which affected the quality of management negatively.

The president sought to decentralize programs to the states, which increased the number of actors and fragmented authority further. Not only did the shift create initial confusion, but it made it more difficult to supervise expenditures and see that they were in accordance with the law. It is much easier to prevent waste, fraud, and abuse when a single organization has total responsibility for a program.[36]

Second, the president's goal of deregulation led to simplification of grant application processes. Simplified procedures, combined with reduced eligibility requirements for funding, mean less thorough examination of proposed projects for suitability and conformity with the law. The result is likely to be an increase in the amount of money spent on inappropriate projects, and hence an increase in waste.

Third, the President's continuing goal of reducing the number of nonmilitary employees is likely to exacerbate the problems of lack of supervision concerning how federal money is spent.

In addition to these three goals, other presidential strategies and tools had negative effects on agency management. For example, the president's use of rescissions and deferrals and threats of budget vetoes led to a situation in which budget levels changed with great frequency during the year; many agencies had little idea how much money they could spend from one month to the next. The increased levels of uncertainty affected the quality of decision making in some agencies.

A second example of how the president's strategy affected the quality of management was his effort to take control over agencies through reorganizations and reductions in force. The result was initial confusion and a more long-term schism between career personnel and the political levels of the agency. The schism negatively affected the morale of those upper-level officials who were excluded from the policy process and reduced the amount of information available to the political levels in their decision making.

A third example of how cutback strategy affected agency management was the choice of reductions in force rather than attrition as a tool for reducing staffing levels. Reductions in force are controlled by Civil Service Regulations, which are written and monitored by the Office of Personnel Management. At least through November 1983, the process was complicated, cumbersome, and somewhat unpredictable in its outcomes. It was costly to use and hard to target on particular individuals, and it reduced productivity. In addition, the procedures had a built-in bias against women and minorities.

The regulations required that reduction in force begin with the selection of positions (not persons) to eliminate. The occupants of these positions were then temporarily without a job, although they may have had rights to jobs already occupied by other persons. Rights to occupied positions were determined by a series of rules, which resulted in an overall retention status. Generally speaking, those with a higher retention status "bump," or replace, those with a lower retention status. However, one person could replace another with a lower status only if the new job required skills similar to those he or she had performed in the previous job. Ultimately, someone would be released from a position and have no one to bump. Unless that person also had "retreat rights"—that is, unless he or she could return to a formerly held position—he or she would probably be forced to leave the organization. Thus the people out the door were not necessarily the people whose position were initially eliminated. For each position eliminated, a number of people could be negatively affected through federal transfer, demotion, or termination of employment.

Under the regulations in effect during 1981 and 1982, retention status depended on four factors: career tenure, seniority, military experience, and performance evaluation. Career tenure is the status an employee has after having served a probationary period and become a career civil servant. Probationary personnel were let go before career civil servants. Nonveterans were let go before veterans. Those with less seniority would be let go before those with more seniority. Performance evaluations could add several years of seniority if a person had a rating of "outstanding." Performance was thus the least powerful determinant of retention status. If the reduction-in-force procedures were rigorously followed, they were unlikely to weed out the incompetent or protect the productive.

Overall, reductions in force create managerial nightmares. Not only is much time and effort involved in determining retention rights, calculating severance pay for separated employees, and tracing through the bumping and retreat rights of each affected employee (many agencies did this process by hand), but once the reduction is over, many employees are left in new positions. Old work teams are broken up, people have new bosses, and some people are demoted to positions they formerly held but for which their skills are rusty.

To add to the work and confusion created by the reduction in force itself, there is often a period before and after the reduction that is characterized by its own brand of preparation and recovery. The period before is often characterized by high rates of attrition (people leave as they get new jobs). The period after is usually characterized by informal trading and loaning of personnel and more formal detailing (loaning between units) of personnel back to their old jobs, temporarily or for an indefinite time. According to the regulations, if a person is not traded back to his or her old job, he or she can take up to ninety days to learn the new job. In short, the obstacles posed to good management by the side effects of cutback processes were formidable.

The President's Strategy

The president's strategy to improve management as part of the cutback program was aimed partly at techniques to save money and partly at reducing the worst of the side effects of the cutback process. The plan to save money had to do with improved techniques for handling money and new methods of reducing fraud. In addition to relying on the inspector general system for detecting fraud and abuse, the president called for more computer equipment and better data bases to check applicants for aid for program eligibility. He argued in the 1984 budget proposal that the administration had gone as far as it could go with outdated equipment and methods. The president also emphasized 1) new procedures for handling cash flow that would get money deposited more quickly and would therefore reduce the amount of borrowing required; 2) collecting bad debts owed to the government, even if that meant selling the loans or turning them over to professional collection agency; and 3) revamping the procurement system.[37]

To ameliorate the negative effects of deregulation on fiscal control, the administration sought to uncover fraud through high-level audits. Its response to weakened requirements for obtaining federal grants was to hold out the threat of a federal audit. The simplified application procedures were in effect long before new audit procedures were worked out, however, leaving grant recipients uncertain as to the basis of a later audit. Nor did the general audit strategy speak to the difficulty of recovering misspent funds.

The major action taken by the administration to lessen the negative managerial impact of cutback was the issuance of a new set of regulations for the reduction-in-force process. After a lengthy battle, the Office of Personnel Management published final rules on 25 October 1983. According to the argument the OPM published in the Federal Register, the purpose of the new rules was to 1) give more weight to performance in the reduction-in-force process, 2) minimize agency disruption, 3) limit negative effects on employees, and 4) preserve for veterans their preference in determining retention standing in accordance with law.[38]

The new regulations increased the number of years of seniority that an employee could earn through good performance evaluations, with a maximum of ten years' additional service for ratings of "outstanding." This rule change thus increased the importance of performance relative to seniority. The new regulations also limited demotions, so that a person could not drop too far below his current rank, even if he could do the work of a person considerably below him. This change will have the effect of reducing the number of people to be affected by any reduction in force and will reduce the productivity loss of, for example, having upper-level officials operating as mail clerks. If there are no appropriate positions into which an employee can bump, he or she will be separated from employment. The reduced extent of bumping also makes the outcome of the reduction-in-force procedure easier to calculate and predict.

Not only were the new rules intended to reduce damage to the agency using reductions in force, but they were clearly designed to make reduction in force an easier tool for the administration to use. Personnel ceiling reductions had not been a legitimate ground for a reduction in force under the old regulations but were included in the new regulations. That means that if the Office of Management and Budget or the secretary decides to lower the personnel ceilings, the agency can run a reduction in force to get down to the new lower ceiling. The former grounds for reduction in force included reduction in budget, lack of work, and reorganization. Some agencies apparently used reorganization as a reason to use the reduction in force process when Congress would not cooperate and reduce the budget for personnel. Under the new rules, agency heads will not have to reorganize unless they want to.

The new rules also sought to handle the problem of people's being unqualified for the jobs into which they had bumped or retreated. Occasionally employees had performed a job several years earlier, and, under the old rules, that fact alone was sufficient proof of competence. The new rules allowed the agencies to apply a recency-of-experience criterion to guarantee the ability of the employee to perform the work in the job he or she was about to enter. The result of the rules change will be a reduction in the loss of productivity due to rusty skills but also a marked reduction in the number of positions which an employee is able to bump into. That change might be good for the organization, but it is likely to be bad for the employee.

The Office of Personnel Management sought to combat the unions' strategy of appealing reduction-in-force actions by limiting the possible grounds for a hearing. Employees could still write an appeal but would not be eligible for a hearing unless there were material issues of fact in dispute. This measure will undoubtedly reduce the administrative cost of the reduction-in-force procedure as well as the importance of the one tool the unions used extensively.

The Success of the President's Strategy

Although it is too early to tell how successful the new reduction-in-force regulations will be, they have provoked great deal of opposition, some of it based on the self-interest of employees who saw reduced job security, some based on the technical grounds of measurement problems associated with performance evaluation.

The new regulations were seen as an attempt to make the reduction-in-force procedure easier to use, thus making employees more vulnerable. The increased emphasis on performance evaluation was seen as increased ability of the managers to pinpoint whom they wanted to keep and whom they wanted to fire. The general consensus was that the performance-evaluation procedure did not measure performance well. Hence the new procedures would not be able to perform as claimed, to protect the hard-working and able at the expense of the lazy.

The new reduction-in-force procedures gave employees fewer alternate jobs within agencies and in general reduced the security of employment, but procedures that would help protect the jobs of federal employees through improved placement programs and rehiring programs were conspicuous by their absence. Members of Congress sympathetic to civil servants tried to block the new regulations[39] and promulgate their own version, but OPM director Donald Devine was determined to put the new management procedures in place. Though there was still controversy in the fall of 1983 over some of the revisions, OPM did promulgate the new rules.

There was some opposition to other presidential initiatives to improve management, but it was scattered. For example, one congressional committee, the House Committee on Public Works, took exception to the Economic Development Administration's action in selling the portion of its loan portfolio that was difficult to collect.[40]

The initiative to improve procurement was probably not very successful, since after the president issued Executive Order 12352 (on procurement procedures), "working level procurement personnel perceived efforts to orient contracts more politically."[41]

Agencies did not react negatively to the president's efforts to improve management; rather, they sometimes tried to supplement it by efforts of their own to minimize damage to programs and productivity.

The final test of whether the president's strategies to improve management in spite of cutbacks were successful is whether the agencies were able to minimize the negative consequences of cuts and policy redirections while improving their management. Chapters 3–7 discuss the effects of cuts and policy redirections on the management of five federal agencies.

THE CASE STUDIES

The cases were chosen to illustrate different aspects of the political process described in this chapter.

Chapter 3 describes what happened to the little Bureau of Health Planning when the Office of Management and Budget tried to terminate its health planning program. The case illustrates several themes. Though the administration wanted to terminate the bureau, Congress took no action on termination and took unpredictable action on budget levels. The bureau's leadership was loyal to its program and would have liked to fight for continued existence, but it lacked the political support from interest groups and Congress. The level of uncertainty harmed the agency's ability to make decisions and take action. The case illustrates themes about the controllability of the bureaucracy, the importance of interest groups (or lack of them), and the negative effects of cutback on management.

Chapter 4 describes events in the Employment and Training Administration, which lost one program completely and was severely cut back in budget and personnel. The case of ETA is one in which Congress and the administration agreed on the cuts, and it illustrates how reduction in force is carried out when there is a real fiscal emergency. It also illustrates the formation of a separate political leadership at the top of the organization, which excluded the union and many upper-level officials from decision making.

Chapter 5 is about the Community Development and Planning Program. Unlike the Bureau of Health Planning and the ETA, this program had strong interest-group support and, within careful limits, fought termination proposals. Partly because of its high level of support from Congress and interest groups, the agency got caught between the administration and Congress, to the consternation of its career-oriented officials who were trying to satisfy both Congress and the president. The Community Planning and Development case also illustrates a department-wide reduction in force for reasons that were probably determined by the president's policy to reduce staffing levels.

Chapter 6 is about the Urban Mass Transportation Administration, an agency with considerable interest-group support, which the administration sought to control. This chapter illustrates the use of reorganization and reduction in force to take control of an agency and make it more responsive to the president's policies.

Chapter 7, the last of the case studies, is about the Office of Personnel Management. This study is really two related stories: one about the effects of the president's cuts and policy redirections on the agency and its management and the other about the OPM's implementation of the president's personnel policies across the government. Of all the case studies, this one deals most directly with the question of whether the president was able to improve management while cutting back nonmilitary agencies.

NOTES

1. Herbert Kaufman, *Are Government Organizations Immortal?* (Washington: Brookings Institute, 1976), p. 9.

2. Aaron Wildavsky, *The Politics of the Budgetary Process*, 2d ed. (Boston: Little, Brown, 1974), pp. 102–8.

3. Herbert Kaufman, *The Administrative Behavior of Federal Bureau Chiefs* (Washington: Brookings Institution, 1981), p. 161.

4. Thomas Cronin, "Presidential Departmental Relations," in *Current Issues in Public Administration*, 2d ed., ed. Frederick S. Lane (New York: St. Martin's Press, 1982), p. 90.

5. Richard Nathan, 'The 'Administrative Presidency'" in *Current Issues*, ed. Lane, p. 79.

6. *Ibid.*, pp. 76–86.

7. *Ibid.*, p. 81.

8. *Ibid.*, p. 80.

9. *Ibid.*, p. 81.

10. Chester Newland, "A Midterm Appraisal—The Reagan Presidency: Limited Government and Political Administration," *Public Administration Review* 43, no. 1 (January/February 1983): 1–21.

11. "Cut 40,000 Middle Level Bosses," *Chicago Tribune*, 17 November 1983.

12. House Subcommittee on Human Resources and Subcommittee on Census and Population of the Committee on Post Office and Civil Service, *Reductions in Force at the Census Bureau: Joint Hearing*, 97th Cong., 2d sess., 10 June 1982, p. 9.

13. See Allen Schick, *Congress and Money* (Washington: Urban Institute Press, 1980), for a richly detailed discussion of the congressional budget process since 1974. The reader is referred to that book for either clarification of the present discussion or additional information.

14. For more information on the reconciliation process and how it works, see Allen Schick, *Reconciliation and the Congressional Budget Process* (Washington: American Enterprise Institute, 1981).

15. Martha Gottron, ed., *Budgeting for America* (Washington: Congressional Quarterly, 1982), p. 69.

16. Jeffrey Straussman and Barry Bozeman, "Shrinking Budgets and Shrinking Budget Theory," *Public Administration Review* 42, (November/December 1982): 509–15.

17. General Accounting Office, *Recent Government Wide Hiring Freezes Prove Ineffective in Managing Federal Employment* (FPCD-82-21) (Washington: Government Printing Office, 1982), p. 2.

18. A detailed description of how the reduction-in-force regulations worked during this period was contained in the federal personnel manual, chapter 351, Reductions in Force. To see the old regulations, see an older manual (1982 or earlier).

19. Office of Management and Budget, Budget of the U.S. Government, 1983. Special Analysis "I," Civilian Employment in the Executive Branch, 1982.

20. Edward B. Fiske, "Top Objectives Elude Reagan As Education Policy Evolves," *New York Times*, 27 December 1983.

21. Kaufman, *Are Government Organizations Immortal?*, p. 21.

22. General Accounting Office, *Department of Housing and Urban Development's Fiscal Year 1983 Reductions in Force* (GAO RCED-83-47) (Washington: Government Printing Office, 29 October 1982).

23. General Accounting Office, *Savings from 1981 and 1982 Personnel Ceiling Reductions* (FPCD-82-23) (Washington: Government Printing Office, 1982), pp. 1–4.

24. This restriction appeared in Title 1 of HUD's 1983 appropriation act, Public Law 97–272, 30 September 1982.

25. The department's case was presented in a press conference I attended at

HUD in the fall of 1982. The conference was called to explain the results of the court case and to announce an immediate reduction in force.

26. Kaufman, *Are Government Organizations Immortal?*, p. 11.

27. *Ibid.*

28. "Many Invincible Programs Are Spared the Budget Ax. In Spite of Reagan Campaign," *Congressional Quarterly Weekly Report* 39, no. 29 (18 July 1981): 1271.

29. Robert Behn, "Twelve Hints for the Would Be Policy Terminator," *Policy Analysis* 4, no. 3 (1977): 393–413.

30. Floyd Abrams, "The New Effort to Control Information," *New York Times Magazine*, 25 September 1983.

31. Fiske, "Top Objectives Elude Reagan."

32. *Ibid.*

33. Allan Rosenbaum, "Federal Management: Pathological Problems and Simple Cures," *PS*, Spring 1982, p. 189.

34. *Ibid.*

35. On the effects of uncertainty on decision making, see Irene Rubin, "Universities in Stress: Decision making under Conditions of Reduced Resources," *Social Science Quarterly* 58, no. 2 (September 1977): 242–54. On the personnel problems created by decline, see Charles Levine, "Organizational Decline and Cutback Management" in *Managing Fiscal Stress: The Crisis in the Public Sector*, ed. Charles Levine (Chatham, N.G.: Chatham House, 1980), p. 15.

36. Allen Schick, "Contemporary Problems in Financial Control," *Public Administration Review* 38, (November/December 1978), p. 513–19.

37. Newland, "A Midterm Appraisal", p. 14.

38. *48 Federal Register* 49462 (1983).

39. "Stevens Seeks Compromise on Federal Employee Rules; House May Block Changes," *Congressional Quarterly Weekly*, 4 June 1983, p. 1119.

40. This information was presented in a discussion between staff members and representatives of the Subcommittee on Oversight and Investigations and the Subcommittee on Economic Development of the House Public Works Committee on 30 November 1983. The discussion was part of a hearing on the effects of the president's budget cuts on the Economic Development Administration. As of the early 1984, the hearings were being printed.

41. Newland, "A Midterm Appraisal," p. 14.

3

The Bureau of Health Planning

The Threat of Termination

INTRODUCTION

In 1981 and 1982 (when the field work for this case study was being carried out), the Bureau of Health Planning was a small bureau in the Health Resources Administration of the Public Health Service, in the Department of Health and Human Services. Its function was to administer a grant program to a nationwide network of local health planning agencies (called Health Systems Agencies, or HSAs), which in turn carried out the bureau's mission, to improve access to quality health care for all citizens.[1]

The local health planning agencies had (and still have) two major functions: 1) to evaluate local health conditions and, in conjunction with individuals and community groups interested in health care, draw up a plan for improvements; and 2) to implement that plan by reviewing hospitals' requests for expansion, proposed uses of federal funds in health care, and the appropriateness of local medical services and costs. If the state health agencies uphold the local agencies' recommendations, it is possible for a local HSA to deny a hospital permission to expand or purchase new equipment. Neither the local health systems agencies nor the Bureau of Health Planning has provided any direct services to the public.

The Bureau of Health Planning experienced a series of budget cuts, beginning with President Carter's budget for 1981, proposed in 1980. The program was targeted for termination by the Reagan administration in 1981. The Office of Management and Budget gave the bureau a personnel ceiling of ten for 1982, down from over three hundred in 1981, and gave the bureau a budget of zero for 1983.

According to the administration's plan, the fate of the bureau was negative but certain. The bureau would have one year to wind up its affairs, with greatly reduced budget and staffing levels, and then would close down. But though the administration's plan was definite, congressional action on budget levels was unpredictable. It was possible that the bureau would have more money than staff to administer it. Moreover, when the program came up for reauthorization in 1982, it was not formally reauthorized but was allowed to continue spending under consecutive continuing resolutions.

Thus the agency was caught between the administration's mandate to terminate and congressional inaction. The bureau tried to carry out the administration's policy to terminate itself without foreclosing the possibility of future congressional rescue. At the same time, it was dealing with budget reductions, continuing resolutions, rescissions, and reductions in personnel ceilings.

The case study of the Bureau of Health Planning illustrates two themes developed in the first two chapters. First, it describes the president's ability to control an agency in a situation calling for the agency to terminate itself. Second, it describes the impact of retrenchment and the threat of termination on agency management and decision making.

To illustrate the degree to which the President controlled executive agencies for the purposes of cutback, the case study describes the response of bureaucrats, in this case primarily program loyalists, to the policy requiring them to terminate their own program. The chapter describes the bureau's power to resist the termination policy, especially its ability to call on interest groups and Congress to reverse the termination decision, as well as the decisions made and actions taken to resist or adapt to the policy.

To illustrate the impact of retrenchment and the threat of termination on management and decision making, the chapter describes the impact of uncertainty on morale and on the ability to make and implement decisions and make progress toward stated goals.

AGENCY RESPONSE TO THREATENED TERMINATION

As pointed out in Chapter 2, the literature assumes that agencies are not passive pawns in power struggles and that when threatened with termination they will take an active role in defending their agencies and programs. If, however, all the leaders of an organization were appointed by a president or secretary eager to terminate the program, and those leaders promoted and supported subordinates who agreed with them, the axiomatic wisdom that agencies always take action to defend themselves might not apply. The first question, then, in examining the response of the Bureau of

Health Planning to proposed termination, is to what extent was the agency leadership loyal to its program? Did the president's control extend to the appointment of bureau policy makers loyal to *his* program?

The Bureau of Health Planning, with an employee roster of a little over three hundred employees, was too small to warrant a new appointee as the agency director to enforce the president's views. The bureau director from the Carter years was allowed to stay on. Moreover, a group of program loyalists had been recruited internally into policy-making positions when the bureau was organized in 1974; bureau staff who had less enthusiasm for the program, and perhaps more exclusive concern with their careers, were to some extent shunted aside. This cadre of program loyalists still dominated the program when President Reagan was elected. It is natural to assume, therefore, that they would have wanted to fight for the continued existence of the program.

However, the ability of the bureau's leadership to fight back, directly or indirectly, was highly constrained. The bureau was not a politically powerful agency, and it had little autonomy over the program it managed. Moreover, the President exerted effective control over the agency through the secretary for the Department of Health and Human Services and the assistant secretary for health, further limiting the Bureau's options.

Political Power

Partly because the health planning program had a regulatory function and partly because of some characteristics of the legislation creating the program, the Bureau of Health Planning never achieved much political power.

The health planning program was designed to help put hospitals where they were needed and prevent excessive hospital and equipment expansion in areas that were already well served. Local HSAs together with state health agencies could veto hospital expansion and new equipment purchases and control the increase in new programs. Hospital administrators reportedly resented both the control and the paperwork, especially the need to apply to local health planners and then again to state decision makers. Doctors and their medical societies seemed to resent any interference in their decisions, no matter how it was done.

Hospital associations and medical societies provided an active constituency against the health planning program. In many parts of the country, where federal grants flowed directly to the HSAs, local governments had no interest in maintaining the grants; and in those areas where local officials controlled the program, it was usually because they wanted some of the grant money for other purposes or because they wanted to control the decisions of the HSA, not because they approved of the program. In short, the program generated a lot of hostility and no supportive constituency.

Before 1974, under an earlier health planning law, the Bureau of Health Planning was combined in one administrative unit with a hospital construction program. Not only was this arrangement beneficial for the planning program because it related construction and needs assessment, but it was also good for health planning in a political sense. The hospital construction program (the Hill-Burton Act) was highly popular, providing millions of dollars to local areas for construction and jobs and pleasing both hospital administrators and doctors. At first the health planning program could take advantage of the political popularity of the hospital construction program, but in the 1974 legislation, the health planning program was separated from the physical facilities program and lost the major portion of its political support.

As a regulatory program, health planning could still have generated popular and legislative support if it could have demonstrated its effectiveness in providing better access to medical care and holding medical costs down. However, several circumstances prevented the Bureau of Health Planning from being able to demonstrate major successes.

Part of the problem was that the 1974 legislation included extremely detailed instructions to the Health Systems Agencies on the composition of their community boards. Many hours were spent in the early years of the program finding appropriate board members, educating them to their roles, and working out politically acceptable plans. The outcome was that more attention was absorbed in the process of planning than in the product. To add to this difficulty, a portion of the legislation requiring implementation of plans was never funded, curtailing the ability of HSAs to improve local health care or reduce costs. This made it difficult to show Congress and the General Accounting Office what the program was accomplishing.

The problem of evaluating the program's accomplishments became more acute under Secretary Califano of the Department of Health, Education and Welfare (the Department of Health and Human Services was formerly called the Department of Health, Education and Welfare, before the Department of Education was created). Secretary Califano emphasized almost exclusively the goal of reducing the cost of health care.[2] The HSAs, designed as multifunctioned agencies, were ill equipped to reduce health care costs singlehandedly. They had limited authority over capital increases, less over existing capital plant, and none over personnel costs. Because rising personnel costs are a major factor in rising health care costs, the HSAs were bound to be considered ineffective when judged solely from the perspective of cost containment.

The continuing loss of political power of the health planning program was suddenly accelerated by the election of President Reagan. The director of the Office of Management and Budget, David Stockman, had opposed health planning when he was in Congress[3] and brought to the office a determination to end the health planning program. The Reagan administration opposed health planning because it had a regulatory approach to cost containment.

Given its general lack of political power, the Bureau of Health Planning did not have the ability to force the administration to retract its termination proposals. Moreover, the agency did not have much autonomy with which to either get around the policy or minimize its impact.

Autonomy

Although the bureau could not force a reversal of the president's termination policy, if it had had sufficient autonomy, it could have fought to minimize the effects of cuts and to delay termination. It could have tried to target cuts in such a way as to save some parts of the program or some agencies, in case Congress later saved the program, and to reorganize itself to function at a lower level with a smaller staff and carry on until the end.

However, the agency lacked sufficient autonomy to carry out most of these tactics. Part of that lack was due to the original legislation of 1974, in which Congress created a program that permitted managers little discretion, but part reflected the president's success in taking control of the executive branch agencies. The agency was blocked at almost every turn.

The 1974 legislation that created the health planning program was passed at a time when Congress was trying to wrest control back from the executive branch by writing extremely detailed laws that in essence took discretion away from administrators.[4] The health planning law is thus extremely detailed. It not only outlines the purposes of the law but also specifies that there be a nationwide network of HSAs and includes details on how the boundaries of each HSA are to be drawn up. The law also includes requirements on the composition of governing boards for HSAs and restrictions on sources of income other than the federal government. The minimum number of staff for each local agency is listed in the law along with the formula for allocation of the grants. Though the Bureau of Health Planning administered the law, it was not granted much discretion as to how the program would be run.

The lack of administrative discretion came up frequently as bureau staff wrestled with retrenchment decisions. Could they close down some agencies which were not performing well in order to save some money to give to other agencies that were performing better? The law specified very limited grounds for breaking the contract between the bureau and the HSAs. An extensive and time-consuming appeals process (also written into the law) made timely action difficult. Moreover, formula allocation gave money to more heavily populated health services areas, not to those HSAs that performed better or that had a better chance of survival.

The bureau sought some relief from the constraints in the law when the program was threatened by extensive cutbacks and termination. Some of these requests were granted by Congress. But the most important request, to be allowed to run a discretionary program if funds were cut drastically, was denied. Under the discretionary program proposed by the bureau, the local agencies would compete for grants and the decision to allocate would be made by the bureau. Bureau staff wanted the freedom to use the money more efficiently if only a small amount was available. Spending a tiny bit on each HSA was a waste of money because then none of them could function properly, but if money could be withdrawn from the least effective agencies and allocated to the more effective ones on a competitive basis, the result would be improved use of resources. However, the bureau was not allowed to deviate from the formula.

Autonomy was curtailed not only by the health planning law but, more important for the purposes of this study, by the Department of Health and Human Services as a matter of policy. The bureau was forbidden to submit a 1983 budget proposal for any programs then in existence. Any kind of budget strategy was ruled out in a single stroke. Also, and probably with the same goal in mind, the bureau was required to plan as if the worst-case staffing scenario given by the Office of Management and Budget were going to materialize. It was not granted the autonomy to plan for a more realistic scenario or to devise a new internal structure for proposed reduced staffing levels.

Agency Strategies

Within the constraints posed by a lack of political power and limited autonomy, the bureau tried to respond to threatened termination, but in a low key and generally constrained fashion. The lack of visible activity was due partly to the formal constraints on lobbying and the limited number of staff assigned to legislative liaison activities but also to the sense of hopelessness that assailed staff members each time they tried to preserve themselves. The OMB seemed implacably opposed to the program, the Public Health Service (of which the bureau was a part) was at best lukewarm, and the bureau's congressional supporters seemed paralyzed by the conservative budget-cutting mood that prevailed after President Reagan took office.

Within this policy of toned-down efforts to survive, the agency tried to avail itself of the channels left open to it by the department. The bureau had been instructed not to include any currently funded programs in its 1983 budget request but had been informed that new proposals were acceptable. It accordingly drew up its new proposals, somewhat similar in philosophy to what was already in existence but with more emphasis on voluntary compliance and competition to reduce health costs. These modifications were intended to make the program more acceptable to the administration.

The bureau gained some outside support for its new proposals (from organized labor), but this apparently had little effect, and the proposals were rejected. The Bureau then managed to get enough support from its immediate superiors to appeal the decision inside the department, but the appeal was turned down, and there the matter rested.

Because of the lack of support for the program in the Public Health Service and in the Department of Health and Human Services, the bureau's strategy for survival had to focus on Congress. Although lobbying from bureaucratic agencies is formally discouraged, there was clearly some communication between congressional committees (or their staffs) and bureau personnel. Some of this was via the formal channels, in which agency officials recommend to congressional committees technical amendments necessary for the administration of the program. When Congress eliminated the minimum funding requirements in the formula for allocation of grants, thereby permitting even very small amounts of money to be allocated by formula, bureau staff managed to convince congressional committee staff that chaos would result. Minimum levels of funding were restored.

Some of the contact with Congress was less direct. Most of the lobbying was probably done informally by the local HSAs. One political advantage of a nationwide network of HSAs should have been a broad base of political support in Congress. Even though such a base did not develop, it was still possible for HSA staffs to exert considerable political pressure on congressional delegations. The bureau used this capacity in a nondirective and nonattributable manner. For example, the policy of not refunding the first grant-renewal applications to come up in fiscal year 1982 was reportedly intended to mobilize the affected HSAs to activate their representatives.

The bureau staff watched Congress closely and almost continuously. Because the program was funded under continuing resolutions and was subject to rescissions, there were numerous times throughout the year when the budget for that year could be determined. And for each of these four or five key decisions, there were subcommittee votes, committee votes, full house votes, and conference committee (both houses) votes, each of which could raise or lower budget totals. Bureau staff watched the process closely, not only because the program's funding levels were at stake, but also because they hoped that Congress would give them a sign as to its intention to go along with or defy the administration's proposal to terminate the program.

On one occasion, in May 1981, it did appear that Congress sent the bureau a message concerning its future fate. A Senate committee put in a report (which is not legally binding) a request that the agency document its efficiency by 15 June. The wording was taken as an indication that if only the bureau would do some particular things, Congress would support the program. The wording of the Senate committee's request sent the bureau into a hopeful flurry of activity. The director forwarded an evaluation plan to the committee, and the bureau staff tried to sort out inefficient HSAs to terminate as a signal to Congress of increased efficiency.

While the bureau struggled for some support to continue operations, it simultaneously assumed that federal funds were going to drop for 1982 and perhaps disappear in 1983. The urge to keep health planning alive in some form gave rise to the adoption in January 1981 of "transition strategies," a policy designed to keep local agencies alive without much federal funding. This step was difficult for agency staff to take, because it implied that federal funding would soon disappear and the program as it was then would die.

In encouraging the HSAs to adopt transition strategies, the bureau advised them to do a self-assessment, plan survival strategies, reorganize, and focus on some activities at the expense of others. Of these four tasks, the bureau provided additional guidance in two areas, survival strategies and task priorities.

With respect to survival strategies, the bureau advised HSAs to foster or participate in various health care coalitions. Many of these coalitions were dominated by business or insurance companies who had a deep and abiding interest in reducing health care costs. The policy of encouraging coalitions left the bureau's staff feeling "schizophrenic" (staff member's vocabulary). On the one hand, they felt that consumers would lose their voice in health planning and that equal access to quality health care would not be the goal of the new coalitions. On the other hand, private sector coalitions seemed to be the most likely successors to publicly supported health planning. In supporting coalition strategies, the bureau was encouraging HSAs to become something quite different from what they had been in order to survive.

With respect to task priorities, the bureau urged HSAs to de-emphasize some (legally mandated) functions and emphasize others. Most HSAs had already devised their health plans—creating new plans could be deemphasized. The bureau advised agencies to concentrate on high-impact areas—reviewing expensive hospital projects and implementing the plans already devised.

The emphasis on plan implementation served a triple function. With respect to transition activities, plan implementation could be used to attract positive attention in the local community and create a group of allies who could serve as the basis for a non-federally funded program. With respect to phaseout activities, plan implementation could serve as a way of creating a visible accomplishment as evidence that the program had been effective. Simultaneously, the effort to implement plans was a response to critics of the program who argued that HSAs only created plans and had no effect on either health conditions or health costs. There was an effort to bring seven years of work to fruition as evidence of bureau successes in a bid for reauthorizing the program.

The bureau put considerable effort and resources into implementing this transition strategy for the HSAs. It reduced its reporting requirements from the HSAs to free up resources for transition activities. It began a research project on business and community coalitions for health care. The bureau pressed for and received from Congress two important new areas of flexibility to help HSAs cope with declining resources and transition planning: the ability to drop certain functions and a broadening of the sources of revenue permissible to the HSA while it was still a federal grantee. The bureau contracted with its technical assistance arms (private contracting firms) to provide transition advice and assistance. It also managed to get permission to write some new regulations (a difficult task, given the administration's opposition to new regulations) to allow states to redraw the boundaries of and combine HSAs. This regulation would allow states to enlarge the area of one or several HSAs to include that of HSAs going out of business.

Clearly, the bureau took much more policy leadership in the area of transition planning for HSAs than it did in transition planning for the bureau or for the program itself. The policy was formulated earlier and was more consistent in its application than survival strategies for the bureau. The bureau staff came increasingly to believe that all the major outside actors who could have supported them were either implacably opposed to the program or temporarily helpless. If health planning were to survive, it would have to be because the HSAs were given the freedom, the technical assistance, and the resources to find their own way without federal funds.

THE EFFECT OF CUTBACK AND THE THREAT OF TERMINATION ON MANAGEMENT AND DECISION MAKING

The Reagan administration, through its own efforts and because of the bureau's lack of autonomy and client support, did succeed in limiting the defensive responses of the Bureau of Health Planning. The uncertainty, the cutbacks, and the threat of program termination had an enormous impact on the quality of management and decision making.

Uncertainty

The effect of the administration's decision to terminate the program and congressional reluctance to take definitive action was to create an almost unbelievably high level of uncertainty, magnified by the effect of budget cuts as they filtered through the congressional budget process. After the Health Planning Program's authorization expired, continuing resolutions controlled not only funding levels but also program authorization. In essence, the program was authorized for only a few months at a time.

Estimates of both staffing and funding levels went up and down, some-times hourly, depending on reports coming from Capitol Hill. Every time budget and staffing estimates went up or down, a different group of staff (larger or smaller) felt that they would either lose their jobs or be bumped.

Agency-wide reduction-in-force notices were sent out to all personnel in August 1981, giving warning that individual notices could come within a month. At the end of September, just before individual notices were to be issued, they were postponed by Secretary Schweiker until November or December. The appropriation level was still unknown but would probably be higher than that implied in OMB's recommended staffing levels, which were used to plan the reduction in force. If the department went through with reductions in force on the scale envisioned by OMB and implied in the president's budget request, and if Congress appropriated a larger sum of money, there would have to be rehires. Consequently, the reduction in force was delayed.

Such episodes increased the personal insecurity of the bureau's staff and stretched out the period of intense anxiety, preventing the agency from recovering. Many staff members began to look for and move to other jobs, making the staffing level even more unpredictable than before. Farewell parties were held amost every day for a while. And each time someone left, it reminded the others of how insecure they were.

All the cutback and termination decisions at the bureau were colored by this overwhelming uncertainty. For example, the decision to allocate 1982 funding by formula or by competitive grant depended on the level of funding, yet the bureau did not know what the level of funding would be. Bureau officials could not decide whether or not to gear up for a competi-tive grant program. During the study, estimates of funding varied by a factor of ten. When estimates were low, the discretionary program seemed likely; when estimates were high, it seemed unlikely. Thus bureau staff members picked up and dropped plans for a discretionary program.

Uncertainty about staffing levels made it almost impossible to fill out work plans designed in accordance with "Management by Objectives" (MBO). MBO requires employees to negotiate with their bosses an amount of work for which they are responsible; their personal merit evaluations for salary increments are based on whether or not they accomplish these objectives. For middle-level managers, the amount of work they can promise depends on the number of subordinates they have —a number that was absolutely unpredictable. Work plans and evaluation of the performance of middle- and upper-level managers proceeded as if all were normal in a situation in which they could not possibly work. The use of salary increases as a motivation to work harder and more efficiently collapsed amidst these extremes of uncertainty.

The uncertainty about the number of people who would remain on board was acute just before the beginning of fiscal year 1982, when the bureau still did not have a budget, and the assistant secretary for health was still arguing that the reduction in force should take place immediately, before the Congress had acted. The following excerpt from field notes taken at an operations staff meeting on 30 September 1981 illustrates both the uncertainty and its effects on decision making and management.

E: Is anyone thinking of furniture, the master files of the agency, plans, applications? Where will ten or fifteen people be located? P— suggested the telephone closet on the fourth floor. We can't keep them all on this floor with all the empty offices.

L: Has the Health Resources Administration [the agency of which the bureau was a part] addressed these issues? There was a story that people were RIFfed and their personal possessions were immediately removed.

P: I can't deal with equipment. But speaking from previous experience with cutbacks, except for working files for ten or fifteen people, the burden of proof for keeping something should be on an exception basis. Don't waste time sorting papers. Leaving paper and data is not a legacy.

L: Do we have responsibility to get the grant file from the regions? Does it have to get shipped here, because there is no staff there?

B: If we have ten people, ten people on board can't do it. It will require either other HRA positions here or in the regions.

E: I'm looking at it from a mechanical viewpoint. Where will things and contents of programs go? I haven't heard any discussion. Implications cannot be solved in the next month.

L: What you are saying is that we haven't done strategic long-term planning.

E: (grinning at the understatement) Yes. What if we need seventeen people instead of fifteen, what are the mechanics of hiring consultants? My staff wants to know.

L: We haven't thought about it.

Director: But if there are 110 positions ...

E: Tomorrow we will know.

?: No.

B: The organizational decisions will be made by Brandt et al. [the assistant secretary's level].

E: Don't we still make recommendations, or do we get it from on high?

Note that none of the issues raised got any kind of answer. This portion of the meeting closed with a request by the director for a memo from his staff members on the issues raised.

Fluctuations in Morale

Personal insecurity about jobs and collective uncertainty about staffing and funding levels and the future prospects of the program had a devastating impact on morale. Morale ebbed and flowed, depending on recent events. Sometimes staff members quarreled with one another because they were insecure or upset about the future prospects of the program. Sometimes they could not deal with closeout issues at all. For example, one office director reported he was getting some ideas on closeout from his staff in "dribbles." He indicated he was afraid to ask them point blank "because they would freeze." Individuals sometimes withdrew their efforts to order to concentrate on finding new jobs. The low level of morale in general made it difficult for staff to seek out trouble spots in advance or design alternative modes of response depending on contingencies.

One staff member described the motivation problem as follows: "We are all like starving people crawling across a desert. One person falls down, and someone else picks them up. Then the second one falls down. We are kind of limping along like this."

The ebb and flow of morale caused alternation between attempts to control retrenchment, termination, and survival activities and a general attitude of relinquishing control to others both above and below the bureau level. Though it is clear that some bureau staff members favored a laissez faire attitude while others pushed for more activity, more control, and more autonomy over decisions, the division of the bureau into factions who expended more or less effort is not enough by itself to explain the bursts of action followed by policy reversal or moderation. Individual spokespersons for each view sometimes had the motivation to fight for their perspectives and sometimes did not. The whole tone and atmosphere of the bureau changed with external circumstances, now favoring more activity and now less.

For example, as soon as President Reagan took office, it became clear that the administration opposed the health planning program. The director began to take actions to help the HSAs make the transition to nonfederal funding. Morale at the bureau dropped. Despite the need to help some HSAs survive, the general consensus at that time was not to make difficult reallocative decisions. According to one informant,

> Staff contemplated giving up. The policy under consideration was to fund each agency at its level—why review anything? There was no sense of responsibility. My staff came up faster than most; we fought hard not to make any irreversible decisions. That picked up the bureau. Then we fell apart again. There had to be a critical mass of motivational energy. If not, there are wide fluctuations [in policy].

Interestingly, it was not the case that when morale improved, the staff's energies were directed only toward survival; rather, there was an attempt to do all the bureau's tasks well, including preparation for termination.

Pursuit of Separate Goals

To add to the problems created by high levels of uncertainty and shifting levels of morale, the agency also had to deal with the necessity to pursue three somewhat antagonistic goals at the same time, namely, termination, cutback, and survival. The result of trying to deal with all these problems at the same time was that the bureau developed an odd style of decision making. Not only did it alternate between goals, but sometimes in the effort to anticipate opposite outcomes, the bureau pursued several different goals simultaneously, either by giving a single message to different actors at the same time, or by giving the same actor two different messages. Sometimes policies were articulated that served both the termination of the federal program and program survival.

Decisions were often made after considerable analysis of the alternatives, with well-thought-out criteria for judgment, but after all the analysis, the implementation tended to be limited and incremental. Bureau staff could not go too far in any one direction lest the opposite set of conditions immediately appear in the environment. Thus the bureau maintained itself in a state of readiness for anything but could do very little to achieve any particular goal.

An Example of Bureau Decision Making

These characteristics of bureau decision making—frequent reversals of decisions, using one message to convey several different policies, and comprehensive consideration of alternatives followed by limited implementation—are all illustrated in the bureau's efforts to reallocate resources from some local HSAs to others as part of an effort to help some HSAs survive. This issue will be described in some detail in this chapter because it not only illustrates what happens to decision making in agencies threatened with termination but also describes the impulse to reallocate in declining agencies and the conditions under which reallocation is likely (or not likely) to take place.

There were three factors that affected the willingness of staff to reallocate. The first was the perception of what funding levels would be for fiscal year 1982. If funding levels were very low, many HSAs would die that might be able to survive if they had a little bit longer to look around for other sources of funding. The need to help these agencies lent strong impetus to a reallocation policy. The second factor influencing the decision was the perception of the amount of autonomy the bureau had in allocating funds and in retaining saved funds. The greater the perception of autonomy, the more likely the bureau was to try to reallocate. The third factor was the perceived likelihood of the federal program's survival. Whenever it appeared that the program was going to be terminated, morale plummeted and there was no desire to cause any of the HSAs any more pain by terminating their funding before the federal program did so.

There were several options for reallocation. One was to reallocate from weak to strong agencies by terminating weak agencies for non-performance, allowing a larger pool of funds to be distributed by formula to other agencies. A second reallocation scheme was to apply to Congress for a discretionary grant program for 1982, to bypass the formula allocation altogether and award grants on the basis of excellence of the local agencies or on the basis of the greatest likelihood of surviving the termination of federal funds. A third strategy was to try to terminate agencies (or press them to terminate themselves) during the fiscal year 1981, to save some money for fiscal year 1982. This strategy required the cooperation of the secretary, who could reprogram the funds internally and prevent the bureau from using them on the HSAs. The fourth strategy required the bureau to refuse to renew some agency contracts when they came up for renewal.

The issue of reallocation first came up in January 1981, after President Reagan took office. The administration's determination to eliminate the program led to a drop in morale and a refusal to reallocate. Staff decided to support an across-the-board refunding policy—that is, refunding an agency on schedule, regardless of its performance.

The issue came up again in May 1981, when a local HSA, anticipating that the president's request to rescind much of the bureau's funding would be successful, volunteered to close down. The voluntary action suggested that other agencies might want to close and implied the need for the bureau to have some kind of reallocation strategy. Further, the president's proposed rescission for 1981 suggested that 1982 funding would be minimal and reinforced the staff's motivation to reallocate.

In accordance with rational comprehensive decision making, bureau staff considered several techniques of reallocation. The first was the possibility of terminating some HSAs for nonperformance, which would free up some additional funds for the remaining agencies. Second, staff considered but rejected the possibility of not renewing the contracts of some of the HSAs. This option would be less painful than terminating agencies for nonperformance but was considered impractical because so few HSAs were coming up for renewal. Clearly, the simplest option for the bureau would be to encourage more voluntary closures by the HSAs, but staff reported that they had a hard time asking HSAs to "shoot themselves." What gradually emerged from the meeting was the desire to sort out and shut down the few agencies that were not performing well.

Less than a week later, the bureau director reported to his operating staff that the Senate had asked the bureau to demonstrate its efficiency by

15 June. The Senate language was seen as providing explicit support for a policy of pruning out the weak HSAs as a signal to Congress of increased efficiency.

The general mood at this meeting was hope for the future combined with low expectations for funding in 1982. This combination created the maximum impetus for reallocation. Morale was high enough that the staff members were willing to make difficult decisions, and anticipated revenue was low enough to make it plausible that Congress would grant the bureau authority to run a discretionary program. The staff decided to reallocate to keep some HSAs alive until a discretionary program could be implemented. The director of the bureau assigned staff the task of preparing a list of crippled agencies for possible termination. The staff picked the first two from the list of possibles.

As the following excerpt from an interview illustrates, this policy was seen as delivering different messages to different groups:

> *Q:* How many HSAs will be on the list?
> *A:* It will be a short list. It's a signal to Congress and to the field that we'll take a tough stand and we aren't wedded to a policy of national coverage. We want to act responsibly, but to get rid of the deadwood.
> *Q:* Then the strategy is primarily to give a signal to Congress for *survival?*
> *A:* The signal to decision makers is one signal. It's also a signal to the field [HSAs] that tough times are coming, and we're going to be tough. They might feel. I'd like to get out of this.

The message to Congress was part of a survival strategy; the message to HSAs, encouraging them to close voluntarily, was part of a reallocation scheme.

Concurrently with selecting agencies to eliminate, staff continued to work on a project that would sort out the best agencies for possible refunding or additional funding. One project included ranking health service areas according to health care needs and the quality of the local HSAs.

Over the next week, the criteria for selection of agencies to terminate were polished up. A list of troubled agencies was drawn up, and then three major criteria were applied to each case. One of the criteria was the adequacy of staff. Did the agency have a regular or acting director? Did it have the minimum number of professional staff? Were enough staff assigned to legally mandated tasks? A second criterion examined the adequacy of the governing body—its composition, its community support, and its support of the HSA. The third criterion was adequate performance, including the quality of the agency's health plans and its performance on review of proposed hospital projects. This information was culled from a variety of sources available at the bureau.

The staff proceeded to discuss all the agencies on the list with respect to these criteria and any additional knowledge they had about those agencies. Agencies that looked weak after examination were starred for further action, and those that would almost certainly be given notice of termination were given double stars. After going through the list and coming up with recommendations, staff members were instructed to go back and make a second list, using as a first cut those seventeen agencies that had had restrictions put on their funding, indicating some kind of performance problem.

All this activity took place in order to free up some funds for reallocation, but it was unclear how much if any money would be released by terminating an agency in the middle of its contract year (not the same as the fiscal year). The one agency that had volunteered to close was planning to use the whole year's funds in less than a year, using the surplus over normal expenses to liquidate closeout costs. This problem put the bureau in a bind: it was not clear that the bureau had a legal right to give an entire year's funding to an agency for half a year's services, yet closeout costs had to come from the regular budget. If the bureau gave the agency a full year's funds, there would be no money released for reallocation. Staff members were personally torn between sympathy for an agency forced to close down and desire to close it down sooner so that there would be enough money saved to provide both closeout funding and funds for reallocation.

By the end of May, the environment had changed. On 29 May there was a general staff meeting, followed by a meeting to discuss termination and closeout plans. During the meeting, the director told the staff that the department had instructed them to take the worst-case personnel ceiling, given by OMB, as the basis for planning. Fundamentally that meant there would be only ten people in the bureau in 1982, and by 1983 there would be no staff at all. The director indicated that this scenario might be improved but also noted that legislation might soon be introduced to repeal the health planning program.

This news had a negative effect on morale and destroyed the staff's motivation to make difficult decisions. All the arguments *against* selective termination of agencies were raised. Staff questioned whether any money could be recouped from such a policy and whether the case-by-case approach would stand up in hearings. The director, distinctly annoyed, began to back down, arguing that the policy was only to examine, not to terminate, agencies and that only a few—perhaps only two or three—were involved. He reported that on closer examination several on the original list turned out not to be candidates.

Shortly after this meeting, the bureau received two more pieces of news: that the expected level of the rescission was only two-thirds as deep as they had expected for 1981 and that their proposal for a budget for 1983 had been turned down at the Public Health Service level. The willingness of Congress to defy the president on the level of the rescission in 1981 was seen as an indication that the 1982 budget would also be higher than the president's request. However, it still appeared that the program would be terminated in 1983. This combination of moderate funding in 1982 and none in 1983 favored an across-the-board refunding approach, because it simultaneously lowered morale and reduced both the need for and the likelihood of getting a discretionary program.

On 11 June, a time at which all those staff members who favored selective allocation were on vacation, the director called another meeting. The timing of the meeting combined with recent news to determine the outcome. The decision was made to refund all HSAs for six months, regardless of whether or not they submitted a revised work plan based on new lower funding levels. There would be no effort to allocate selectively in 1982. This meeting therefore completed the policy turnaround.

Over the next couple of weeks, the news worsened. It now seemed that the appropriation for 1982 was in fact going to be toward the low end of earlier projections. Worse than that, it was rumored that a cost overrun at the National Institutes of Health had resulted in the secretary's obligating more than half of the bureau's anticipated 1982 appropriation to pay for the overrun. That meant almost no money in 1982.

Ironically, far from creating a mood of indifference, the news created a small burst of reallocative activity, reversing yet again the policy on reallocation. The director determined that the amount of money likely to be available for 1982 was too small to allocate according to formula. He believed that the bureau would get the requested authority to run a discretionary program and that some criteria had to be established for allocating the funds. Efforts were made to refine the HSA staffing study done by the regional offices and the planning division of the bureau, to use it as a basis for selective refunding. (No criteria for allocation were formally announced, but the improvement of the survey instrument suggested that the bureau intended to use staffing levels as the basis for terminating agencies.) The selectivity principle was alive again but with a changed set of criteria.

Efforts were also taken to close down certain portions of the program in states that had never complied with the health planning legislation. These terminations did not recover any funds, however; the action was taken too late and the funds were taken over by the secretary for use in 1982.

By 23 June 1981, reinforced by the bureau's new determination to allocate 1982 funds selectively, some of the program loyalists reopened the argument to try to save money in fiscal year 1981 for fiscal year 1982. By now, more than a month had gone by since this issue was originally raised, and time was indeed growing short if any money were to be recovered. The director suggested they stop trying to reallocate funds from this year to next year and made another suggestion instead. The following excerpt from the field notes indicates the relationship between the changing expectation of funding levels, and the impetus to reallocate.

> *Director:* On October 1 [the beginning of the 1982 fiscal year] issue a ninety-day nonrenewal [notice]. If you want to contest it, you have to show you have a full-fledged program plan.
> *E:* Why not do it now? It may give us some money if there is no money.
> *Director:* I am banking on there being some money.
> *T:* I'd support it [reallocation from this year to next year] if we could get it to the agencies we want to get it. . . .
> *E:* You'll help some that don't deserve it, it's not an unmitigated good . . . . But if you see more money coming, I'll close down the argument. My hypothesis is that the Brandt [Assistant Secretary for Health, who favored the OMB scenario] outcome will happen. . . .

The underlying theme of this meeting was that the purpose of saving money was to help those agencies most likely to survive, and current procedures and restrictions made it very unlikely that the bureau could do it. Even if it did, there was a possibility that any savings would be absorbed again by the secretary. The program loyalists who favored selectivity yielded to the vision of more funds; the issue was closed, and they lost the argument.

Toward the end of July 1981, the Omnibus Reconciliation Act was passed, and it bore out the director's vision of more money for 1982 than proposed in the president's budget. The bureau's plans to allocate selectively in 1982 were then dropped because bureau staff correctly anticipated that Congress would not allow it the discretion to allocate the larger sum. This decision completed another reversal on the reallocation issue.

What actually occurred in September and October of 1981 was that 1) several of the first agencies that came up for renewal were given a ninety-day notice of nonrefunding, and 2) five state governments chose to eliminate their HSAs in favor of a state health planning agency. The result was hardly the outcome of a systematic policy of selective refunding, but it does reflect the ambivalence of agency staff members toward reallocation and the uncertainty about survival and termination.

Although the bureau did issue notices of nonrefunding to the first agencies to come up for refunding in fiscal year 1982, it did not do so on the basis of any of the criteria of merit or likelihood of survival that it had been considering earlier. The first agencies to come up for refunding were severely understaffed, but not all understaffed agencies were given notice of termination. The language of the letter to these agencies indicated that they were being given notice not because they were understaffed but because the amount of funding was not yet clear. (The bureau was operating under a continuing resolution, and the amount of the 1982 appropriations was still unknown in October 1981.) The bureau argued that it needed to give the HSAs ninety days' notice in case there were no funds. Although the statement in the notice to these agencies was undoubtedly true, it probably had another purpose than the stated one. These notices were examples of the tendency to undertake activities that had dual messages, either to different audiences or for different goals. In this case, the bureau on the one hand was telling the HSAs they were not being refunded because there might be no money; this was a phaseout activity. But on the other hand, it was motivating these agencies to storm Congress; this was a survival strategy. One informant at the bureau explained the policy in the following terms:

Q: What was the response to the [nonrenewal] letter?

A: It raised fury. Congressmen have been writing and calling. We said, "Look, the law says ninety days' notice. This is notice in case we default. It's like a general RIF notice." It was an important message. It should tip agencies and bureaucracy. It took a lot of hassle here and up the line to the assistant secretary [to get the nonrenewal notices approved].

Q: How are the HSAs reacting?

A: Good. They made a lot of noise. They made congressmen aware. It was a smart move. L.A. is Waxman's district.

Q: Ahaaa.

A: The strategy wasn't so much a countermove to the administration—that was a byproduct. It was a legal administrative move for due process. I'm not trying to help the program by doing this. It has taken me nine to eleven months to look for a job, and I still don't have it. I'm being humanitarian. Trying to give the HSA directors some time. The quicker you give certainty on intentions, the better. I would rather get my specific [reduction in force] notice now. Give me a month's notice, not five days.

In the fall of 1981, while the bureau was sending out notices of nonrenewal, the governors of a handful of states closed their local HSAs in favor of a state program. Though this action achieved part of what the bureau was trying to do—reducing the number of HSAs so that more money would be allocated to the remainder—the action was taken by the governors and not by the bureau. Moreover, the bureau had adopted a policy of not encouraging the state governments to terminate their HSAs. This state action cannot be taken as a sign of successful implementation of bureau policy.

It was not until February 1982, after the bureau had experienced a reduction in force and the bureau director had resigned and was replaced, that it returned to the policy of selective termination for understaffed agencies. Unless the bureau could close a number of agencies by 1 July 1982, it could not succeed in carrying many dollars into fiscal year 1983. There was a strong protest on this policy from the HSAs, and the health planners professional association was instrumental in negotiating a delay in deadlines for conforming with the policy. The professional association eventually persuaded Congress to change the staffing requirements, taking away the bureau's rationale for selective termination. Over the long run, the bureau's policy to close down agencies for understaffing was not successfully implemented.

SUMMARY

The leaders of the Bureau of Health Planning were very committed to their program and would have liked to reverse the termination decision, but they had little independent power and were constrained by lack of autonomy. They continued to follow the law and tried to conform with presidential and departmental policy as well as they could under the circumstances. Although they did not dramatically oppose the president or militantly defend the bureau or the program, they did violate the intent of the administration in trying to ease the transition to private funding for the HSAs and keep health planning alive in some form.

The bureau staff wanted very much to help the HSAs that were most likely to survive by giving them a little more funding or funding them a little longer, which they could do with a policy of selective reallocation. For a brief period, it seemed as if the selective reallocation policy had congressional support. The bureau went about devising its reallocation policy in a rational way, exploring alternatives, devising criteria, finding or developing systematic data bases that would provide legal grounds for what it wanted to do.

But there were several obstacles to this emerging policy. The data base used to select agencies for termination was technically legal, but it did not seem to measure the excellence of the agency or its likelihood of surviving the end of federal funds. The bureau's autonomy to carry out reallocation was questionable. When morale was low, staff tended to let things go, unwilling to make painful decisions, especially those involving the termination of agencies' funding before the termination of the federal program. Looking back over the bureau's responses to declining political and financial support, one finds a distinct pattern characterized by vacillation between policies, by reluctance to terminate HSAs, and by incremental but highly symbolic decisions.

The goal of the bureau during the period of decline was to keep the HSAs and health planning alive, no matter what happened to the federal program. On the one hand, this goal led to a policy of reallocation, closing out some agencies to provide others with sufficient time and resources to find their own funding. On the other hand, the desire to keep the HSAs alive created a general reluctance to deal with closeout issues, especially if they involved terminating an agency's funding before all federal funds were gone. Because of this contradiction, the bureau could not take much action in either direction. Staff tended to vacillate between alternatives and take only limited steps to implement either reallocation or closeout policies.

Key decisions cycled back and forth between major alternatives not only because of the contradiction in strategies to keep planning alive but also because of constant changes in the environment. For example, the changing perception of how much money would be provided for 1982 altered decisions to allocate funds across the board or selectively. Also, as the perception of the environment changed, the morale of actors ebbed and flowed. Actors were sometimes willing to take on the bureaucracy around them to make something happen and sometimes unwilling to fight a structure which gave them little discretion.

Despite its vacillation between policies, the Bureau of Health Planning was not immobilized during the period of sharp resource decline and uncertainty. It continued to carry out its duties and attempted to make decisions in a rational and comprehensive manner. It laid out alternatives, devised decision-making criteria, and gathered evidence to make its decisions. Nevertheless, the outcomes of decisions were incremental, making only small symbolic changes from the status quo.

CONCLUSION

As of the beginning of 1984, the health planning program was still alive, although in a greatly reduced form. The bureau had undergone a reduction in force, which was not so severe as the administration wanted but which did substantially reduce staffing levels. Attrition continued as staff members found other jobs. Eventually, the bureau was reorganized and demoted to an office.

From the beginning of 1981 until 1984 the health planning program had persisted without clear direction or knowledge of its future. The program now is neither dead nor alive. There is talk in Congress of reviving it, as no effective alternative scheme for controlling health care costs has appeared. The problem of rising health care costs has become not only an immediate political issue but also a financial one for the federal government, which struggles with medicare and medicaid payments. Some of the regulated hospitals, including some hospital associations which benefited from the restraint of competition, have come forward to petition for some kind of health planning. Any new program is likely to have few regulatory teeth, however.[5]

While the fate of the bureau is being resolved, it remains moribund, unable to recover or adapt. As one staff member put it at the end of September 1981, after only one year of threatened termination, "The HSAs, even with all the weaknesses in their retrenchment process, are doing better than the bureau. The bureau has no idea of what it is to become and has made no effort to retain particular staff to make it happen."

The kinds of problems encountered by the Bureau of Health Planning are probably typical of those faced by agencies caught between the pre sident and Congress. The president was certainly able to control the agency; it neither defied his policy nor evaded it, although the bureau violated the spirit of the policy a bit by trying to keep the HSAs alive. But even though the bureau was basically docile in the face of the policy to terminate itself, the outcome over a three-year period has certainly not been a leaner, better-run organization. Threatened termination (as op- posed to actual termination or cutback) does not seem to improve manage- ment or increase efficiency.

NOTES

1. The legislation creating the health planning program is entitled, "The National Health Planning and Resources Development Act of 1974" (PL93-641).

2. Bruce Rocheleau describes the change from a multigoal health planning program to one more narrowly focused on cost control in 1977. See his paper, "Bargaining Theory and a Minimax Approach to Federal Bureaucracy" (Delivered at the Midwest Political Science Meetings in Chicago, 1979), especially p. 21.

3. Linda Demkovitch, "If the Health Planning Lid is Removed, Will a Hospital Boom Erupt?" *National Journal*, 20 June 1981, p. 1110.

4. Congress reacted to President Nixon's unilateral rescissions not only by changing the congressional budget process, as described in Chapter 2, but also by passing program legislation that gave the executive little autonomy over programs and built in limitations on funding. Thus the health planning law had built-in mini- mums for both staffing and funding levels of the HSAs.

5. Elizabeth Wehr, "Health Planning Lacks Friends, but Its Enemies May Save It from Extinction" *Congressional Quarterly Weekly*, 5 June 1982, p. 1335.

4

The Employment and Training Administration

Budget Cuts by the President and Congress

The Employment and Training Administration (ETA), a major agency in the Department of Labor, was responsible for a number of programs, including the Comprehensive Employment and Training Act (CETA), unemployment insurance, employment services (job placement), veterans employment programs and apprenticeship training. The ETA had a marked social service bias. Many of its programs were targeted to the poor; training, counseling, and job placement were seen as a way of reducing poverty. The programs were also designed to aid the unemployed. For example, Public Service Employment, a CETA program, provided the unemployed with work in public sector organizations. Other programs in CETA were designed to help particular classes of hard-to-employ people, such as housewives suddenly thrust into the marketplace, or youths from central cities who lacked skills and had no experience to offer employers.

The ETA generally did not provide services directly to the public but funded programs that were staffed by other levels of government. For example, the employment service is funded by the federal government but run by the state governments. CETA was a block grant program awarded to "prime sponsors" who were usually city governments or consortia of local governments. The prime sponsors contracted with private industry for training the unemployed and often ran Public Service Employment programs themselves.

The CETA program expanded rapidly for several years, increasing much faster in program dollars than in staff at headquarters. Given the complexity of the ETA's mission, the range of programs offered, the complexity of the arrangements for service delivery, and the relatively small staff to supervise all this activity, it is not surprising that the ETA gained a reputation in some quarters for being poorly managed and "flying by the seat of its pants."[1]

During the Reagan administration, the Employment and Training Administration experienced massive program cuts as well as extensive cuts in its administrative budget. The CETA program was due to expire in 1982, and though it seemed likely that some kind of program would be authorized to take its place, until the new legislation was passed, it was unclear how big the replacement program would be, how much administrative burden it would place on the central office, and how many people would be required to run it.

The ETA thus wrestled with both budget cuts and uncertainty. However, unlike the Bureau of Health Planning, the ETA was not confronted by a gap between the administration's intent and congressional action or inaction. Congress sided with the administration and sharply curtailed the ETA's budget. Later, Congress passed a reauthorization of the CETA program (the new bill was called the Job Training Partnership Act) that addressed many of the administration's concerns. The ETA case, then, is one in which the president both cut the agency and redesigned programs with the consent of Congress.

This chapter describes the relative roles of the president and Congress in cutting back the ETA, the agency's response to that effort, and the impact of budget cuts, personnel cuts, and reorganization on the management of the agency. Because interest groups were not particularly active in this case study, their role is sketched only briefly.

BACKGROUND

Agency Loss of Political Support

The Employment and Training Administration experienced a loss of political support over several years that led to continuous erosion of personnel levels and eventual budget reductions. In the mid 1970s there were a few well-publicized cases in which local officials ignored CETA regulations, creating scandals. These scandals created the impression that the agency was poorly managed.

For example, one involved the widespread practice in which city officials abused the Public Service Employment funds. Some cities reportedly fired their own employees to reduce payroll costs and then hired them back under grant funds as PSE employees because they were unemployed.[2] This practice was called "fiscal substitution." In essence, cities were substituting grant money for regular revenue.

There was also considerable publicity about improper expenditures by CETA sponsors and subcontractors. The result was several hundred million dollars of audit exceptions. An audit exception is a query by an auditor. It may mean that some data are unclear, a problem easily resolved, or it may indicate underlying and systematic management problems. Regardless of how many of the audit exceptions were cleared away, the number of dollars involved gave the impression of gross mismanagement.

In 1978, Congress acted to amend the CETA authorization act in an effort to reduce the number of abuses. The amendments were intended to "increase its targeting toward the poor, eliminate fiscal substitution by recipient jurisdictions, increase the amount of emphasis on transition to unsubsidized jobs, and reduce the levels of fraud and abuse."[3]

These improvements did not raise the political support levels of the agency, however, especially with respect to Public Service Employment. The new restrictions were adopted by local governments, but they made the program much less attractive to local officials. As a result, the program lost the support of much of its urban clientele. In fact, when Congress gradually cut back the program's funding, there was little protest. The coup de grâce in the president's March 1981 proposed budget reductions was only the culmination of a decline in support and funding of several years' duration.

The Reagan administration opposed CETA on ideological grounds, arguing that training should be separated from any kind of support payment. The combination of work training and payment made the program too much like a welfare program, and the public service aspect of the program was creating meaningless and dead-end jobs for PSE trainees, who were being trained for permanent jobs in the public sector that they might never fill, instead of jobs in the private sector. Finally, the politically conservative Heritage Foundation found the whole ETA badly run and recommended a total overhaul in administration:

The Employment and Training Administration is currently one of the poorest managed, confused and directionless agencies in the government. The agency pursues three sometimes contradictory missions—social, economic, and political—and constantly shifts direction in response to the changing whims of Congress. It is an agency that flies by the seat of its pants, and does even that poorly. Major changes are required in the legislation that provides the agency its mandate; in the agency's administrative personnel (from top to bottom) and in its management techniques.[4]

Erosion of Personnel and Funding

Over time, the result of the loss of political support was a loss of personnel positions and funding, eventuating in the loss of programs in ETA. The reductions in personnel began in 1977, when the official staffing ceiling was at 3831 permanent positions. By 1979, this had dropped to 3562. In 1980, the ceiling was down to 3185, and in 1981, there was an additional drop, to 3126. As of June of 1982, the agency-reported ceiling was 2750, while the official OMB ceiling for 1982 was 2557.[5]

Informants in the budget office at the ETA reported that these personnel reductions would continue in 1983 and 1984. They reported that the agency was expected to reduce another three hundred positions in 1983 or possibly spread out the drop over two years. The formal OMB-reported ceilings asked for a reduction of another three hundred positions in 1983 and an additional two hundred in 1984.

The continuing drop in personnel reflects both budget reductions and program changes. In the Omnibus Reconciliation Act of 1981, the Public Service Employees program was completely terminated, while other CETA programs were drastically cut back. Budget authority for CETA (budget authority is the legally mandated spending limit for the program) was reduced about 53 percent, and actual outlays for 1982 were reduced about 40 percent.[6]

It was not long after the omnibus reconciliation of 1981 that the president asked for a second round of budget cuts for the 1982 budget. In September 1982 he asked for an additional 12 percent budget cut for all agencies. This cut was concentrated primarily in salaries and expenses; that is, there would be a reduction in the cost of administering federal programs rather than in the size of payments to individuals or to state and local governments. Along with the requested 12 percent budget cut, the president called for a reduction of seventy-five thousand civilian employees over a two-year period. It was clear that he expected much of his budget cut to result in personnel reductions and layoffs.

Congress approved almost all of the additional 12 percent cut that the president requested for the Employment and Training Administration. It cut the Employment Training program an additional 10 percent after the omnibus reconciliation. Further, the Congressional Budget Office (CBO) estimated that for the following fiscal years, 1983 and 1984, the funding outlays would continue to drop, assuming the program was reauthorized (which it was).[7]

Although the president's personnel reduction targets called for about 6–6.5 percent across-the-board personnel cuts, the Department of Labor was reportedly cut about 10 percent in personnel levels. The ETA initially took the heaviest brunt of the cuts, with early proposals for personnel reductions running as high as 38 percent, or about twelve hundred jobs. After extensive negotiation, the final reduction in force was reduced to about five hundred employees in the ETA, which was closer to a 15 percent reduction in staffing levels. Given the size of the budget cuts, these layoffs, as great as they were, were proportionally moderate.[8]

After all this budget struggle, the CETA program was reauthorized, as the Job Training Partnership Act. This new law solved some of the difficulties that the Heritage Foundation had pointed out in its evaluation of the CETA program. The new law decentralized much of the program control and oversight to the state governments as part of the president's overall decentralization strategy. The expectation was that as the state governments took control over the program, there would be less and less work at headquarters, and the size of the staff would continue to shrink.

THE SOURCES OF THE CUTS

As the preceding account suggests, the ETA was cut back at several different times and in several different ways. On each occasion both the president and Congress played a role, although at each point one or the other may have been dominant. These relative roles can be illustrated by a more detailed examination of the sources of budget reductions in 1982.

The Omnibus Reconciliation

The major program cuts in the ETA occurred in the congressionally passed omnibus reconciliation. Although Congress cut the budget, the omnibus reconciliation was seen as the result of presidential policy. An assistant secretary for the Department of Labor described the origin of the ETA cutbacks in the following terms:

> There was a policy to terminate Employment and Training activities. It was a high-level decision, political, and made very early. Presumably, the decision flowed from the "mandate," if you want to talk of such things, of the 1980 elections.

The omnibus reconciliation of 1981 was described as originating with and being controlled by the administration:

> It was a top-down process. [Budget Director] Stockman and OMB determined where, quickly, and I might say, efficiently. There was not a lot of appeal [from their decision]. Cabinet officers were in sync with the philosophy; it was not a normal policy review. It was almost done by fiat.

When asked to compare the roles of Congress and the president, the assistant secretary described how the reconciliation process was used to bypass the Department of Labor's traditional support in Congress:

> The House struggled over the issues a little, but the president kept winning. The committee chair, Gus Hawkins, is a traditional, liberal L.A. Democrat. He could not bring himself and the committee to make the changes required

by the budget resolution, and they got "rolled over," beaten. It was Gramm-Latta [the OMB-initiated Gramm-Latta amendment.] And Stockman negotiated with the appropriate coalitions.

We did not go through the process of legislative changes. If we had relied on that [process]—subcommittees, hearings, etc., [the drastic cuts and program changes] probably would not have happened. Liberal Democrats controlled the Education and Labor Committee [but they were bypassed].

One of the features of the budget process is that it forces action by Congress around the traditional budget process. The reconciliation bill [1981] made all kinds of changes that the traditional workings would not allow. It couldn't have been done as swiftly without the Budget Reform Act [1974] and the vehicle of reconciliation.

To summarize, the president and OMB dominated and directed the omnibus reconciliation of 1981. The "new" congressional budget process (which was passed in 1974) allowed the president and OMB to bypass the traditional linkages between congressional committees and executive branch agencies.

The President's September Call for 12 Percent Reductions

The omnibus reconciliation in July 1981 was orchestrated by the president and the Office of Management and Budget, but it was executed by Congress. Theoretically, the president's September call for an additional 12 percent cut could have been handled in a similar way, but in fact the administration did not wait for Congress to act before it took action to implement the new round of cuts.

Considerably before Congress had taken final action on the 1982 budget, the ETA was told it would have to take the 12 percent cut. Because the cut was so large and because it was targeted to salaries and expenses (administrative costs), the ETA was forced to take immediate action to plan reductions in force. Since officials at the department level insisted that the ETA balance its budget, the proposed shortfall could not be ignored or even delayed. The agency was informed by departmental officials that it should accept the worst-case scenario for planning purposes. On 19 October 1981, before the battle between the president and Congress over the 1982 budget had been resolved, the assistant secretary for the ETA issued a general notice of anticipated reductions in force.[9]

The preparation for the reduction in force had to begin before Congress had acted on the budget because, first, Congress was passing continuing resolutions rather than a complete budget and, second, the agency needed to carry out the reduction in force in the first quarter of the year in order to save enough money. A reduction in force late in the fiscal year does not save very much money; firing an employee in the last month of the fiscal year would save only one month's salary. To save the same amount of money in the last month as would result from firing one person in the first month, twelve people would have to be fired.

Since preparations for a reduction in force take about three months and the effective date for the reduction was 31 December (the end of the first fiscal quarter), the preparation had to begin by early October. The agency was well along in implementing the president's budget request *before* Congress voted on that request.

Funding the Salary Increases

The third source of deficits for the 1982 fiscal year was the congressionally mandated salary increases. Congress voted during the continuing resolutions to allow salary increases for federal employees but did not include the cost of the increase in the continuing resolution. The result was that each agency had to decide whether it would fund the salary increase by further cutting the agency's expenditures (particularly personnel) or whether it would later request a supplemental appropriation from Congress to cover the increase. Congress had to act on each request separately and might grant it to some agencies and not to others.

If the ETA assumed that the administration would allow it to request a supplemental appropriation and that Congress would grant it, only to find out later in the fiscal year that these assumptions were wrong, the agency would have to find millions of dollars late in the year to cover the salary increases. Although, as noted, late reduction in force does not save much money, a furlough saves the same amount of money whenever it occurs, and everyone can participate in it. Thus if the agency had to save money late in the year, it would have to run a massive furlough.

Administrators at the ETA took the risk and asked for permission to apply for a supplemental appropriation. Officials at the departmental level approved the ETA's request. In case they did not get the supplemental appropriation, ETA officials planned a furlough, but this was cancelled just before it was to begin, when Congress granted the request.

The issue of the salary supplements involved both the administration and Congress, since the administration had to allow the agency to request a supplemental appropriation and Congress had to grant the request. But the dominant role in this financial problem was played by Congress, which, fearing that the president would veto its continuing resolutions because of the total cost, passed a resolution calling for salary increases without including their cost in the resolution.

To summarize, the budget reductions were directed primarily by the administration rather than Congress, even though Congress did eventually approve the devastating budget cuts. Congress was responsible for only one of the three cuts that occurred in the 1982 budget, and that one occurred because the Congress was trying to resist the president's pressure to cut and feared a presidential veto. Later, the one cut that Congress initiated was reversed when the supplemental appropriation was granted. But although Congress did not generally direct or determine the cuts, neither did it oppose those made by the president. At least during the budget cycle for fiscal year 1982, the president had enough control over Congress to cut back the ETA's programs, budget, and personnel.

THE PRESIDENT VERSUS THE AGENCY

President Reagan and OMB Director David Stockman had little trouble getting Congress to go along with budget cuts for fiscal year 1982. And when Congress lagged behind the administration's schedule, the administration took action on its own. But how did the agency respond? Had the president taken sufficient control of the department to prevent a major rebellion? Was the ETA able to reach Congress or interest groups with a protest? Were any of the cuts overturned? Did the agency disobey any of the president's cutback directives?

The President's Control over the Agency

One way of judging the degree to which the president controlled the agency is to determine whether officials at the top policy-making levels of the department were presidential nominees and, if so, whether they followed the president's policy for cutting back the agency.

Both the secretary and the assistant secretary for the ETA, two key positions for the agency, were loyal to the president. There was no indication that the secretary opposed any of the cuts, and the assistant secretary carried out OMB's policies to the fullest extent possible. The assistant secretary for administration, however, was a holdover from the Carter administration and a career official. Thus, since President Reagan did not initially select all the assistant secretaries for the Department of Labor, his political control was not complete.

The assistant secretary for administration did leave office (voluntarily) after the initial cutback period, but while he was in the assistant secretary position, he helped to maintain norms of impartial (nonpolitical) administration of the department. He did not specifically oppose or resist the president's policies; rather, he consistently advocated positions that would keep the appearance of politics out of administration.

It is not clear that the president's initially incomplete control of the policy level of the Department of Labor harmed his effort to cut back the agency. The ETA was cut back successfully and avoided the appearance of using the reduction in force for political purposes.

A second way that the president can take control of an agency is to cause a reorganization in which those most responsive to his policies are promoted into a leadership group, while program loyalists are demoted from policy-making positions. Though the ETA is not an extreme example, it exhibited some elements of this pattern.

When the agency reorganized, it reduced the number of GS-14 positions and demoted the incumbents of those positions. Because a number of GS-15 positions had been eliminated during the reduction in force, the combined effect of the reduction in force and the reorganization was to reduce the number of middle-level managerial slots and hence the number of middle-level managers. Since GS-14s and 15s are high-level civil service positions that normally involve policy-making responsibilities, the outcome was to weaken the ability of program loyalists to determine policy. Circumstantial evidence suggests that this outcome might have been the result of a conscious decision, since the administration later informally announced a policy of reducing the number of middle-level managers.[10]

Regardless of how the purpose of the reorganization is interpreted, it is clear that an invisible line was drawn around the top policy-making group and that, by comparison with the Carter administration, contact between it and ordinary employees was reduced. The labor union which had participated in management decision making found itself outside the decision-making group and seldom consulted for advice. Other employees complained that the assistant secretary for the ETA seldom came to the building in which the ETA was located, and one speculated that the top administrators did not want to get to know them because that might make it more difficult to terminate their jobs.

To summarize, although the agency was not overwhelmingly politicized, and the reduction in force was not used to fire program loyalists or retain those more responsive to presidential policy initiatives, the president had a firm control over the top level of the Department of Labor and, in particular, over the assistant secretary who supervised the ETA. Decision making was concentrated in a policy-making elite at the top of the organization, and career civil servants who had had a role in decision making during the Carter years were excluded.

Given the level of administrative control over the agency, there was not an enormous amount the agency could do to protect itself against cuts. The ETA was not in a position to rouse its constituents to fight for threatened programs either within the administration or in Congress. CETA, and the Public Service Employment program in particular, did not have many friends inside or outside Congress. Its traditional supporters in Congress were outvoted and outmaneuvered by OMB and the president.

Though program administrators at the ETA sensed that their major avenues of response were cut off, they did not simply accept whatever cuts were assigned to them. The agency tried to delay or reverse the initial cuts in the spring of 1981, offering to meet a 2 percent cut by cutting back two programs that were highly popular on Capitol Hill. The hope was that Congress would reject the proposal, and the agency would escape that round of cuts.

One of these programs was the Veterans' Employment Service. The matter came up at Senate Budget Hearings, where the strategy was questioned and explained. Senator Burdick asked Secretary Donovan, "Why would the Department of Labor propose this reduction since Congress so strongly disagreed with this proposal two years ago, and in fact included language in the appropriations bill which mandated the Department of Labor to retain these positions?" Mr. Zuck, assistant secretary for administration, answered, "Obviously, if we were not faced with the need to make the budget reductions, that may not be the approach we would have taken, but every program in the department obviously was subject to being reviewed to determine whether or not some possible reductions could be made."[11]

In the end, the agency's strategy did not work. All it achieved was a short delay. Congress did reject the cut, as the agency intended, and the Office of Management and Budget restored the positions which the ETA had offered to cut. However, OMB did not restore the funding for those positions in the 1982 budget. In essence, it told the agency to take the cuts elsewhere.

Other than that effort, there were no reported attempts to avoid or reverse budget cuts. Managerial strategies focused on carrying out the required reduction in force in an equitable and cost-effective manner. In particular, administrators in the ETA sought to minimize the number of personnel separated through reduction in force. They also sought to minimize the damage done by the reduction by shifting people around and returning them to their previous positions, but all this was done without a hint of defiance or resistance.

Minimizing the Number of Personnel to Be Terminated

The response of a number of ETA career officials (civil servants) was to accept the cuts as either inevitable or necessary or both. Within that acceptance, however, was a belief that reductions in staffing levels should continue to be by attrition, as they had been since 1977. Reductions in force should be avoided, but if they could not, the number of people involved should be kept to a minimum.

Since departmental officials prevented the agency from running a dollar deficit, there was no possibility of spreading out the time for personnel reductions so that attrition could carry more of the burden of reducing the work force. One of the alternatives left to the agency was to reduce the nonpersonnel operating costs as much as possible.

Administrative costs were the major target of President Reagan's proposed 12 percent reductions in September of 1981. Since salaries and expenses are lumped together in the federal budget as administrative costs, a reduction in nonpersonnel administrative costs (operating expenses) would minimize the need to cut staff. These items included travel, printing, space rental, and other overhead items.

Cutting the operating budget presented a formidable task, one that challenged the managerial capacity of the agency. The cost of items like printing and rent had recently doubled, with no allowance from OMB for the increases in cost. In effect, OMB's action forced the agencies to cut their budgets in these operating lines by about 50 percent. On top of that, the ETA tried to squeeze additional savings to reduce the need for personnel cuts.

One budget official in the ETA described the process of putting together the salaries and expense budget for 1982. He said, "It was like a puzzle, with known quantities and estimates of unknown quantities to fit in. It was difficult because of the restrictions on the agency." He explained that the nonpersonal service items in the salaries and expense budget were pared "to reduce the number of people to be RIFfed." Then once the number of people who had to be separated was established, the costs for the reduction in force had to be estimated, and further cuts had to be made to produce enough funds to carry out the reduction.

In addition to trying to squeeze more money out of the expense budget, agency officials tried to minimize the number of layoffs by requesting supplemental appropriations from Congress. As suggested earlier, this strategy required the cooperation of the assistant secretary for the ETA, who eventually endorsed it. The Office of Management and Budget sent a signal of possible support for a smaller reduction in force. The assistant secretary accepted this signal as an indicator of the administration's policy and went along with the ETA's requests for supplemental appropriations. The planned number of jobs to be eliminated was thereby reduced from twelve hundred to five hundred.

The signal sent by OMB was a reduction in the size of the drop in personnel ceilings for the ETA. In October 1981, OMB issued the new personnel ceilings for ETA, at the level of 2750 positions. That was a drop of only 500 positions. The budget cuts required a drop of 1200 positions. Normally, if budget cuts are greater than ceiling reductions, the cuts determine the size of the reduction in force. The amount of money available to pay for salaries is a limiting factor. In this case, however, the ETA chose to use the ceiling level for a guide instead of the budget cut. The reasoning was that the smaller-than-expected ceiling reduction indicated that OMB supported a smaller reduction in force and that it might support ETA's request for supplemental funds. This argument was accepted by the assistant secretary. Why OMB relented on the personnel ceiling was never explained.

The ETA put in two requests for supplemental appropriations, one to cover the salary increase, one to reduce the deficits resulting from the higher staffing ceiling. Between the two supplemental requests, the ETA asked Congress for about $14 million. If Congress did not come through for the agency, the shortfall would require thirty–forty days of furlough. The impact would be a substantial salary reduction for all employees, to avoid terminating the employment of an additional seven hundred employees.

For many months the agency did not hear from Congress on its requests. In April and May of 1982, furlough notices were sent to employees. Congress did pass the supplemental appropriations in time to prevent the furloughs, however. To this extent, then, the ETA strategy was successful.

Keeping the Reductions in Force Nonpolitical

The career officials at the ETA, in cooperation with the assistant secretary for administration, strove the keep the reduction in force free from political manipulation. The ETA administration succeeded in running a neutral RIF, by the rules, but it is not clear whether the president and his appointees were trying to use the RIF politically. Hence it is not clear how much defiance of the administration was involved in these tactics.

In order to understand what the agency did to prevent politicization of the reduction-in-force regulations, the reader needs to know a bit about how the regulations can be used for political or personal purposes. The regulations that were in effect until the fall of 1983 left much room for administrative discretion. (The changes introduced in the fall of 1983 have only added to that discretion.)

For example, administrators could hold out some positions from the reduction in force, not allowing affected employees to bump into them or retreat into them. Those employees might then be laid off. After the reduction in force, the positions which were held out could be filled by selecting favorites in the organization or by recruiting from the outside.

A second technique—one not formally advocated by the Office of Personnel Management, but not strictly illegal—was to separate and demote more people than necessary based on finances and then after the reduction in force to repromote or rehire those that were favorites.

A third technique was to define the competitive levels (the groups of people with similar skills) narrowly, so that there were only one or two or three people in a given competitive level. When that happened, if a position was eliminated, the administrator could be fairly certain who in that competitive level would be affected and who would lose their jobs. If competitive levels were broad, then bumping was likely to be extensive, and predicting the impacts on individuals could be difficult, if not impossible.

A related technique was to run practice sessions, or dry runs, of the reduction in force. In this technique, managers made recommendations for the original positions to be eliminated and then watched for the outcomes of the simulations to see who would finally be separated from employment. If managers did not like the outcomes, they could choose a different "seed," or position, to eliminate and see who would be affected by the resulting chain of bumping and retreating.

The great discretion allowed by the rules required the secretaries of the departments to specify how decisions ought to be made. In the Department of Labor, the assistant secretary for administration drew up a list of rules for running the reduction in force, many of which were designed to prevent the kind of tactics mentioned above.[12] The assistant secretary set up an appeals procedures within the Department of Labor on whether the RIF was run according to the regulations. He received no procedural appeals from the ETA.

It is also clear that the ETA had no intention of overfiring and then hiring back. Much of its goal in designing the reduction in force was to reduce the number of people involved. The agency separated many fewer people than initially indicated by budget constraints. Moreover, managers anticipated further reductions in staffing over the next two years, making it difficult to hire anyone back.

Nevertheless there were some accusations that the discretion was abused. The unions complained about the practice of running reductions in force on a trial basis, but agency managers argued that the trial runs very seldom led to any changes, because managers were usually not convinced that choosing another "seed" would produce a better outcome. Managers reported that they used the technique to prevent employees with absolutely indispensable skills from being separated from employment. Employees did not seem to feel that the criteria for selection of individuals to lay off were political; even the union did not charge that the choice of whom to separate had been based on political loyalties.

A second area in which questions were raised about the way discretion was used was in the merit evaluations. Civil service procedures allowed four years of seniority to be granted for outstanding performance ratings. Beginning in 1980, the top-level managers were to be rated in performance, while other employees could be evaluated if the agency wished. The system was implemented in 1981, and the evaluations of senior staff were completed just before the reduction in force. The rest of the employees were not evaluated before the RIF (because they had not been covered by the system for ninety days) and so had no possibility of receiving additional seniority.

The proximity between the performance evaluations and the RIFs put enormous pressure on managers to use the evaluations to protect selected employees from the danger of RIF. A much larger number of people were in fact judged outstanding in 1981 under the new system than in 1980 under the old system.[13] This change suggested some manipulation of the system.

In response to a wave of union protest, the evaluations were reviewed by support staff, office directors, and the assistant secretary and pronounced generally defensible. Reportedly, the evaluation system was less abused in the ETA than in sister agencies.

Not only were the merit evaluations sustained on review, but analysis of high ratings shows that they did not reflect attempts to protect some individuals so much as they reflected rater bias. Some bosses simply gave higher ratings to all their employees than others did. There was great variation from office to office. This is a weakness in the evaluation system and does not reflect a political use of the reduction-in-force procedures.

To summarize, presidential control over the ETA was substantial. The agency had little interest-group support to manipulate and was unable to reverse major cuts or program changes. The ETA tried a classic budget maneuver with Congress, offering programs to satisfy a budget cut that Congress would not accept, but the effort backfired when OMB restored the positions but not the funding in the 1982 budget. Thwarted in external strategies, the agency focused on reducing the size and maintaining the political neutrality of the reduction in force, tactics the administration accepted.

Though the Office of Management and Budget backed off from its worst-case scenario and allowed the ETA to ask for supplemental appropriations from Congress, the administration enhanced its control over the agency. Many of the agency's middle-level managerial positions were eliminated during the RIF and in the reorganization that followed. This action may have been part of a general strategy to create a politically loyal cadre at the top of the department and to remove program loyalists from policy-making positions.

CUTBACKS AND MANAGEMENT

The entire cutback process, including budget cuts, reductions in force, and reorganization, imposed new managerial complexity on the agency, absorbed time and attention, and lowered morale. Some of the managerial impacts were temporary, while others were longer lasting.

Budget Cuts

The budget cuts affected not just the programs in the states and cities but also the management of the agency itself. The uncertainty imposed by the president's budget battle with Congress was reflected in the budgetary process at the ETA. The president's targeting of administrative costs guaranteed that internal agency management would be affected. In addition to difficulties in the budgetary process created by uncertainty and reductions in force, the budget cuts created bottlenecks.

The uncertainty in the congressional budget process combined with the financial complexity of running a reduction in force to create a chaotic situation in the budget office. RIFs are financially complex because it is difficult to estimate both savings and expenses.

One budget officer at the ETA described the budget process as it was supposed to work and as it actually occurred in the fall of 1981:

> We normally prepare a budget estimate in August. The salaries and expenditure budget depend on the decisions of the assistant secretary, who makes decisions on staffing and on program areas. [Given that we had no decisions from the assistant secretary] we could not do anything. It should take four–five weeks to do a salaries and expense budget. We complete it, and it is submitted for departmental review, and then it goes to OMB. We get it back at the end of September. We change it, to reconcile it [with comments received] and print it for the president's budget in January. [Last year] we did a budget each month practically—one in August, one in September, one in October, and one in December. All told, there were five or more revisions of the budget. Probably all agencies did the same thing.

The fact that the salaries and expense budget changed so many times understates the impact of uncertainty, because each budget was treated as a puzzle, with some knowns from which the unknowns had to be deduced. When the size of the budget cut was announced, the budget officers had to decide where the money was to come from. They first cut the non-personnel lines, as far as they could, to determine how much they would have to save by reductions in force and/or furloughs. They then estimated the number of positions that would have to be cut to yield the necessary dollar savings. Then the costs of the RIFs had to be estimated by figuring severance payments, lump sum payments for unused leave, and expected unemployment payments. That amount had to be made up by more separations or by furloughs, in a repeated process.

The budget process had to be carried out in August after the omnibus reconciliation, when the first budget figure for cuts was "known," and then had to be repeated in September, after the president's request for an additional 12 percent cut. These were the figures that led to estimates that over twelve hundred people would be laid off. Then OMB reduced the personnel ceiling by five hundred, and five hundred became the operating number for position reductions. Estimates from savings from a reduction in force of this size had to be made in order to come up with the appropriate figures for a request to Congress for a supplemental appropriation and to estimate the size of the furlough if Congress did not approve the request. Uncertainty about the supplemental appropriations lasted into July of 1982.

In addition to affecting the budget process, the cuts also affected routine administration. Because of the desire to squeeze every possible cent out of the nonpersonnel budget items, many routine operating expenditures were severely reduced. The agency lost two floors of space, which caused employees to move all over the remaining floors. The amount of chaos is not hard to imagine, as files were temporarily inaccessible and telephone numbers changed quickly, with no provision for forwarding calls. It became difficult to know who was employed, let alone how to reach them.

Travel was cut back to the point of making it difficult to monitor what was occurring in the field. The travel constraints also affected morale. Employees were not only unable to carry out their normal responsibilities, but they were trapped in Washington, in the middle of reductions in force, watching their programs and agency shrink and, in some cases, disappear. As soon as possible after the reduction in force, the freeze on travel was lifted in an effort to improve morale, but other cost constraints remained in place.

Another item that was cut that had implications for management was the incentive system for outstanding performance. The incentive system was intended to identify outstanding workers and gave them a financial bonus. When money to fund the system was withdrawn to help limit the size of the reduction in force, the effect was to substitute for a positive incentive system a negative one based on the fear of job loss.

Reductions in Force and Reorganization

The managerial problems caused by budget cuts were as nothing compared with the problems introduced by the reductions in force. Each phase of a reduction—the preparation, implementation, and recovery—introduces its own managerial difficulties.

The preparation of a reduction in force is an extremely time-consuming task. It normally takes about three months of work by the entire personnel office, plus considerable time on the part of the office managers. The office directors must review the position descriptions for every position in their offices in order to match people to jobs. Employees have to update their work histories to demonstrate what jobs they had done and what work they can do.

The personnel office has to draw up competitive levels—that is, clusters of jobs with similar skills—and has to prepare retention registers, which list employees according to their rights to claim available jobs. When the office directors pick the initial positions to eliminate, the personnel office must prepare individual letters to affected employees, telling them whether they have been separated from employment or whether they are eligible for another position. That means that for each affected person a total search must be made of other jobs for which the person is eligible.

The letters informing employees that they have been separated include calculations of severance benefits and lump sum payments. When the RIF is actually administered, many of the letters must be amended. Sometimes amendments are required because of mistakes, but more often changes occur because new positions come open or people who have been offered alternative jobs refuse them. Thus the personnel office must be able to calculate retention rights and severance benefits immediately, as new people are affected during the reduction in force.

Besides the overwhelming mechanics of a reduction in force, there are other tasks associated with the preparation for it. For example, as already mentioned, as the ETA managers decided to do trial runs, to see who would be affected in the end if a particular positions was eliminated. Also managers had to be trained in how to inform employees of their rights and how to deliver the reduction-in-force letters. The employees themselves were trained in the RIF process so that they would know what was happening, what the rules were, and what the managers could and could not do for them.

In addition to the normal activities associated with the management and mechanics of RIF, the procedure was made more complex by the changing size of the planned reduction. The choice of twelve hundred positions to eliminate had already been determined and the people involved decided on when the reduction to five hundred was announced; thus the agency had to prepare the reduction in force again with fewer positions. The agency contract with the union specified that the union would be informed two months in advance of a reduction as to the job series and location of cuts, which put additional time pressure on the already hasty RIF.

The ETA official in charge of running the reduction in force described the process that went on:

I called the office managers in and explained to them the need for speed, and asked them how to allocate the position reductions. There was some turf protecting and fussing. They recommended that I just prorate the cuts. I went along. Some of the managers opposed my decision. My boss [the assistant secretary of ETA] said a few offices should be protected. There should be lesser cuts in unemployment compensation and some national program accounts. I didn't agree, but ... the rest was across the board. Twelve hundred positions. By December 31.

As soon as the RIF for twelve hundred was prepared, the five hundred figure was accepted, and the reduction in the number of positions to be eliminated was prorated. The official in charge of the RIFs described this phase:

Quick! Back to the drawing board. Prorate the reductions. Then share the information with the unions. And then put out the RIF notices. There was no time to fuss around. There was *tremendous stress*. Seven hundred people's jobs. Keep them, or drop them. [Seven hundred was the difference in size between the first estimated reduction in force and the second and actual RIF.]

Because the agency had focused on reducing the number of employees to be affected by the reduction and tried to run a RIF that conformed to the letter and intent of the civil service regulations, little attention was paid to trying to rig the reduction to minimize its impact on program management. As a result, employees were bumped all over the organization, and nearly every office was affected in some way. Old work groups were broken up, and new people unfamiliar with the work were bumped in.

Though considerable attention was given to the technical qualifications of employees for their new jobs, there was no attempt to match jobs to personalities. Thus some programs lost the people who were necessary to get programs started, and even though they were sometimes replaced, the new people could not necessarily carry out the project. For example, office automation was halted after word processing equipment had been purchased, because the person who had been responsible for getting employees to adopt word processing had been transferred, and the replacement reportedly did not have either the personality or the skills to sell a new technology.

Another aspect of the RIF implementation that affected the agency management had to do with the seniority of employees. Because the agency had been cutting back personnel levels since 1977, there were few employees with low seniority. That meant that employees with many years' experience in the agency were likely to be separated from employment because there was no one below them to bump. For those who did bump, especially for those who were able to retreat to former positions, the demotions tended to be very severe. The result was that managers were sometimes demoted to clerical positions while maintaining their old salary. The effect on both morale and productivity was dramatic and negative, while savings were minimal. (According to the RIF rules then in effect, the salary stayed with an official who was downgraded in a reduction in force for a period of two years.) The greater the demotion, the greater the loss of productivity, as highly trained, highly paid employees did work that less experienced, less well-paid employees could have done.

Because the RIF had been run with more attention to political neutrality and position preservation and less attention to managerial damage, the initial outcome was that people were scattered all over the organization, assignments were interrupted, and people were working in jobs well below their skill levels. Estimates were that between one hundred and fifty–two hundred people in the central office were shifted to new jobs and new supervisors. Very few offices were untouched. As a result, the activity level during the recovery period was almost as intense as in the period before the RIF.

There are a number of ways of recovering from this chaos, some formal, some less formal. Two bosses can swap employees back to their old positions, or an employee can be reassigned to another job in the same unit in which he is currently working. Employees can be detailed or formally loaned to another unit, usually to the unit they worked in before the reduction in force. The purpose of all the shifting around is to reassemble work teams to finish projects that were interrupted or to regain someone whose skills or knowledge was deemed crucial to the unit.

Not only may people be shifted back to their old positions, but those who were demoted can be repromoted in one of two ways. If the position they have been demoted to is part of a career ladder, they can be immediately promoted up the top of that ladder by their new supervisor. Or if a position opens up between the new low position and the old higher one, the demoted person may compete for the new opening. There is a requirement that demoted employees be considered for these positions, but there is no requirement that they be hired for them. A demoted person has a stronger right of consideration if a vacancy occurs at the level he or she occupied before the reduction in force.

At the ETA, the recovery period began immediately after the RIF, when the freeze on reassignments was lifted. People were traded "like baseball cards." "We traded supervisors, secretaries, etc." Sometimes "you got a turkey" bumped into your office, but "you could not get rid of those, even two for one." "There was some detailing." "One way to accommodate to the RIF was to get people back. Most of the high performers are [now] where they want to be." "We pushed here and there, exchanged lists at all hours of the day." The personnel office reported that there had been between thirty and forty repromotions between January and August of 1982 out of about two hundred demotions.

The personnel office director described the recovery phase in detail:

> The RIF was ETA-wide. The agency had no control over who moved from office to office. Some people may have been key—two managers would negotiate for Mr. X; the result could be a reassignment, temporarily or permanently. Some were detailed. Managers did their own swaps. As long as the two people being swapped are at the same grade level, it's O.K. After the RIF, we could go back to business as usual. There were between fifteen and twenty-five reassignments after the RIF. There were between fifty and seventy-five details, for a period of thirty, sixty or ninety days, as a transition device. Repromotions were allowed beginning three weeks after the RIF; there have been twenty-eight of them so far in the national office [as of July 1982].

AGENCY IMPACTS

Although the personnel director reported that the agency returned to business as usual after the RIF, in several ways the return was not immediate. For example, the freeze on promotions was maintained after the RIF, with the exception of repromotions. And there were problems of managing an operation with people only minimally familiar with their jobs. The recovery period, with all the swapping of personnel, was proceeding well when the reorganization began, which was followed by a second RIF and a round of demotions. The chaos was thus kept going for several more months.

One informant described the continuing chaos after the reduction in force:

> Clearly there is a continuing impact of the shifting. That doesn't seem to stop. The RIF was over in December, but in April we had a headquarters reorganization. We also lost two floors of space and crowded everyone into the remaining space. We tried to fit the reorganization that was coming, but people couldn't report to their new supervisors. It's about done now.... Our boss likes to juggle the organization around a little. It's perceived as totally unorganized, and it's disruptive.

Another factor which slowed down the recovery was that repromotion of all demoted personnel dragged after a brisk start. The problem was that so many GS-14 and 15 positions had been eliminated during the RIF and reorganization that there were not enough positions remaining at that level to accommodate all the demoted employees.

Moreover, the threat of further RIFs and demotions remained, since the agency was basically watching over the transition to block grants run by the states. The agency was gradually reducing its own workload. Thus employees were never able to completely recover from the shock of budget cuts and reductions in force. Although the agency was able to overcome much of the immediate negative impact, it took many months. Eight months after the RIF and some three or four months after the reorganization, several managers expressed the view that the agency had sufficiently recovered to take on a new mission, if the RIF and reorganization did not become recurring events.

Adding the three months of preparation to the eight months of recovery, it took the agency nearly a year to return to a reasonable working level. Because the RIF and reorganization took so much time and effort, many other essential program activities were temporarily set aside. In particular, the agency had difficulty carrying out monitoring activities. As one administrator described it:

> The agency shut itself down. Those demand things we had to do, we did. But other things, such as assist in the management of programs, we didn't do. I asked the regional administrators about the impact [of the reduction in force.] When regional administrators resumed work in January, they found some messes. For example, a big city prime sponsor had spent money on wrong items. If there had been monitoring, it would not have happened. You

have to dig. The city owed us money and paid us back. There was also staff turnover among the grantees; we didn't know the new staff. The CETA system was also RIFfing. They tried to reinvent what they had already done. One of the things that bothered me about the RIF was that all my discussions with the regional administrators were about the RIF, not about the program.

Even after the recovery period was over, some employees reported a continuing effect on morale. "We get our work done," reported one employee, "but we get it done more slowly."

Besides some of the short-term effects on the organization of the reductions in budget and staffing levels, the cutback process at the ETA had some broader, longer-term effects. One of the most important of these was the evolution of the relationship between management and labor. The unions, accustomed to a cooperative relationship focused on work satisfaction and the quality of work life, found that management had ceased to consult with them and rejected the results of their research. Because of the break in communications with management, the unions gradually retreated to the more formal posture imposed on them. They became more concerned with contract rights and the defense of those rights.

One union representative reported,

> The union strategy has been to outmanage management. I am less inclined now to try to convince managers and more inclined to state a position. I used to try to help them find a way. Now I am saying, 'It's crazy.' It's given me an ulcer. I don't trust the assistant secretary, and I don't think the employees do. He hasn't met with the employees. He hardly comes here. We are losing the cooperative relationship. There is no more romance. We are playing by the book. It's a shame. Management loses more than the employees.

A second change that occurred during the cutback period is that many managers who felt they could gradually win over the new administration found that they could not. As a result, they began gradually detaching themselves. Although they did not defy orders or try to delay, they became more frank about indicating where particular decisions had been made. The union leaders reported that many managers had become more sympathetic to the union, sharing information with them in a way that did not used to occur. One informant reported, "They [the program managers] have more allegiance with the union than with the administration."

Even more important than the tendency to detach themselves from decisions they had to implement was the psychological isolation of middle-level managers who opposed the administration's plans for the agency:

> Some managers now are very afraid. Those who are vocal are being isolated. Another layer is being put on top of them, or they are being transferred. There has been some attempt to squeeze some of those with twenty plus years of service, so they can bring in new people. They put the person in a job they know he can't do and let him fail and give him a poor evaluation.

Another long-term impact on the agency was felt by high-seniority employees who were demoted:

> We had an upward mobility program. Those women are now back to typing. Work ethic values are destroyed. That is not effective resource management. Management says the RIF procedures do not provide the opportunity to do otherwise. They may be right, but it can be helped now, and there is no effort to do so. With no expectation of growth or movement, it's frustrating and difficult. I don't know if we will ever recover from that.

For employees, as noted previously, a negative incentive system was substituted for a positive one. The positive incentives included a financial bonus for outstanding performance, the satisfaction of working to benefit the lives of the unemployed and poor, and the general quality of work life. The financial bonus was temporarily eliminated. Agency leadership downplayed the importance of the quality of work life. Some employees came to fear being put into jobs they could not perform and receiving poor job-performance evaluations. They feared that political criteria might be used for reductions in force, and they feared to take a stand lest they be "shelved" (removed from policy positions) or fired. Whether or not these fears were justified, some employees believed they were.

Finally, the reduction in force further depleted the ranks of younger people and female managers. The younger people were disproportionately affected because of the importance of seniority in the calculation of retention rights; women managers were affected by both seniority rules and veterans' preference. Often women have been in their managerial positions for a shorter period than men, and because they normally do not have military service, veterans (mostly males) are more likely to be retained. The outcome for the agency of the RIF regulations is an older, less varied, and less vital work force. This impact on the agency will probably last for years.

SUMMARY AND CONCLUSIONS

Cutbacks at the ETA were designed and dictated by the president and the Office of Management and Budget. Congress generally went along with the president. Individual congressional supporters of the program were bypassed in the reconciliation process when they were unwilling to make cuts in accordance with instructions. The Office of Management and Budget successfully lobbied the right people in Congress to get its measures passed. When Congress did not act quickly enough, the administration moved on its own.

The ETA had few resources with which to fight the cuts. It did not have sufficient interest-group or popular support to reverse the cuts either in Congress or in the administration. Both the secretary and the assistant secretary of the ETA supported the president's policies. Accepting the inevitable, the agency took the cuts with good grace. It made only one effort to enlist congressional support to reverse a minor cut; Congress did reverse the cut, but the OMB forced the agency to take the same size cuts in ways more acceptable to Congress.

Rather than spending its energy fighting the cuts, the agency tried to minimize the size of the reduction in force. This it succeeded it doing, after obtaining administration support.

The cuts caused considerable damage to the agency's management. The speed, severity, and targeting of the president's cuts virtually guaranteed that they would necessitate reductions in force. The reduction procedure, even when followed to the letter, created continuing disruption for many months. The union was alienated and forced into a combative role, women were disproportionately threatened by demotions, and some managers withdrew some of their effort and loyalty from the administration. They were not in open rebellion, but they were cut adrift, and their efforts were not fully tapped.

It took the ETA nearly a year to recover an adequate level of functioning. The CETA program was redesigned by the administration in reauthorization legislation, but there is no indication that the new program (the Job Training Partnership Act) will improve management at the federal level. The new program should, however, reduce the responsibilities of the Washington office by shifting responsibility for program management to the states.

In sum, although the agency was pared down, it was not stabilized at a smaller size with less fat and better management. Despite the administration's goal of improved management and the elimination of waste, it seemed to pay little attention to managerial problems. The cuts and reorganization were not designed to solve these problems. The president and OMB focused more on terminating programs and bypassing the agency by giving new programs to the state governments to administer. OMB may have shown some sensitivity to managerial need in paring back the size of the proposed personnel reductions. Agency managers in Washington did what they could to recover from the reduction in force and reorganization with a system of informal and formal swapping and repromotions to keep work teams together.

NOTES

1. Robert Hunter, "Labor," in *Mandate for Leadership*, ed. Charles L. Heatherly (Washington: Heritage Foundation, 1981), p. 476.

2. See, for example, "Detroit Allowed Funding for Hiring," *New York Times*, 13 April 1976, p. 11, which describes the Detroit case. The Department of Labor

reportedly allowed Detroit to rehire laid-off employees, although the city violated regulations.

3. John William Ellwood, ed., *Reductions in U.S. Domestic Spending: How They Affect State and Local Government* (New Brunswick, N.G.: Transaction Books, 1982), p. 213. The authors cite the Congressional Budget Office, "An Analysis of President Reagan's Budget Revisions for Fiscal Year 1982," March 1981, pp. A–49.

4. Hunter, "Labor," p. 476.

5. The OMB-mandated personnel ceilings are taken from the U.S. Budget, appendix; the agency-reported ceilings are from personnel figures at ETA.

6. These percentage reductions are computed by comparing 1982 authorizations and outlays with the Congressional Budget Office (CBO) estimates of how much it would cost in 1982 to provide the level of services provided in 1981. This calculation tends to make cuts look larger than if 1982 figures were just compared with 1981 figures, but comparisons based on "constant service levels" are more realistic and meaningful.

7. For CBO estimates, see Ellwood, *Reductions in U.S. Domestic Spending*, p. 215. Using the previous year's actual appropriation as the basis for calculation, there was a 50 percent program funding reduction for CETA in 1982. See the U.S. Budget for 1983 and 1984, appendix.

8. There was considerable pressure against the administration's proposal to cut more positions from the ETA because of evidence that the agency was already seriously understaffed and hence unable to monitor grantees adequately. For example, even the conservative Heritage Foundation reported in the spring of 1981 that the ETA might have been cut back too far. The Human Resources Committee recommended overriding the president's recommendation in the spring of 1981, even before the president's second request for cuts, when reductions in ETA were expected to be considerably less severe than they eventually were. See Senate Committee on Appropriations, *Departments of Labor, Health and Human Services, Education and Human Services, Education and Related Agencies Appropriations, Fiscal Year 1982: Hearings*, 97th Cong., 1st sess., Part 1, 1981, p. 620.

9. Memo to all national-office ETA employees from Albert Angrisani, assistant secretary of labor, "General Notice of Reduction in Force," 19 October 1981.

10. "U.S. to Cut 40,000 Middle-Level Bosses" *Chicago Tribune*, 17 November 1983. The article quoted a White House spokesman to the effect that the Reagan administration planned to eliminate forty thousand middle-level management government jobs by forcing federal agencies to abolish or downgrade senior positions when they were vacated. The spokesman indicated the incumbents of those positions would not be demoted or fired but that the positions would be eliminated taken when they became vacant. Though the stated policy involved reduction by attrition, departmental officials could have been overzealous in carrying out this policy, or they could have received another, less formal communication to the effect that reductions in force or reorganizations could be used to force out incumbents.

11. Senate Committee on Appropriations, *Departments of Labor, Health and Human Services, Education and Related Agencies Appropriations, Fiscal Year 1982: Hearings*, 97th Cong., 1st sess., 1981, Part 1, p. 555.

12. Memo for agency heads from Alfred Zuck, assistant secretary for administration and management, "Reduction-in-Force Decisions," 4 November 1981.

13. The numbers involved were provided to me by the union local at ETA.

5

Community Planning and Development

Proposed Termination, Resistance, and Deregulation

The Community Planning and Development Program (CPD), a major component in the Department of Housing and Urban Development, is responsible for a variety of programs aimed at stabilizing changing neighborhoods, eliminating slums and blight, and providing housing and increasing the number of jobs for the poor and those of moderate income.

During the Reagan administration, some of CPD's programs were terminated, while others were threatened with rescission (the withdrawal of legislative approval to spend money) and termination. The number of its regulations was reduced and its capacity to oversee its programs dramatically curtailed. Some programs were turned over to state governments to run. With a streamlined operation and reduced responsibility, the agency was threatened with reductions in force and reorganizations, in the field as well as in headquarters.

The CPD resisted some of these pressures, moderated some of them, and yielded to others. It tried to respond to the president and the Congress as well as to interest groups. When there were contradictions between these pressures, the agency had to negotiate a middle path. The process by which bargaining positions were outlined and compromises reached illustrates much about bureaucratic politics, about the implementation of the president's program, and about the limits of power of the president, Congress, federal agencies, and interest groups.

BACKGROUND

CPD houses a number of programs, the largest and best known of which are the Community Development Block Grant (CDBG) and the Urban Development Action Grant (UDAG). The purpose of the Community Development Block Grants is to stabilize deteriorating neighborhoods through funding local capital projects. The program has also funded some neighborhood-based social services. CDBG requires considerable neighborhood input in the selection of projects. The UDAG program is more oriented to facilitating large capital projects that will generate jobs in low-income neighborhoods; it has been somewhat more concerned with benefiting business than with aiding the poor. This range of programs helped to create a broad base of interest-group support.

CPD, like much of the rest of HUD, was run internally by career officials who believed in the agency's programs and wanted to contribute to the well-being of the poor. Cutting back a program which is run by career officials who are so loyal to their programs can present problems to a president. To counteract these officials, the president needs tight control over the top levels of the department. It helps if the program has little congressional or interest-group support. In the case of HUD, the president enjoyed neither of these advantages.

The President's Control over HUD

The Reagan administration chose a secretary, an undersecretary, and assistant secretaries who were loyal to its program. These appointed officials in turn selected from career officials those more in tune with the president's philosophy and made them part of the decision-making corps of the department. The process was much like that advocated by former President Nixon to take over agencies, which was outlined in Chapter 2.

These officials at the top of HUD presented the Congress the reduced budget requests worked out between themselves and the OMB and defended the reduced requests in the face of harsh congressional questioning. To that extent, they were loyal to the president, but their loyalty was not complete.

The secretary and the assistant secretary for CPD were at least partly convinced of the value of the programs they were supposed to cut. They fought inside the administration to preserve programs and protest staffing levels.[1] While carrying out the president's program, they sought to moderate some parts of it.

The Level of Congressional Support

Part of the resistance of the president's agenda for HUD occurred in Congress. HUD in general, and Community Planning and Development in particular, enjoyed considerable congressional support, especially in the House of Representatives but also, to a lesser degree, in the Senate.

Support for HUD was part of the general congressional reaction to the president's domination of the budget process during the omnibus reconciliation. Initially Congress approved large parts of the president's program in the omnibus reconciliation of 1981, which bypassed the normal processes of committee deliberations. But committees that had been bypassed did not necessarily accept what had been done and sought occasions to help remedy the damage. For example, Congress responded to the president's September 1981 requests for an additional 12 percent cut with a cut averaging only 4 percent.

The House appropriations subcommittee that dealt with HUD (and related agencies) was sympathetic to HUD's programs and helped to stabilize funding levels. Both the House and Senate appropriations subcommittees agreed to temporarily restrain HUD from spending money on a reorganization, as a result of a union-inspired effort to prevent reductions in force at headquarters. In addition, HUD was required to take only a 4 percent cut, when some other agencies had to take the full 12 percent.

The authorizing committees in both houses were even more supportive. The House Banking, Finance, and Urban Affairs Committee and its Subcommittee on Housing and Community Development were extremely loyal to programs they had helped to design. They held hearings on proposed reorganizations and reductions in force, had meetings at HUD with assistant secretaries, contacted interest groups, and invoked the General Accounting Office to do studies and provide arguments against reductions. The subcommittee plagued the department with requests for documentation and tried to delay implementation of new regulations and alter their content.

On the Senate side, it was the ranking minority member of the Senate authorizing committee for HUD, along with three other Senators, who requested the GAO to investigate the Reduction in force at HUD headquarters.[2]

The Level of Interest-Group Support

The third source of resistance to the president's programs was interest groups. Public interest groups, representing cities, counties, and state officials, and representatives of business all fought together to protect programs from termination. Neighborhood groups testified on the harm caused by program cutbacks and the damage likely to be caused by changing regulations. Bankers, builders, and developers testified against closing area offices and merging them with regional offices in a field reorganization; they were joined by local unions representing career employees.

The interest groups represented a wide geographic area. The neighborhood associations and their national umbrella groups came from all over the country, as did the associations of city and county officials. The regional office reorganization threatened new groups throughout the country, developers, union locals, bankers, and builders. This broad geographical base, representing a variety of classes and groups, helped make interest-group opposition effective.

What made this opposition even more effective is that the different groups were allied with each other. Business leaders and city officials fought for UDAG and CDBG programs. City officials and neighborhood associations, often antagonists, joined together to fight the new CPD regulations that weakened programs aimed at the poor. These unusual alliances left the administration without anyone to argue for reduced regulation, reduced targeting, or program termination.

The interest groups supporting CPD's programs were easy to rouse. Like most such groups, they followed key budgetary events carefully and watched for the issuance of new regulations. Once they sensed an issue pending, they took action, testifying before Congress, writing letters to the agency, and arguing with the president.

Though interest groups usually knew what was going on and decided on their own course of action, they did not always learn about policies that were kept secret by the administration. The proposal to terminate the UDAG program, for example, was kept quiet. Then officials in CPD had to inform the interest groups of the danger and urge them to act. On the issue of a reorganization in the field and on the issue of targeting programs to the poor, congressional committees helped to orchestrate the interest groups to make the maximum impact.

Interest groups were not, then, an entirely independent force, exerting pressure in their own behalf; they were also a means by which both the congressional committees and the agency could speak to the administration and argue in political terms the administration could respond to. Once the interest groups were unleashed, however, the agency was caught between the interest groups and the administration and had to find a position for itself between the various demands.

THE PRESIDENT'S PROGRAM AND AGENCY AND DEPARTMENT RESPONSE

The president's program involved budget and program cuts, deregulation, and decentralization to the states. The actions taken to achieve these aims created a certain amount of chaos and required some managerial adjustments, such as reorganizations and personnel reductions. The administration also sought to reduce personnel and reorganize for other reasons, including the political goal of "taking the bureaucrats off the backs of the people," and the administrative goal of increasing the agency's policy responsiveness.

Budget and Program Cuts

Community Planning and Development first came under budgetary attack during the Carter administration in the 1981 rescission proposals, but the problem became more acute under the Reagan administration, which proposed the total cancellation of first the UDAG program and then CDBG. The agency fought these proposals inside the administration, with some degree of success.

Why cut UDAG and CDBG? The Reagan team targeted its cuts early in the administration to discretionary programs over which the administration and Congress had direct control. Both UDAG and CDBG were considered discretionary. In addition, these two programs were targets for ideological reasons.

The UDAG programs was considered a subsidy for redevelopment projects in inner-city areas. Administration strategists opposed the subsidy nature of the program as a threat to free markets. Moreover, the expenditure was seen as a waste of money because the projects would (arguably) be built even without UDAG funds.[3]

Underlying much of this criticism may have been a political argument. The program was created in the Carter administration, and awards had been made to solidly Democratic mayors who supported that administration. Those cities could not be expected to support the Reagan administration.[4] Therefore, the Reagan administration had no desire to support them.

Objections to the Community Development Block Grant program were a little different. One argument was that CPD did not keep good enough data to know whether the program was achieving its goals.[5] Politically, the issue had to do more with targeting the program to the poor and the regulations and application procedures for such targeting. Later, when the administration found that it could not just terminate CDBG, it decided to attack these issues of regulations and targeting more directly.

The UDAG program was attacked first, when OMB proposed a rescission of the program in February of 1981. CPD's response was to try to fight the termination proposal inside the executive branch, but in order to gain any support inside HUD, CPD needed the support of Secretary Pierce. This was a level of support never gained by the Bureau of Health Planning in the Department of Health and Human Services or by the ETA in the Department of Labor.

Program officers and CPD leadership managed to convince the secretary to support the program. Informants described the process of winning over the Secretary:

In February of last year, there was a rescission proposal for UDAG. There was a great debate between us and OMB. Stockman's [the director of the Office of Management and Budget] black book was all over the city. The secretary was reasonably convinced, but not overwhelmingly, that it was working well. He ordered a major study. He ordered a cabinet meeting, which is a forum for budget discussion for the departments. The president had met with the mayors who supported it. The decision was made by the president not to rescind it.

My informants described the gradual involvement of Secretary Pierce in the administration of CPD programs and his consequent support for those programs. The secretary was particularly involved in making decisions on UDAG funding.

> The secretary hears of each UDAG. It goes all the way up. We take the marginal ones up. The secretary picks up on them. . . . He is very involved. . . . The secretary used that experience to argue for the program. He argued, "I see the cases, these deals are the ones that should be funded. The least [possible] amount of government money is going in."

The study ordered by Secretary Pierce was also an important part of winning him over, since it was basically favorable to the UDAG program, finding most of it good and suggesting some improvements, which were adopted. The program had a good track record, with concrete, observable results—over three hundred projects completed—and this factor reportedly was important in winning the secretary's support. Once Secretary Pierce's assistance had been enlisted, he become a vocal spokesman, appealing the OMB decisions and reversing Stockman's decision at the cabinet level.

As suggested above, there was also active interest-group pressure directly on the president at this time. Richard B. Williamson, spokesman for the administration on urban and state funding cutbacks, described the president's response to this lobbying: "The Mayors' strong praise for UDAG has caused Reagan to remove it from his list of cuts, at least temporarily, and to order Meese, budget director David Stockman and Secretary of HUD Samuel Pierce, Jr. to examine ways in which its valuable elements might be saved."[6]

An informant in CPD described the role of interest groups in turning the president around on the issue of program termination. He felt that the president was convinced because of the business backing for the programs. The informant argued that the involvement of these big corporations in UDAG-sponsored projects paid unexpected dividends when the presidents of the corporations went to bat to save the programs:

> City interest groups of course supported the programs, but others did as well. The governors, for example. The presidents of Prudential and General Motors liked the programs. That has turned out better than expected, in terms of their participation in the program.

The battle over the proposed rescission of fiscal year 1981 funding was soon followed by a skirmish over the proposed 1982 budget. Coming only a few months after the political battle over rescission, the results confirmed what the administration had learned, that the UDAG and CDBG programs had considerable political support. Both UDAG and CDBG were cut slightly in program dollars in the Omnibus Reconciliation Act in 1981, but the programs were basically left intact.

It was only a few months after the omnibus reconciliation, in September, that the president called for a new round of budget cuts of 12 percent, more or less across the board. UDAG lost almost nothing in this second round of cuts for 1982, but CDBG program funds were cut about 6 percent from the reconciliation level.[7]

At first, CPD leadership thought that 12 percent would be taken across the board in salaries and expenses, since Secretary Pierce had indicated that if the cuts were to be that deep, they would be shared equally. The salaries and expense cuts were not that deep, however, and were not allocated across the board. CPD experienced only about a 2.5 percent reduction in salaries and expenses in this second round of cuts.

All of HUD averaged together reduced its salaries and expenses only 1.28 percent for 1982.[8] HUD had requested of OMB that the cut be taken disproportionately in program funding and that salaries and expenses be relatively protected. OMB went along with the proposal.[9] Up until this point, at least, the secretary and the assistant secretaries had been successful in trying to protect the department from budget-driven reductions in force.

The president, as represented by OMB, did not give up his efforts to terminate UDAG and CDBG, even after the considerable demonstration of interest-group support for both programs. The battle was refought over the proposed 1983 budget. Initially in that request UDAG was terminated again, and CDBG was to be phased out over a three-year period.[10]

In early December, CPD spokesmen appeared at meetings of interest groups, suggesting that the program was under attack and that interest-groups representatives needed to tell the president they supported UDAG.[11] Governors' associations, business groups, and cities' representatives met with the president and indicated the political costs of eliminating the program.

Against this background of lobbying within the executive branch, Secretary Pierce and the assistant secretary for CPD did battle again with David Stockman, and they won again, at least to the extent of stabilizing the 1983 appropriation at the 1982 level and stabilizing the estimated budget (but not staffing levels) for the next few years.[12] The extent of the success was tempered slightly by OMB's request for a deferral of some CPD funding in the fall of 1983 of about $500,000,000. (Deferral is the temporary denial to an agency of the right to spend a particular sum of money.) The deferral was of carryover funds the program had been unable to commit in earlier years. The administration wanted to be sure that there was no program expansion using leftover funds.

Almost all of this process was fought out within the executive branch, including the mobilization of interest groups. The administration proposed termination of these programs and then withdrew the proposals, all before the budget was presented to Congress. The following exchange, at a budget hearing, clarifies the administration's position and the history of the budget request for the UDAG program, while illustrating the extent to which Congress was excluded from the process.

> *Mr. Boland* (Congressman):   Is the Department aware of any information that came from the OMB that this program [UDAG] will be phased out in 1983?
>
> *Mr. Dodge* (from CPD):   I am aware that OMB originally had proposed it be eliminated in FY 1982. However, it was decided during a cabinet meeting to be carried throughout this year as well as in fiscal year 1982.
>
> *Mr. Kliman* (budget officer for HUD):   Yes, there are documents in blue-covered books which call for the program to go only through 1982. Many of those documents have been published. For instance, there is another document which announced a Community Development Program with different percentages than in the legislation which is going forward at this point. The undersecretary testified before Mr. Gonzales on this very subject that those documents represented the thinking of OMB at a point in time, but did not represent final decisions. No final decision has been made at this time on the UDAG program for 1983 by the administration.[13]

This focus on the executive not only underscores the proper behavior of executive branch agencies during cutback (no end runs to Congress, no opposition to a decision of the president once it has been made) but also suggests where budgetary power lay at that time.

As other analysts have suggested, budgeting became more of an executive and less of a congressionally controlled process under Reagan.[14] Interest-group activity reflected that shift. There was very little congressional lobbying during this budget battle. There may have been an iron triangle of sorts operating, but the corners of the triangle included the agency, the interest groups, and the president (sometimes represented by OMB), not the agency, the interest groups, and Congress. Congress played a role in the budget, of course, but the interest groups focused primarily on the White House during the budget battle.

Deregulation

The second major portion of the president's program involved deregulation. With respect to CPD, that activity had three parts: 1) dropping the application procedures for CDBG grants, 2) reviewing existing regulations, and 3) promulgating new regulations to implement the changes in law in the 1981 omnibus reconciliation. The new regulations were to be less restrictive and burdensome than the old ones.

The first step in deregulation was to eliminate or greatly simplify the application procedure for the Community Development Block Grant. In the 1981 omnibus reconciliation Congress approved the administration's request to drop most of the application procedures. Since the review of applications was CPD's way of ensuring compliance with the intent of the law, the elimination of applications eliminated CPD's effective control over how the grant money would be spent. The administration offered postaudits as a substitute for prior project approval.

The postaudit route is likely to be a difficult one to implement. CPD was unable to put together any regulations regarding postaudits at the time when it presented (nearly a year after the legislation passed) regulations to implement the other changes, such as removal of the application procedures. Also, CPD's information base concerning grantees was very dependent on the information provided in the applications. Without applications, CPD will have to gather data for postaudits in some other way. OMB has approval and veto privileges on all agency requests for information. In fact, HUD had an information collection budget, like a financial budget, which was cut back each year by OMB in an attempt to reduce the paperwork burden on the public. It is therefore possible that OMB will block the gathering of data to evaluate program conformity.

The second part of the deregulatory effort was to review existing regulations. This review began on 6 April 1981, when Secretary Pierce established a departmental process intended to carry out the deregulatory objectives of the administration. Three-quarters of the regulations in CPD were designated for review, and new regulations were slowed down.[15]

In CPD, the review of existing regulations took several forms. Handbooks were inventoried to see if policy had crept into them. According to agency officials, policy was sometimes intentionally issued in this manner to get around the clearance procedures. "One hundred and eight of those [it is not clear whether handbooks or policies is the referent] were rendered obsolete. There were 2000 pages of obsolete or redundant paper." About 1600 pages of missives were inventoried. The impact of this purge of regulations was estimated for the small-cities program alone to save about 457,000 "burden hours" (burden hours means the number of hours citizens spend filling out forms).

According to an informant in CPD, the program for the entitlement cities (the larger cities funded by a formula) went through a mandated review. "OMB was pleased. Now the regulations are ready to go to OMB [for approval]. There has been a 50 percent reduction in regulations. A lot of it was deadwood, clutter. They were regulations for programs we no longer had. Those were easy."

Although there was clearly much effort involved in cleaning out regulations and reducing their numbers, given this description of the process, it is difficult to judge how meaningful or important this deregulatory effort has been.

The third part of the deregulatory effort in CPD involved issuing new regulations to implement the changes and simplifications in the omnibus reconciliation and to continue to broaden the autonomy of grant recipients in the use of funds. One informant gave an overview of this process:

> We had difficulty with the new regulations. We were involved in the deregulatory effort. We put the new regulations through their rigorous process. There was a big debate with OMB over what it should be like. It was improved but still too prescriptive. The process with OMB was tense at times. But we came to a reasonable agreement and shipped it on up on the Hill. On the Hill, some were happy, others were not. They asked the secretary for changes. The regulations were published last November [1982];[16] we put them in effect March 8 [1983]. Then we made some changes in April in line with congressional concerns.

What the informant described as a "reasonable agreement" involved a major reinterpretation of the law, backing down from the overall requirement that the CDBG program benefit primarily low- and moderate-income people. The response, both from the House authorizing committee and from interest groups, can only be described as intense. Having gone through a bargaining process with OMB which made the program more like revenue sharing (that is, grants with no strings attached on how to spend the money), the agency had to go through a round of negotiations with Congress and interest groups.[17]

CPD proposed revisions which divided the distance between OMB and the interest groups. Assistant Secretary (for CPD) Bollinger argued in a hearing in December 1982, "We believe that the proposed changes represent a good faith effort to respond to the concerns that have been brought out regarding the published rules. The proposed changes reflect considerable movement on our part to accommodate these concerns"[18] A few examples from the proposed regulations and CPD's revisions of them after the hearings illustrate how far CPD moved.

For the UDAG program, the proposed regulations approved by OMB indicated that any projects which retained or generated jobs would be considered to benefit low- or moderate-income people. The new rule would end any targeting of the UDAG program on the poor. CPD changed the rule back to its old wording after the hearings, so that a majority of jobs created or retained would be available to poor or moderate-income people.

The OMB-approved version of the regulations had proposed to make housing eligible for Community Development funding if as little as 20 percent of the units were occupied by low-income people. The agency modified the rule, still allowing funding to such buildings but reducing the amount of funding as the proportion of units occupied by the poor decreased. This was a compromise that preserved the principle of aiding mixed-income housing projects without abandoning support for lower-income people.

Most important, the regulations approved by OMB proposed dropping entirely a review of whether grantees were using funds to benefit low- and moderate-income people. Under pressure, CPD restored a moderate provision for review.

Some of the proposed regulations were restored to their original wording, some were weakened, and some were left as negotiated with OMB. Overall, however, members of Congress and the interest groups were very effective in reversing the most dramatic attempts to alter programs intended for the poor.

What made congressional and interest-group opposition effective is that the interest groups that were supposed to benefit from the increased freedom from regulation—the local governments and local officials—opposed the essence of the change. Representatives from the American Planning Association, the National Association of Housing and Redevelopment Officials (NAHRO), the National Association of Counties (NACo), the U.S. Conference of Mayors, and the National League of Cities all testified against the proposed regulations.

Because of this reaction, CPD was able to argue that the more extreme forms of changes in the regulations were simply not politically acceptable. Despite the apparent success of the program officials in finding a middle ground between Congress and the president, CPD was put in an extremely delicate position on the issue of these regulations, because it could be accused of marshaling support against the administration's position. The agency's defense was that interest groups needed no prodding to protect their perceived interests.

Decentralization

Part of President Reagan's program was to give programs to the state governments to run. In the 1981 omnibus reconciliation, the Small Cities Program, which had been a program of discretionary grants run through CPD, was turned over as a block grant to the states, if they chose to take it over. The states would then decide how to allocate the money to their local governments.

This part of the president's program, relying as it did on legislation passed in July 1981 (before Congress got obstinate about passing his proposals), was very successful. The state governments generally liked the new discretion, and thirty-six states and Puerto Rico opted to run the Small Cities Program themselves in its first year. That left CPD with only fourteen states that it was still administering directly. Officials at CPD indicated that they believed the other states would take over the program soon, leaving CPD with virtually no discretion over this program.

The result of the effective program to decentralize the Small Cities Program was that after the transition period, there would be less work for headquarters. This factor created a long-term morale problem and a sense that whether or not reductions in force occurred in the near future, the threat would continue to hang over the agency for several years.

MANAGING RETRENCHMENT

Many of the cutback decisions which affected CPD were made at the departmental level and involved units other than CPD. The proposed field reorganization, for example, affected all HUD programs. As a result, the following description shifts between the departmental level and the agency level.

Field Reorganization

The department proposed a plan for reorganization the field offices, for example, which affected housing programs as well as community development programs. The department argued that partly because of declining workloads and because the field structure was clumsy and in need of an overhaul, it would close many area offices and merge them with the regional offices nearby. The area offices served much smaller areas than the regional offices but were not supervised by them; they each performed separate functions. The reorganization proposal would result in reductions in staffing levels and rent, and the savings were estimated to outweight the costs associated with reductions in force.

Although reorganizations of this sort are normally considered within the scope of the executive rather than the legislation branch, there was an outcry of protest from the House authorizing subcommittee, the Subcommittee on Housing and Community Development.

These representatives reacted to the proposed reorganization much as they would to a military base closing, insisting on a community-by-community impact analysis. HUD officials responded that the impact on the cities' economies was too small to measure. Representatives invoked the GAO to check the department's estimates of savings; the GAO found them quite inflated.[19] In hearings, representatives tried to ferret out what the effect would be on program delivery. Since the area offices were the ones doing the work of carrying out programs and the area officials knew the local bankers and local markets, some of these representatives foresaw a deterioration of service.

As they worked around the issues, some committee members became suspicious that the real reason for the field reorganization and reduction in force was not reduced workload (which was never documented to their satisfaction) but a shift away from career officials to political appointees. The area offices, though staffed with career officials, made policy decisions; the regional offices, although headed by a political appointee, were more involved in grants management and less in policy. A merger of the area offices into the regional offices would give political officials more power.

The chairman of the subcommittee, Henry Gonzalez, was extremely negative toward the whole presidential program for HUD, including the field reorganization. He charged, "The reorganization is merely a method for justifying large-scale staff cuts. Likewise, the reduction in force seems to have more to do with the overseer's desire to impress the leaders at OMB than it does with helping the field hands do an efficient job."[20]

Chairman Gonzalez was just warming up with that bit of inflammatory prose. He called another hearing in May of 1983, on the impact of the reorganization, during which he declaimed, "I would not want to stand mute and idle in the face of what amounts to guerrilla warfare by departmental administrators against their own employees, their own agency, and their own mission."[21] He argued,

> Even if the reductions in force, personnel reassignments, and reorganizations of the department in recent months might individually be defended as sound, taken together, they amount to clear evidence of a blitzkrieg launched to destroy the effectiveness of the department, or at least to eliminate any real or imagined opposition to the administration's ideological goals.[22]

Chairman Gonzalez and Secretary Pierce opposed each other so emotionally in hearings that it was difficult to figure out how much truth there was in Chairman Gonzalez's charges and how much was simply personal animosity. However, Congressman Hoyer, who had a special interest in reduction-in-force procedures but no known animosity toward Secretary Pierce, pursued the question of the reason behind the field reorganization and reduction in force and got an interesting answer.

> *Mr. Hoyer:* Mr. Secretary, I understand you want to strengthen the role of the regional administrator, which is a schedule C appointment. Are we trying to strengthen the political pressure on HUD career employees to succumb to the Reagan philosophy of cutting out all regulations and nonteam players? ... The thrust of the question is this: by taking the action you suggest, are we not making more political the decision-making process at HUD?
> *Secretary Pierce:* I wouldn't like to put it that way. I think this is good management. This is just sheerly good management. You want the people under you who carry out your policies to be—really be your people, to be the

people who you really know can do the job and will follow through on your policies, and will get the job done the way you think it should be done. And that is what you would do in any company, and that is what you should do in government, and that is just a process of good management.[23]

Despite the rather indirect way that he put it, the secretary affirmed that his aim was to make the agency more responsive to policy. Though there is no evidence that either the president or OMB designed this reorganization (as they had the new regulations), there is evidence that Secretary Pierce generally agreed with the president on matters of policy and was a team player. OMB had certainly encouraged the agencies to reorganize. It seems likely, therefore, that this reorganization was part of the president's attempt to increase administrative control over the executive departments for the purpose of cutback and deregulation.

Reductions in Force

The possibility of reductions in force hung over headquarters at HUD as well as over the field offices. As the financial situation stabilized, some employees began to think that reductions at headquarters might not be necessary, or might be necessary only as an accompaniment to the gradual transition to state control. There were a variety of reasons for thinking that HUD would be able to continue to avoid reductions in force, at least through 1982, but in June 1982 a reduction at headquarters was announced for the fall.

The rationale for reductions in force was somewhat obscure. Not only had program funding stabilized, but the threatened 12 percent reduction in the salaries and expense budget, which would have caused RIFs, did not materialize at HUD. Because the final cut at HUD in the salaries and expense lines was much smaller, HUD could afford to keep its current staffing levels. There was no reorganization at headquarters which could have served as either a pretext or a cause of a reduction in force.

Moreover, the department as a whole was reportedly below its personnel ceilings at the time the reduction in force took place. The secretary of HUD allocates ceiling levels to agencies inside the department. Some of these agencies were reportedly over ceiling, but since the department as a whole was below ceiling, all that was required to avoid a reduction in force was for the secretary to reassign ceilings internally. Such a procedure might have resulted in some imbalances between workload and staffing levels, but presumably these problems could be handled with transfers.

Since the determination of whether or not to use reduction in force was made by the secretary, and the more traditional reasons for reduction in force were ruled out, the reduction appeared politically motivated and hence, as far as employees were concerned, unnecessary.

The rationale given for the RIF was that certain offices had exceeded personnel ceilings. During the budget battles, several programs had been terminated, but the department had not experienced a reduction in force at that time. The remaining pieces of terminated programs had been scattered to other programs, their staff gradually reabsorbed. The offices which had absorbed these pieces had been given permission to remain over ceiling. The department adopted a policy of encouraging attrition. It seemed that attrition would be able to take care of this small number of extra persons. Secretary Pierce had decided that a reduction in force was not necessary.

The secretary changed his stance on reductions in force some time in May or June 1982. According to a time line provided by the union, Harold Henry, director of headquarters operations, Office of Personnel, proposed a strategy for reduction in force for 1982 in a memo to Secretary Pierce dated 8 June 1982. The memo stated that if current rates of attrition continued, some offices would be over ceiling at the end of the year, and it suggested encouraging attrition by announcing a reduction in force by 30 September, identifying by name personnel who were over ceiling and using an aggressive outplacement program. The number of persons to be separated would be amended based on actual attrition between June and September.

According to the time line, the next major event occurred on 16 June, when Judy Tardy, assistant secretary for administration, sent a memo to principal staff members, informing them that the secretary had selected a strategy to ensure that all principal staff units reach authorized ceiling levels by 30 September. The major elements in the Tardy memo were the same as those in the Henry memo: maximizing attrition, continuing the hiring freeze, outplacement to stimulate attrition, and later evaluation of the need for selective reductions in force in some principal staff functions. The Tardy memo reportedly asked principal staff to submit a plan by 30 June, combining known attrition with the abolishment of encumbered positions.

Principal staff members were asked to distinguish between whether positions were being eliminated because of a skills imbalance or in order to get down to ceilings. The positions to be abolished were to be listed by name of incumbent, reason, and proposed disposition. Staffers were also told to consider abolishing positions occupied by low-tenure employees to minimize displacement and disruption, and to respond to the need for adequate secretarial support.

HUD made every effort to encourage employees to leave "voluntarily." According to the union time line, letters were sent to those whose positions were being abolished, telling them their rights to other jobs had not yet been calculated and that this was not a formal reduction-in-force notice, but that they might wish to take advantage of outplacement counseling. The letters indicated that some positions opened by attrition might be filled by "surplus" employees—that is, employees whose positions had been eliminated.

On 10 August, according to the time line, all headquarters employees were sent a note reporting that a job abolishment list was available in the HUD employee information center. The list included the names of 146 employees whose positions had been abolished and 20 who had retired or otherwise vacated positions.

Shortly after this list was made public, general reduction-in-force notices were sent to all employees. Within a few days after that, the (unverified) registers listing employees by retention status were made available to personnel. (Retention status is the order in which employees will be let go.) The reduction in force was set for the last day of the fiscal year, 30 September. The initial timing of the reduction suggested the desire to get under personnel ceilings for the end of the year. It also maximized the possibility of attrition and minimized the number of people who would have to be separated from employment. Somehow, the date for the reduction in force slipped, and specific notices (notices to individuals of termination, transfer, or demotion) were sent out in September for the end of October. The delay may have been due to the personnel office's lack of experience in constructing retention registers, the consequently large number of amended letters which had to go out, and the general reluctance to carry out the reduction.

The rather absurd result was that a reduction in force occurred in fiscal year 1983 to reduce staffing levels for 1982. Moreover, the possibility was created that HUD would experience two reductions in force in 1983, the one originally set for 1983 and the leftover one from 1982. The timing of the RIF became more problematic still when on 31 October, in the middle of the afternoon, the HUD union managed to get a court order delaying the reduction while certain issues of legality were examined by the courts.

The timing delays were only one indication of the difficulty that HUD had in actually administering the reductions in force. For example, the position descriptions, which are at the heart of the RIF mechanics, were reportedly poorly drawn up. When position descriptions were initially verified as part of the RIF procedure, the descriptions were not shown to the office managers as a check.

Good position descriptions are necessary in order to draw up competitive levels—that is, form groups of positions requiring similar skills. They are also necessary in determining employees' bumping and retreat rights. Employees whose positions have been eliminated can retreat to positions they held in the past or they can bump someone else (who is lower on the retention register) out of a position if they can show they have done that kind of work in the past.

The personnel office searches for new positions for people whose jobs have been eliminated. This task involves matching of position descriptions with employees' past experiences. If the position descriptions are not well drawn up, it is possible that people will lose their jobs unnecessarily or will be transferred to jobs they do not know how to do. More likely, the result will be many mistakes, amended notices of reduction in force, and appeals.

In the event, the HUD reduction in force was plagued with mistakes. The number of amended letters was so great that the entire reduction was delayed. Not only were individual RIF notices challenged, but office directors complained that employees bumping into new positions were unable to perform the new tasks. The confusion was compounded by making available to employees an *unverified* retention register prior to the RIF. Thus employees who were not involved in the reduction in force thought that they were, and those not involved sometimes turned out to be affected.

There was considerable opposition to the reduction in force at HUD. The union, which eventually merged with several other groups of personnel opposing the RIFs, linked up with sympathetic congresspersons on capitol hill. The results were a congressional committee ban on reorganization for several months,[24] a court-ordered delay in implementation of the reduction in force,[25] and a GAO study of the department's RIF procedures.[26] Opposition remained strong despite the efforts of management to minimize the effects of the reductions on both employees and programs.

HUD managers tried to reduce the effects of reductions in force on employees by minimizing the number of people affected. Thus they encouraged attrition and retirement and reduced the number of positions to eliminate in the reduction in force by the number of vacant positions. They emphasized outplacement, to get threatened staff new jobs.

To minimize damage to programs and management, officials tried to minimize the length of bumping chains by encouraging the selection of positions to eliminate in which the incumbent had no one else to bump. (A bumping chain occurs when one person without a position replaces someone else who does have a position, and then the person who has been replaced finds someone else with lower retention status to replace. A long bumping chain has five or six links in it.)

Officials also defined the competitive levels narrowly, to avoid disruption of programs and help improve the predictability of the reduction in force. (Competitive levels are groups of positions which have similar skills levels. Basically, people can take new jobs only in their competitive levels. A personnel officer cannot replace a computer programmer because they will be in different competitive levels.) The personnel office drew up competitive levels along program and office lines, which means that not only could personnel officers not replace computer programmers, but that a personnel officer in housing could not replace a personnel officer in community development.

The personnel office sent its proposed designation of competitive levels to the office managers for review, where the tendency was to make them even narrower. The average was three people per competitive level.

With such narrow competitive levels, when a position was eliminated, the incumbent had almost nowhere to go. A manager could look at the incumbents of three positions and work out who had greater retention rights and hence who would be fired if one of the three positions was eliminated. Narrow competitive levels thus aided predictability.

For a variety of reasons, these efforts to minimize the damage done by the reduction in force were interpreted by the union and by some other employees as politically motivated. The fact that the reduction itself was not motivated by financial pressure and seemed to have been avoidable was taken as proof that it was political.

It was a small step from assuming that the reduction in force was politically motivated to interpreting the behavior of officials in narrowing competitive levels as an attempt to target individuals to be fired or demoted. Even relatively benign strategies such as encouraging retirement were interpreted as age discrimination, and the effort to encourage attrition was described by some as persecution, an attempt to make employees feel insecure and voluntarily quit.

HUD's history during the Nixon era probably contributed to the willingness of employees to respond skeptically to the department's procedures. During the Nixon era and for several years thereafter, the department had been politicized, with a large number of political hires and rather blatant rejection of civil service procedures.[27] The department had been caught in its illegal practices and had stopped them, but the whole episode left a legacy of distrust and made the HUD union more militant and active than those of other agencies.[28]

The union strategy focused on motivating Congress to take some action to block the reduction in force. An unidentified HUD employee is credited with beginning the strategy of linking up to Congress. As a result, in the appropriation for HUD for 1983, a committee restriction had been written to restrain HUD from using any of the 1983 appropriation to plan or carry out a reorganization without prior committee approval, until 1 January 1983. The union argued that since a reduction in force could not be done without some kind of reorganization, it would be covered by the committee language. When HUD carried out the reduction in force, the union took the issue to court after gathering some congressional assistance. Congressman Sabo, who was on the appropriations committee, agreed to join the suit.

HUD argued that its RIF did not involve a reorganization and hence was perfectly legal. HUD held scrupulously to the policy of not reorganizing before 1 January. The reorganization, when it came, would be considerably after the reduction in force. Unless one defines the elimination of positions without any coherent plan as a reorganization, there was no reorganization during this period. HUD also argued that congressional committees and subcommittees did not have the right to administer executive agencies through such oversight and veto activity. Only both houses together had that right, according to the courts. HUD won its case in court.[29]

As soon as the court decision was announced, HUD reinstituted the reduction in force planned for 31 October. The reduction finally took place 10 December 1982. CPD and other HUD programs were affected. In CPD thirteen people were fired and twenty-seven were transferred or demoted.[30]

Once the reduction in force had occurred, opposition shifted to the composition of those separated and demoted and the apparent disproportion of women and minorities. Sympathetic journalists were primed by union representatives to ask questions about possible discrimination. HUD spokespersons argued that the fact that OPM's RIF procedures happened to work against women and minorities had little to do with HUD policies. However, the department's presentation of statistics concerning the effects of the reduction in force on the racial and sexual composition of the workforce was so misleading that it was not convincing.[31]

OUTCOMES

The Reagan program for shrinking the Community Planning and Development Program had a number of outcomes. The outcome on budget levels was an immediate but not drastic reduction in funding, followed by a stabilization of funding as Congress gained confidence in its ability to resist the president. This stabilization and the increased role played by Congress were facilitated by the activity of interest groups. The president's control of the top levels of HUD turned out to be less than perfect, as the secretary and the assistant secretary became advocates of CPD programs.

The result of continuing negotiations between the Office of Management and Budget, HUD, Congress, and the interest groups was a number of compromises. Instead of terminating the UDAG and CDBG programs, headquarters' control over those programs was reduced. The application procedures for grants were dropped, new regulations were promulgated that loosened spending guidelines, and portions of the program were decentralized to the state governments.

Throughout the process, though the agency was not passive, it was caught between Congress and the president. One CPD official described this situation as follows:

We are not only caught, we are ground up between Congress and the president. You have to reconcile the ideological thrust of the administration—the president and the department—and the pragmatic impact of Congress—the politics of what sells. You want to go according to the law, *and* follow the direction of the president. When there are differences, there is trouble. You do as much as the president can cope with, and try to sell it on the Hill. There has to be compromise; no one wins.

Inside the agency, the effect of the threatened budget cuts and the reductions in force was to exacerbate old, barely healed wounds. The disproportion of women and minorities who were affected by the reduction reinforced tension based on race and sex. The union's skepticism about the RIFs rekindled the distrust which was rampant during the Nixon era.

The increased polarization between management and the union was another important outcome. Moreover, one of the effects of the reduction in force was to broaden the use of the union, making that polarization even more important. Several other ad hoc groups of personnel fighting the reductions eventually merged into the union. Employees from many administrative levels contributed information and talent to the union and analyzed and reported on current events. These reports were sometimes used by managers in lieu of official reports.

In fact, the union showed itself to be more effective than management in transmitting information to employees, a fact that further broadened its base of support. For example, notices of reduction in force were delivered simultaneously to the office managers and the unions. The union aggregated the information in the notices into a coherent summary before the office managers could, although it was the office managers' role to answer questions and inform personnel. Similarly, information on court proceedings concerning the reduction in force flowed from the union, not from upper levels of management. As a result, many lower-level managers and their subordinates turned to the union for information.

Another internal impact of the reduction in force and budget threats was to lower morale. For many months, employees expected reductions that did not materialize. Then there was a reduction which was announced far in advance in order to make people feel insecure and voluntarily seek other jobs. When the RIF was scheduled to occur, it was twice delayed, once because the personnel office could not act quickly enough and once because of the union's legal challenge. Even when the RIF was finally over, employees sensed that another one might be just ahead. They felt that the shifting of programs to the states had to have an impact on the level of headquarters staff. Because of all the uncertainty and insecurity, morale at HUD, according to one informant, was as low as it had ever been, not only among those affected by the RIF but also among those sympathizing with them and anticipating it would be their turn next. Managers reported difficulty getting employees to concentrate.

The third impact of the RIFs was on management. Despite the department's conscious and successful attempts to minimize damage from the RIFs, there were several negative consequences. Although there was limited bumping, what bumping did occur evoked protests from office managers, who complained that the new person often could not do the job. Since repromotions were delayed until after a reorganized structure could be created, recovery was delayed for an indefinite time. The long delay in the execution of the RIF also prevented a normal recovery period.

The HUD policy of delaying the reorganization until well after the reduction in force at headquarters, while perhaps not of HUD's choosing, led to other managerial complications. Ideally, an agency selects positions to eliminate as part of a larger plan of consolidation and shifting patterns of functional alignment. If reorganization cannot be done beforehand, as in this case (and as in HHS, for different reasons), reorganization should follow soon after the reduction in force, to accommodate the organization's new smaller size. However, reorganization did not follow immediately after reduction in force at HUD. In essence, the organization shrank without thinking about what the smaller organization should look like.

SUMMARY

CPD was in a fortunate position to oppose the administration's plans to eliminate its two key programs. It had active interest-group support and was able to reverse the administration's resolve to terminate funding. Key in this process was the winning over of the secretary. However, the victory was not complete. CPD fell victim to a department-wide reduction in force, despite the opposition of the (politically appointed) assistant secretary for CPD. And the administration managed to weaken CPD's ability to target funds to the poor.

Because CPD's programs were politically popular, CPD got caught between Congress and the president and had to walk a tightrope of compromises to comply with the law and satisfy the president, at least at a minimal level. These compromises took place over the program regulations rather than over funding issues directly.

The fight over the budget and the fight over new regulations took place in different ways. The first battle took place primarily within the administration; Congress was barely aware of what had happened. The interest groups descended on the president, not on Congress. The second fight, however, involved OMB, the agency, Congress, and the interest groups. Congressional committees were instrumental in changing the wording of the new regulations.

The contradiction between winning the funding battles but having to submit to a reduction in force led to the belief that the reduction in force was politically motivated, a belief that helped to polarize opposition within HUD. A direct linkage between the union and Congress was formed. The union then sent a plague of administrative irritants to HUD officials. The reduction in force was delayed for an indefinite period, with negative effects on management and on morale, and the GAO sent an investigative team to HUD to find out what was happening.

The RIF was run with the dual goals of protecting people's positions and protecting program management. However, because of the union's mistrust of management, even the most benevolent of strategies was interpreted in a negative manner. The lack of an acceptable reason for the reduction in force, combined with union hostility and the ineptness of the HUD personnel office (largely due to inexperience with RIF procedures), led to a hotly contested reduction in force.

The fear of future reductions in force and further reorganizations continues to hang over the organization, making full recovery difficult if not impossible.

NOTES

1. "In the case of the Community Planning and Development Office, Assistant Secretary Stephen J. Bollinger apparently registered a cogently argued dissent on the question of whether to proceed with the RIF." This quotation is taken from a memo written by the Federal Government Service Task Force, dated 20 September 1982, to Chairman Gonzalez, concerning the task force review of the proposed reduction in force at HUD headquarters. The memo is reprinted in House Subcommittee on Housing and Community Development of the Committee on Banking, Finance and Urban Affairs, *Impact of the HUD Field Reorganization: Hearing*, 98th Cong., 1st sess., 26 May 1983, pp. 126–27.

2. The two reports requested by the senators are: General Accounting Office, *Department of Housing and Urban Development's Fiscal Year 1983 Reductions in Force* (GAO-RCED-83-47) (Washington: Government Printing Office, 29 October 1982); and General Accounting Office, *Further Information on the Department of Housing and Urban Development's Fiscal Year 1983 Reductions in Force* (GAO RCED-83-80) (Washington: Government Printing Office, 23 December 1982).

3. See, for example, Robert Poole, Jr., "Community and Regional Development," in *Agenda for Progress*, ed. Eugene McAllister (Washington: Heritage Foundation, 1981), especially page 183. He argued, "In all but the poorest localities, many of the worthwhile projects funded by CDBG, UDAG and EDA grants would have been carried out anyway, using local resources." p. 183. Poole was stating a rather widespread belief within the administration, a belief supported by several key GAO studies.

4. Robert Poole quotes *Business Week*, 12 November 1979. UDAG "was proposed after political sophisticates in the administration and Congress took a searching look at where Carter's votes had come from in 1976." According to Poole, the magazine described the program as "grants that can be used to make the president look good." *Agenda for Progress*, p. 181.

5. See Poole, *Agenda for Progress*, p. 182. Here he cites two other GAO studies as evidence: General Accounting Office, *Management and Evaluation of the Community Development Block Grant Program Need to Be Strengthened* (GAO/CED 78-168) (Washington: Government Printing Office, 30 August 1978); and General Accounting Office, *The Community Development Block Grant Program: Discretionary Grant Funds Not Always Given to the Most Promising Small City Programs* (GAO/CED 78-157) (Washington: Government Printing Office, 31 August 1978).

6. David S. Broder, "White House Opens Drive to Sell Governors and Mayors on Funds Cuts," *Washington Post*, 22 February 1981.

7. See John William Ellwood, ed., *Reductions in U.S. Domestic Spending: How They Affect State and Local Governments* (New Brunswick, N.G.: Transaction Books, 1982), p. 168.

8. U.S. Budget, Supplement, for 1983 and 1984.

9. Reference is made to negotiations between OMB and the department in the House Subcommittee on Appropriations budget hearings for 1983. In that hearing it was established that the initial departmental request was for a 12 percent reduction in salaries and expense lines but that the department argued with OMB to take more off other lines and less from the salaries and expenses, to average total cuts of 4 percent. OMB reportedly agreed to do that. Judy Tardy, assistant secretary for administration, argued that this arrangement allowed the agency to avoid disruptive RIFs. House Committee on Appropriations, *Department of Housing and Urban Development-Independent Agencies Appropriations for 1983: Hearings*, 97th Cong., 2d sess., 1982, p. 16–17.

10. *Housing and Development Reporter* 9, no. 28 (7 December 1981): summarized the OMB proposal for fiscal year 1983.

11. According to the preceding article, several HUD officials, including the assistant secretary, appeared at the National League of Cities' meeting during the previous week. The article indicated that the officials urged the three thousand officials present to lobby the White House. The author quoted the assistant secretary in particular as noting the inconsistency between turning the Small Cities Program over to the states and then eliminating the program. The CPD officials with whom I spoke denied that CPD had stimulated the protest, arguing that the interest groups kept a close watch on OMB proposals and took action without prompting from HUD.

12. *Housing and Development Reporter* 9, no. 30 (December 1981); p. 582, reported that HUD had appealed the OMB proposals on CDBG and UDAG to the White House Review Board and to the president, arguing that such a course (as proposed by OMB) was politically unwise and would antagonize Congress.

13. The source of this exchange is House Committee on Appropriations, *Department of Housing and Urban Development-Independent Agencies, Appropriations for 1982, Part 6: Hearings*, 97th Cong., 1st sess., 29 April 1981, p. 97.

14. Barry Bozeman and Jeffrey Straussman, "Shrinking Budgets and the Shrinkage of Budget Theory," *Public Administration Review* 42, (November/December, 1982): 509–15.

15. According to testimony delivered by Donald Hovde, Undersecretary of HUD. House Committee on Appropriations, *Department of Housing and Urban Development-Independent Agencies Appropriations for 1983, Part 6: Hearings*, 97th Cong., 2d sess., 1982, p. 7.

16. The proposed regulations were initially published in 47 *Federal Register* 43900–43933 (1982) (codified in 24 C.F.R. & 570).

17. The Housing and Community Development Subcommittee in the House held hearings 7 December 1982. House Subcommittee on Housing and Community Development of the Committee on Banking, Finance, and Urban Affairs. *Community Development Block Grant Entitlement Regulations: Hearing*, 97th Cong., 2d sess., 7 December 1982.

18. *Ibid.*, p. 43.

19. See the statement from Dexter Peach of the General Accounting Office in *Impact of the HUD Field Reorganization: Hearing*, 1983, pp. 49–64.

20. House Subcommittee on Housing and Community Development of the Committee on Banking, Finance and Urban Affairs, *HUD Field Reorganization, RIFs, and Pending Legislation: Hearing*, 97th Cong., 2d sess., 21 September 1981, p. 1.

21. *Impact of the HUD Field Reorganization: Hearing*, 1983, p. 3.

22. *Ibid.*, p. 2.

23. *Ibid.*, pp. 59–60.

24. The House report issued after hearings on the 1982 appropriations bill

contained the following language: "The committee is concerned with personnel actions planned for the central office and the field. Because of that concern, a limitation has been included in the bill denying any reorganization without the prior approval of the Committees on Appropriation." House Committee on Appropriations, *Department of Housing and Urban Development-Independent Agencies: Report No. 97–720*, 97th Cong., 2d sess., 10 August 1982, p. 10. The Senate appropriations committee did not agree with this restriction; it worked out a compromise accepting the language but making it effective only until 1 January 1983, which meant the ban was only to be in effect for three months. HUD did carry out a reduction in force during those three months. The union and one of the representatives on the House appropriations subcommittee for HUD brought a case against HUD for violation of the congressional language. It was this case which brought about the court order halting (temporarily) the HUD reduction in force.

25. See Karlyn Barker, "Judge Halts Demotions, Firing of HUD Workers," *Washington Post*, 11 November 1982, for an account of the court-ordered injunction against the reduction in force.

26. The request for a GAO study was reported by Ruth Marlow in "Auditors Probe RIF Plan at HUD," *Federal Times* 18, no. 36 (1 November 1982): p. 1. That article describes the audit as "the latest in a series of challenges from concerned members of Congress and employees to HUD's plans to reorganize headquarters and field operations and reduce staff and programs."

27. For descriptions of the politicization of civil service selection procedures during the Nixon era, see Inderjit Badhwar, "Malek's Ring Exposed: Government Wide Patronage Deals," *Federal Times* (25 September 1974): p. 1 and Inderjit Badhwar, "Insider Tells How Merit Rape Plot Began at HEW," *Federal Times* (19 January 1976): p. 1. For a history of events at HUD during this period, see *Washington Post* columnist Mike Causey's report on congressional subcommittee hearings. "Covert HUD Job Unit Described," *Washington Post*, 26 June 1975.

28. The reaction of the HUD union and the HUD Women's Caucus to the subversion of civil service hiring procedures, is reflected in the undated flyer circulated by the union in connection with the hearings held by the House Committee on Post Office and Civil Service. The flyer probably dates from 1975. The flyer sought evidence of continued abuses after the 1973 reported closing of the Special Personnel Unit. The flyer begins, "Are merit staffing violations still commonplace in HUD? Did ex-secretary Lynn really 'clean up' the system, as he has claimed? Do you really trust 'management' and your supervisors in matters of selection, appointment and promotion?"

29. The reversal of the lower court decision (which had been in favor of the HUD employees) was rendered in the U.S. Court of Appeals for the District of Columbia Circuit, on 8 December 1982. *American Federation of Government Employees v. Pierce*, 697 F.2d 303 (DC Cir. 1982).

30. Memo from Marcia K. Dodge, Office of Management to Rita Grieco, evaluator, resources, Community and Development Division, GAO, dated 18 November 1982. The reduction in force planned for 31 October was the same one that occurred in December; thus this November memo is an accurate description of the December RIF.

31. On 9 December 1982, during the press conference announcing the RIF, one reporter asked whether blacks were treated unfairly. Judy Tardy's response was, "Out of 57 people downgraded [throughout HUD], 19 were dropped more than three grades. Of those 19, only 7 are black." In response to the follow-up question, "Out of 63 people separated, how many were women and minorities?" Tardy answered, "We look at it as [minorities occupied] 53 percent of the jobs abolished. [They constituted] 48 percent of the work force before the RIF and 47 percent of the work force after the RIF. That is what counts. You don't abolish

people, you abolish positions that are excess. Then [each incumbent] exercises entitlements." The reporter, still without an answer, repeated his question, "How many blacks and women out of 63?" Tardy then provided the following information: There were 412 black males before the RIF and 394 after. There were 1323 black females before the RIF and [?] after. There were 38 Hispanic males before the RIF and 36 after. There were 41 Hispanic females before the RIF and 37 after. Among American Indians, there were 7 males and 4 females before the RIF and 7 males and 4 females after the RIF. Asian males remained the same at 33, and Asian females dropped from 19 and 18. White males dropped from 1543 to 1531, white females from 747 to 727. The reporter who was asking these questions calculated that only 12 white males had been separated, leaving 51 out of 63 separations as women or minorities, or 83 percent. When the reporter asked for Tardy's concurrence with his arithmetic, she refused to agree, arguing, "No, this is before and after." The argument went on for several more rounds, with increasing inconsistency, until Tardy agreed to provide the reporter with figures later.

6

The Urban Mass Transportation Administration

Reorganization, Reduction in Force, and Reauthorization

Like Community Planning and Development, the Urban Mass Transportation Administration (UMTA) has enjoyed considerable interest group and congressional support in recent years. Despite that support, the Reagan administration persisted in trying to terminate CPD's programs over time. However, it realized more quickly that it would not be able to terminate all funding for mass transit. Hence it limited its goals for UMTA to eliminating the operating subsidy and cutting out new rapid-transit projects. To compensate for the loss of funding, the administration proposed to eliminate some of the more costly and burdensome regulations associated with the program.

The president had better control over UMTA than he had over CPD. Unlike CPD, the Urban Mass Transportation Administration did not resist the administration's attempts to reduce its budget. Like HUD, the agency carried out a reduction in force when there seemed little need to do so, but unlike HUD, UMTA spent a great deal of energy on a reorganization that centralized policy making and made the agency more responsive to presidential direction.

After both the reorganization and the reduction in force, the legislation for the program expired and had to be reauthorized, prolonging until early 1983 the uncertainty that began in 1981. The battle over reauthorization pitted the administration against the interest groups and Congress.

The UMTA case illustrates how an agency cuts itself back and redesigns its programs in response to the administration's policy and in the face of congressional and interest-group opposition. It indicates the bargaining positions of the White House, the agency, congressional committees, and interest groups illustrating the extent of each actor's power.

BACKGROUND

The Urban Mass Transportation Administration is a highly visible agency in the Department of Transportation. From the standpoint of personnel, it is of moderate size, five hundred to six hundred employees, but in terms of budget, it is a multibillion-dollar agency. (In 1981, its budget was $4.6 billion.) Its function is to aid local mass transportation agencies through innovative research, technical assistance, and direct grants. UMTA helps to build subway systems and buy rolling stock. More controversially, in recent years it has also been giving operating subsidies to local transit systems.

UMTA's visibility is due not only to the total dollar size of its programs but also to the allocation of many of its grants on a discretionary basis rather than by formula. That means there has been much competition for the large grants, as well as an organized interest-group structure to help maintain and direct the flow of resources. And for each large discretionary project, there has typically been one or more interested congresspersons, watching over the agency's shoulder.

The impact of extensive interest-group involvement at UMTA has been mixed. On the one hand, the result has been poor management, overregulation, and slow, often political decision making. UMTA has been buffeted by numerous strong lobbies, which have occasionally pulled it in opposite directions.[1] On the other hand, however, UMTA has had strong and continuing congressional support.

ADMINISTRATION OPPOSITION TO UMTA

With both interest-group and congressional support, it is not surprising that UMTA had a successful track record of budgetary growth from 1972 to 1981. With the election of President Reagan, however, there were intimations of future budgetary trouble. The new administration attacked the program, alleging that it was poorly managed and that its mission was ideologically unacceptable. By attacking the UMTA budget, the administration was also able to make deficits look smaller, as explained below.

UMTA had long had a reputation for poor management in many quarters, not just in the administration.[2] It had grown very rapidly but was still organized in an ad hoc manner. It had been decentralized to regional offices, but the central office and field offices had no clear division of responsibility.[3] Field officers complained that it sometimes took a year or longer to get an answer to a policy question from the central office.[4] Congress complained that the agency had no goals and measures of achievement.[5]

Although there was general agreement that UMTA had serious management problems, there was a disagreement between the administration (the president and the secretary) and Congress as to the reason for the problems. The Subcommittee on Investigations and Oversight of the House Committee on Public Works and Transportation felt that part of the reason for the mismanagement was that as the program grew in dollars and complexity, the staffing level did not grow proportionately.[6] The administration (in this case including the top administrators at UMTA) felt that the agency needed to be reorganized, made more hierarchical, and cut back in staffing levels.

From a more ideological perspective, the Reagan administration indicated a determination to phase out operating subsidies on the grounds that the federal government had no legitimate voice in local issues. Operating subsidies were said to have encouraged inefficiency and allowed transit authorities to keep user fees (fares) artificially low. The administration further argued that subsidies were being used to allow large salary increases in collective bargaining, increases that would not have been allowed on local revenues, and that operating subsidies encouraged buses to run on uneconomical routes.[7]

The Heritage Foundation, which was reportedly influential in setting the administration's domestic policy agenda, roundly condemned UMTA, calling for a phaseout of operating subsidies and eventually of the agency itself. It advised that the function of supporting mass transit be turned over to local governments.[8]

In addition to a marked determination to eliminate operating subsidies, the administration also judged that fixed-rail rapid transit systems were not cost effective, and it tried to prevent any new starts in such systems. Although at first the administration argued that it was just delaying new starts until the economy improved, it gradually became clear when UMTA submitted proposals for reauthorization that the administration had no intention of funding any new starts for fixed-rail projects.[9]

The reason for attacking new starts may have been to manipulate the budget to make deficits look smaller. The UMTA fixed-rail funding had two special characteristics that made it vulnerable to such manipulation. First, each time a new project was initiated, it cost a little the first year and then ballooned to huge payments for the next four or five years. For each new start delayed, the administration could thus claim huge savings for the next few years. That calculation assumed that the project was not just delayed but was postponed indefinitely. To allay opposition, the administration called the projects delayed rather than canceled, but from a budgetary perspective, it treated them as terminated to gain maximum political credit for controlling the deficit.

Second, the rail projects made the budget look huge if several were carried out simultaneously. By delaying the projects and thus avoiding these bursts of spending, the administration reduced the size of the deficit for the years covering the delays. Later, it substituted a formula grant for the discretionary capital grants which UMTA had relied on, thereby further leveling out the lumps in the budget.[10]

THE IMPLEMENTATION OF THE PRESIDENT'S AIMS

How easy or difficult it would be to carry out the president's aims for UMTA depended on three factors: the degree of control the president had over the administration of the agency, the degree of interest-group support for the programs, and the amount of congressional support for the programs.

The President's Control over UMTA

The president's administrative control over UMTA depended primarily on three people, the secretary of the Department of Transportation, the administrator of the agency, and the administrator's assistant for administration. The first two were presidential appointees, and the latter was a career official who was chosen for the spot after demonstrating considerable agreement with the administration's positions. These officials were willing to cut their own programs, reduce their staffing levels, and adhere to the president's policies, but each showed some independence.

Secretary Drew Lewis adhered to the president's program by pronouncing, as soon as he took office, a general personnel reduction that was independent of budget or program changes or work levels. His assumption reportedly was that the work could be done with fewer people. Since he had no time to examine individual programs (in fact, some were known to be understaffed), this reduction appeared to be ideological and in full agreement with the president's program to reduce staffing levels in Washington.

However, Secretary Lewis did argue for mass transit funding for the purposes of capital projects. He argued continuously with the president to increase the gasoline tax and to use one cent of the five-cent increase to fund mass transit capital projects. The president was initially against the proposal, but Lewis eventually persuaded him. This proposal was approved by Congress and was a major victory for mass transit and mass transit funding.

Agency Administrator Teele did not appear to fight the administration's proposals for reduced funding in any way, either inside the administration or in Congress. He defended the proposed cuts against occasionally angry congressional questioning. However, he did concede that the administration's position was difficult to defend. He never hinted that the agency needed more funding, but he agreed with congressional and interest-group estimates of the size of the capital needs of mass transit across the country.[11] These estimates were considerably above the administration's recommendation. In this way Teele seemed to agree with congressional committee members and oppose the administration while defending the administration cuts in operating funds. He made it clear that he himself had not designed the administration's proposals.[12]

The person responsible for administering reductions in force and designing the reorganization was a career official who had written a critique of UMTA that caught the administration's attention. He was placed in UMTA (from the office of the secretary) with the understanding that he would carry out his ideas for improving the agency.

While the administration generally agreed with his ideas, he did not totally agree with the administration on all issues. He privately questioned the evidence behind some of the administration's arguments against the operating subsidies. But more important from an administrative point of view, he, like Administrator Teele, indicated where decisions had been made when they were not his.

Although he carried out the reorganization and the reduction in force with all the skill he had, he made it plain to employees that the RIF was not required by finances but that it was a kind of experiment to see whether the agency could get by with fewer employees. Although he must have been aware that such statements were likely to rouse opposition, he stated what he believed to be the truth, rather than covering up or obfuscating.

In short, each official made the agency cutbacks the president wanted. But the secretary also protected the program by developing a new funding source, and lower-level administrators, who also carried out the tasks assigned to them, separated themselves from the president's policies when dealing with potential opposition. They found a kind of personal middle ground.

Interest-Group Support of the Agency and its Program

The president's strong control of the agency was particularly valuable in view of the agency's strong interest-group support. The Urban Mass Transportation Administration has been supported by a broad coalition including city and county officials, transit unions, construction lobbies, manufacturers of buses and trains, and the elderly and handicapped. In addition to these specific lobbies, there has been general political support for the program as a generator of construction jobs during recessions and as a stimulator of domestic industry.

The construction industry has supported UMTA because it finances new subsidy and rail projects. Manufacturers have been involved because the agency has specified standards for equipment purchased under grants. The elderly and handicapped have supported UMTA because they tend to be dependent on public transportation.

To illustrate the effect these interest groups have had on public transit authorization legislation, one needs only read the laws in effect when the Reagan administration took office. The 1964 authorization act as amended through December 1978 (The Urban Mass Transportation Act) contains a number of provisions that benefit special interests. For example, there is a section requiring all large purchases under the grant to be of materials made or manufactured in the United States (with some exceptions). The law declares as national policy that the elderly and handicapped have the same right as other persons to utilize mass transportation, and it makes funds available for planning transportation facilities to make them accessible to these groups.

Another section of the Act, declaring a national policy to preserve the natural beauty of the environment, requires hearings on environmental impacts of proposed projects. The Davis-Bacon Act requiring that prevailing wages be paid to workers on projects funded by UMTA is also written into the 1978 law. The law also contains a provision to encourage the hiring of women and minorities in the transit industry.

These interest groups continued to fight for mass transit dollars after the Reagan administration took office. They have been active in fighting for program funding, in restoring new rail starts, and in preserving the operating subsidies.

There is no evidence that UMTA encouraged its interest groups to fight on its behalf, but congressional supporters of the program devised a strategy for reauthorizing UMTA that would enhance the power of interest groups. The chairman of the House Committee on Public Works and Transportation, Congressman James Howard of New Jersey, wrapped up the mass transportation reauthorization bill with the reauthorization for the Federal Highway Administration and the National Highway Traffic Safety Administration. The idea was to broaden the base of support for the bill and form a coalition of mass transit and highway lobbies.

This alliance was further cemented by Secretary Drew Lewis's proposal for a gas tax increase, which would be split between highways and mass transit. The powerful highway lobby joined with the supporters of mass transportation to get the tax measure passed. This strategy was successful. It is exactly the opposite of what had happened to the Bureau of Health Planning. When the bureau was combined with a popular hospital construction program, it had plenty of congressional support; when it was split off from the popular physical facilities grants, it lost its major interest-group and congressional support.

Congressional Support

Congressional support for mass transportation was stronger in the House than in the Senate, but even in the Republican-dominated Senate there was a surprising amount of support. As one observer noted, "The support in the Senate was very good throughout. It is clear that Senators were more thoughtful about the transit issue and lent their support well beyond the fact of a large transit constituency within the borders of their states."[13] In the Senate the president was able to introduce his version of the reauthorizing act for UMTA, but it died for lack of support, and several competing, more moderate proposals were circulated.

Ultimately, it was the House version, the most generous of the bills that were circulating, that passed both houses and became law. In addition to a generally favorable reauthorization act, Congress also passed the gas tax increase, which funded a portion of the new legislation.

The support for mass transit was not such that the program could not be touched or changed, however. There was a consensus even among those who supported mass transit that the program had major managerial problems, and that some kind of new approach was required.[14] The split was over the issue of whether more or less funding was going to be the solution.[15] The congressional solution, which managed to get a majority, was to try to stabilize funding at a somewhat lower level.

UMTA managed to avoid the kind of hostility in congressional hearings that the HUD secretary had met at HUD's authorizing committee hearings. The members of the House authorizing committee on mass transit were generally civil to administration witnesses, but they became angry when the administration immediately backed away from the compromise represented by the reauthorization act.

In short, though there was considerable congressional support to start with, it was not overwhelming. The initial congressional decisions were in favor of cuts but with stabilized spending to include operating subsidies. However, positions hardened after the reauthorization in early 1983, when OMB determined to try again to achieve its stated 1981 goals. The House Public Works Committee became balky. It rejected a presidential request for a deferral and held hearings on the implementation of the new law and on the administration's response to it. The rhetoric of committee members became more heated.

THE ADMINISTRATION'S PROGRAM FOR UMTA

The administration's plans for UMTA included budget reductions, program redesign through reauthorization, deregulation, decentralization, reorganization, and reduction in staffing levels.

The Extent of Cutbacks

Even before the president's March 1981 budget proposal for the fiscal year 1982, the administration had obviously tested the political waters concerning the acceptability of reducing and terminating operating subsidies. To allay opposition to its proposal, it decided to phase in the termination of operating subsidies over a three- or four-year period, with no change at all in the first year.

With this soft-pedaling of its goals, the administration's proposals for budget cuts in UMTA were accepted by Congress in the omnibus reconciliation of 1981 and in the fall appropriations. Budget authority was reduced about 25 percent from 1981 to 1982, and actual outlays were reduced about 14 percent.[16]

For the 1983 budget, the administration tried to push home its advantage, recommending a 10 percent reduction in authorizations compared with the previous year, and a 14 percent reduction in program levels (actual obligations). It proposed a 50 percent reduction in operating subsidies.

Congress did not accept this new reduction: authorizations increased 23 percent while program levels increased by about 10 percent. Despite this turnaround, the administration did succeed in reducing the politically sensitive operating subsidies, although not as much as it had hoped. A ceiling on operating subsidies was set at $875 million, although the administration had requested a ceiling of $640 million. Despite the obvious congressional support, operating subsidies were reduced from the 1981 and 1982 level of $1.16 billion.[17]

In fiscal year 1983, just after the new reauthorization legislation was passed, the administration requested a deferral of expenditures for UMTA of $229 million. It was not clear whether this was a technical deferral or a policy deferral because the president opposed the program, particularly parts of the new reauthorization act.

UMTA Administrator Teele presented to a congressional committee the administration's argument that the deferral was technical, based on the startup of the new gas tax trust fund. He stated that the original estimates of revenue to be produced were too high, and when the administration got the revised estimates, it asked to defer the difference between congressionally authorized spending levels and the revised amount expected to come into the trust fund.

Congressmen argued back that other trust funds were not treated in that way, that actual expenses would be paid out later when the money was present, and that the administration was in effect keeping spending way below congressionally authorized levels. Congressmen interpreted the requested deferral in light of the proposed budget reductions for 1984 and decided that the administration was still trying to implement its program of phasing out operating assistance.

Administrator Teele confirmed this impression:

> The authorization would have permitted through discount and transfer provisions up to $1 billion of section 9 funds to be used for operating assistance. Our budget proposes to limit this amount to $275 million. This is the level we originally proposed when we submitted our legislative package last year and this is consistent with our original phaseout proposal announced in February 1981.[18]

The Committee on Public Works and Transportation rejected the presidential request for deferral, and in a highly unusual move, one of its subcommittees called for hearings on the administration's proposed 1984 budget. The House Committee on Public Works is an authorizing committee, and authorizing committees usually deal with issues of program design and administration, as well as legal limits to spending. The appropriating committees are the ones who deal with actual annual funding levels and normally hold hearings on presidential budget proposals. In this case, however, Glenn Anderson, chairman of the Subcommittee on Surface Transportation (and a strong transit supporter) was so concerned that the low funding levels threatened program stability, as well as the authorized spending levels, that he called a hearing on the proposed budget.

The 1984 budget proposal from the administration included further reductions for UMTA. Congressman Anderson summarized those proposed cuts in his budget hearings.

> Public Law 97-424 [the reauthorizing law for UMTA] provides for a fiscal year 1984 authorization of 2.75 billion for section 9. The budget document transmitted to Congress reduced this by 28 percent, to 1.974 billion. And within that amount, the total that is available for operating assistance would be reduced from 873 million, as passed by Congress, and approved by the president, to 275 million, a cut of 68 percent.

Congressman Anderson was irritated that in less than a month after signing the reauthorization bill, the president was seeking again to reduce the amount of funding, particularly the amount of operating assistance.

In sum, the administration set out a position in 1981 and a plan for reduction in expenditures for UMTA and tried persistently to reach that target. It was forced to compromise on the level of funding in the reauthorization bill in order to get some other features in the bill that the president wanted. As soon as the reauthorization bill was passed, however, the administration resumed its efforts to implement funding cuts.

Opposition to the administration's position seemed to be building. Congress moved from easy passage of the president's requests in 1981 to a compromise in the reauthorization act that won by a narrow majority after the president's proposed legislation died in the Senate, and finally to a rejection of the president's request for a deferral of funds. Interest groups which had lined up and mobilized both for the reauthorization and for the new gas tax were in position to fight the administration's 1984 requests.

The Reauthorization Battle

The reauthorization legislation, the Surface Transportation Assistance Act, represented more than a battle over funding levels; it restructured the grant program. In line with the president's goals to reduce the number of strings on grants, the new law was a block grant, giving local governments more choice in how the money would be spent and simplifying application procedures.

The new legislation merged the discretionary grant program, which had been primarily for capital projects and purchases, with the formula grant program, which had been used primarily for operating subsidies. The merged program would result in a totally formula-based allocation scheme, in which funds could be used for either operating or capital projects. This proposal passed Congress and became law, despite the early administration threat that the president would veto any bill that contained operating subsidies.[19] The new legislation greatly reduced the discretionary authority of UMTA and hence reduced the agency's ability to award or deny grants on political criteria.

The administration did not get all it wanted, however. The administration's version of the reauthorization bill (which died in the senate) not only reduced the authorized spending levels dramatically but also eliminated new rail starts and operating subsidies. The House bill, which eventually became law, contained the gas tax revenues as a trust fund for increased capital projects, a fund that would not require annual appropriations and hence would provide both an increase in capital funding and a more reliable source of funding for mass transportation. The bill contained the operating funds that the administration had earlier opposed. It also provided the possibility of new starts in rail projects. What the administration got out of the new law was the new block-grant structure. This was an important change, but it was only a portion of what the administration had been fighting for.

Regulation and Deregulation

A key element in the Reagan administration program was to deregulate—to simplify regulations, making them less costly, less intrusive, and more flexible. It pursued this goal in the Department of Transportation and in the Urban Mass Transit Administration as it did throughout the executive branch. All the "midnight regulations" of the Carter administration were frozen and examined before they were allowed to take effect, and particular regulations were selected for examination because of their cost and the burden they imposed.

In the funding and reauthorization battles, interest groups formed broad coalitions to oppose the administration, but on regulatory matters, they tended to be split. Unlike the HUD/CPD case, in which local governments unexpectedly sided with the representatives of the poor to fight changes in regulations posed by the administration, at UMTA the government representatives pitted themselves against the representatives of the handicapped, and transit operators were lined up against big labor. Though the administration did not achieved all its goals, it did accomplish some major objectives in deregulation, with the help of interest groups.

Two regulations that had the greatest impact and created the most controversy were those dealing with the treatment of the handicapped on public transportation and with the "Buy America" provisions in the authorizing legislation.

The issue of treatment of the handicapped was referred to as "Section 504," a paragraph from the Rehabilitation Act of 1973 (Public Law 93-112 as amended by PL 95-602 in 1978). Section 504 reads in part, "No otherwise qualified handicapped individual in the United States shall solely by reason of his handicap be excluded from participation in, be denied benefits of, or be subject to discrimination under any program or activity receiving federal financial assistance...."

Under the Carter administration, this law was interpreted to imply that all subways must be accessible to the handicapped, even if this meant that new measures must be taken, such as the installation of new elevators. New buses were required to have lifts on them to accommodate wheel chairs. The Reagan administration underlined this regulation as one that needed special examination and should be revised or eliminated.

In May of 1981, a federal court of appeals issued a judgment in a case against the regulation brought by a transit operators' lobby group. The judgment argued that section 504 of the Rehabilitation Act of 1973 did not authorize the department's rule as if affects mass transit. The court did not throw out the regulation as illegal but remanded it to the department for reconsideration. If the department intended to keep the rule, it would have to find a new legal justification.

The Department of Transportation used this opportunity to withdraw the offending regulations and issue some interim rules, which became known as the "local option." They required mass transit operators to certify that they were making special efforts to provide transportation that the handicapped could use. The nature of the effort was up to the local mass transit operator.

The issue of access for the handicapped pitted the handicapped and elderly against the transit operators. The handicapped wanted to be able to get on any regularly scheduled mass transportation. The transit operators, though, faced the possibility of vastly increased costs that would probably not increase ridership substantially, at a time when they were being severely criticized by friend and foe alike as being expensive and inefficient.

The second regulation that had stirred controversy was the "Buy America" provision of the authorizing legislation. This pitted the transit operators against organized labor and U.S. manufacturers of transit equipment. The Surface Transportation Act of 1978 states that the secretary of transportation shall not commit funds unless the items used in the project have been mined or manufactured in the United States. The secretary was empowered under the 1978 law to make exceptions if the law proved contrary to the public interest; if rolling stock would be unreasonably costly; if the items were not made anywhere in the United States, were made in limited quantity, or were of questionable quality; or if the purchase of American-made goods increased the overall project cost by more than 10 percent.

This regulation appeared constantly on the regulatory agenda of the Department of Transportation but was not finally acted on until the 1982 reauthorization. What resulted was a rewording of the law that probably reduced the added costs forced on the transit operators. There was, however, no dramatic backing off from the regulation comparable to the issuance of the "local option" rule.

The new "Buy America" provision allowed the secretary to make exceptions if the goods made or produced in America were 25 percent more expensive than their foreign counterparts; in the case of rolling stock, an exception could be made if U.S.-made goods were 10 percent more expensive than the competition. Rolling stock includes train controls, communications, and transit power equipment. Up to 50 percent may be foreign, with final assembly in the United States.[20] Although these new exceptions may make it easier to buy rolling stock, which is broadly defined, from foreign countries, the regulation can still be described as fairly detailed, constraining, and expensive. The limited changes in this regulation indicate a continuing pressure from U.S. business and labor and from Congress to keep the regulation intact.

The administration made other attempts at deregulation but with no dramatic outcome. There was a flurry of activity after the president first took office. Many of the Carter "midnight regulations" were delayed but then allowed to become effective, since they had more to do with running the program than with major regulatory issues.

The issuance of regulations markedly decreased over the first three years of the administration, but not all of the reduction indicated major deregulatory activity. Some regulations were dropped because they were not required under the new authorization law. A number of proposed regulations were withdrawn and issued as notices instead. In some cases this meant an increase in flexibility and a decrease in the agency's ability to make binding rules, but in a number of other cases, the distinction was meaningless. Guidelines for grant applications, for example, have the same effect whether they are issued as notices or regulations. A reduction in the number of regulations was also achieved by grouping together rules that had initially been considered individually.

The administration did manage to simplify the grant application procedure and planning requirements, especially for smaller localities. It also eliminated most of the proposed requirements for safety reporting and standards and accident investigation procedures. These regulations were potentially very burdensome to transit operators, and there was no substantial support for retaining them; thus deregulation in these areas was relatively uncontroversial. No one argued, for example, for the retention of complicated grant application or planning procedures.

In other areas, the administration had less success. For example, it considered a regulatory reform that would help protect private enterprise in the transit industry, an initiative that came to almost nothing. (The issues included charters and school buses.) Clearly this was an issues that the transit operators were not going to be enthusiastic about and that the administration embraced for ideological reasons. There was no lobby group for private enterprise generally, and private school bus operators and charter operators were not organized into active lobby groups.

The administration also attacked the provisions in the law requiring 10 percent of contracts to be let to minority businesses. UMTA petitioned the department immediately to be treated as an exception to the rule, with the argument that it was not clear that the rule was meant to apply to all agencies in the new authorization law. That argument did not get very far, and UMTA's request was rolled into the department's general consideration of the issue. This is another issue on which there is a clear constituency for and against and a clear legislative mandate that will make it very difficult for the department to make new or different rules.

There is another interesting wrinkle in the administration's attempt to deregulate the mass transit program. The agency itself almost yielded to the impulse to solve a problem through regulation. It tried to make rules requiring transit operators to maintain certain specified standards of maintenance. Such rules would have helped offset the program bias that encouraged purchasing new equipment and allowing it to deteriorate (the agency required fewer matching dollars for purchases of new equipment than it did for repair on maintenance). The administration's proposed elimination of the operating subsidy would probably have exacerbated the problem of encouraging the purchase of new equipment and then allowing it to fall apart. If, however, the agency could have required certain standards of maintenance as a requirement for the receipt of grants, the problem would have been solved in a cost-effective manner.

After outlining some of the regulatory approaches that the agency could take and soliciting comments on the approaches, the issue was allowed to die. Presumably the agency discovered that it could make regulations no better than any one else, and approaches that were likely to be effective and have any teeth were burdensome and would be protested by transit operators. The irony, of course, is that in this case, the regulations would both have made the program more cost effective, and have eliminated a major argument for continued operating assistance.

To summarize, the administration actively sought to deregulate mass transit, as it had sought to deregulate other agencies. It had some major and minor victories and some almost invisible failures. The successes were in those areas in which interest-group support for deregulation was strong and where there was little opposition.

The reduction in the number of rules issued tended not to be meaningful in comparison with the particular rules attacked and eliminated or weakened. In fact, the reduction in the number of rules issued was more of a public relations gimmick than a real effort to deregulate, but the administration was extremely serious and persistent in trying to eliminate or moderate the effect of regulation. It took the whole effort to deregulate so seriously that it hamstrung its own efforts to solve major problems of waste and mismanagement.

Decentralization

The president included mass transportation in his initial proposals to turn back programs to the state governments.[21] He felt that transportation was a local issue in which the federal government had no appropriate role, though he later modified that stance to concede a federal role in capital funding.

Opposition to the president's decentralization proposal was unanimous. The state governments themselves were in sufficient fiscal stress at the time that mass transit operators and congresspersons felt that the program would do better at the federal level.[22] The president withdrew mass transit from his new federalism proposals.

Some decentralization was accomplished in other ways, however. For example, the new reauthorization legislation passed in 1982 was a block grant, which increased local discretion in the expenditure of funds. In addition, agency administrators reported that they were trying to decentralize the structure of UMTA to its field offices. It is questionable how well they had succeeded in this area by the end of 1982.

UMTA had begun such a decentralization under President Carter but never fully implemented it. A number of headquarters staff members were sent to field offices, but decisions were made both in the field and in headquarters, and the responsibilities of the two divisions were not clearly defined.

Part of the reason for the duplication was that the discretionary grants for large projects were treated politically and had to go all the way to the secretary for approval, no matter what formal authority was delegated to the field. Because the 1982 reauthorization reduced the role of the discretionary grants, this source of pressure for centralization at headquarters should be relieved. Also, the reduction in staffing at headquarters, though not great, reduces the capacity of headquarters staff to review applications and proposals. These factors together may encourage a real delegation of authority to the field offices.

The reorganization proposed for UMTA was intended in part to implement that decentralization, but it is doubtful that it achieved this aim. Other than reducing the number of middle-level officials at headquarters and limiting the reduction in force to headquarters, the reorganization did little to clarify responsibilities.

Moreover, some observers questioned whether the impact of the reorganization was in fact exactly the opposite of the stated intent. One informant (who asked not to be identified other than as "a person familiar with the agency and with the industry") argued that fear of accidentally making a decision at odds with the administration in Washington created a *de facto* centralization that hamstrung the field operations during the first two years of the administration.

In 1979 or 1980 UMTA delegated responsibility to the regional offices; then this administration gathered a lot of that authority back in. The program was run by one or two political appointees. The ability of the agency to deliver the program was slowed down by the shift. I think all major grant-making decisions were involved. . . . There is uncertainty in the regional offices that affects their willingness to manage forcefully. They may have had the authority to do that in previous administrations, but the philosophy has changed. They have to keep a close account of what is happening at headquarters and react to that.

There is probably some truth to this description. It is clear that control of the agency was concentrated in the hands of a few political appointees, and it seems likely that officials in the field would be wary of inadvertently diverging from the policies of the new administration. They would be likely to keep their attention focused on headquarters for signals about what they were supposed to do or not do. Presumably, however, this dependence on headquarters for policy guidance would gradually diminish as it became clearer what the expectations of the new administration were.

To summarize, the president did not get very far in decentralizing UMTA. His proposal to turn the program over to the states fell on deaf ears, and he had to retract it. He did succeed in getting Congress to go along with the formula block grant idea, which increased the autonomy of local governments over the grants and paved the way for reduced political distribution of grants by the secretary. Reduced scrutiny of individual grants for political implications leaves open the possibility of really decentralizing decision-making authority to the regions.

Although the long-term implications of the reauthorization are that it may facilitate decentralization to the regions, the administration's policies during its first two years (before the reauthorization) probably had an overall effect of centralizing the agency by concentrating power in the hands of a few key appointees.

The Management of Cutback: Reorganization and Reduction in Force

The Reagan administration did not wait for congressional action on the budget or on reauthorization to make some major changes in the organization of the agency. One of the first tasks given by the new administrator of UMTA (Art Teele) to his staff was to form a study group to design a new organizational structure. This reorganization was eventually linked up with a reduction in force. It took place, at least in part, because "the organizational structure did not relate to new program directions."[23] That is, the reorganization was to aid the agency in carrying out the president's intentions for the program.

The reorganization weakened the unit that dealt with environmental planning, almost to the point of terminating it, in line with the president's effort to deregulate in this area. It also weakened the grant examination function, in anticipation of block grants with simplified applications, and it anticipated the elimination of operating subsidies as a separate program. The staffs for capital and formula assistance were merged before the passage of the reauthorization legislation which combined these two programs. The reorganization also enhanced the ability of the agency to carry out the president's policy directives by centralizing political control at the top of the agency and creating a structure that would be more politically responsive to both Congress and the president.

The reorganization brought about a number of changes. An answer desk was created to combine the record-keeping aspect of handling congressional and field requests for information and the policy-making aspects of responding to such questions. The public relations function was partly folded into this operation. In addition, the number of middle-level managers was reduced from twenty-two to thirteen. A financial management office with a controller was created.[24]

These seemingly disconnected changes to improve management formed a recognizable pattern. The middle level of management was drastically reduced, while the top level of the organization was enhanced. Several new Senior Executive Service positions (a corps of top-level managers who may be either politically appointed or promoted from the civil service) were added at the top of the organization, and the executive secretariat was expanded.

Those changes meant not only increased centralization but also a reseparation of policy decisions from routine administration. It was therefore crucially important to get the *right people* into the newly expanded secretariat and onto the answer desk—people who were knowledgeable and loyal to the administration.

The purpose of the reorganization was described as, among other things, to make the organization "more pyramidal." One top official described the reorganization in the following terms:

> We created a senior management core. UMTA had few SESers. The administrator and I convinced the O.S.T. [the Office of the Secretary of Transportation] that we needed more deputy associate administrators, a hard core of senior managers. We were a mile wide and one inch deep. Counter to organization theory, we created more hierarchy, but we did not make it overly hierarchical. It had begun as nonhierarchical, but it was never well managed. We never had a Weberian bureaucracy. It's not usually appropriate in a professional organization. But we never had discipline to loosen. UMTA's management style had been described as Bohemian. Mostly, stuff got done. But it wasn't responsive. We created more structure and more accountability.

Presumably accountability in this context meant that if you told a subordinate to do something, it would get done. It was not clear that anyone had control over the previous structure.

The plans for the reorganization had to be submitted to a congressional oversight committee. A large pile of documents including a Working Group Report, memos and supporting data, was submitted to Congress just before the reorganization was to take place. There was no way that committee members could really study the proposal and react to it before it went into effect.

The agency's offhandedness bothered some committee members who were pro-UMTA and wanted to guarantee that the agency was not being dismantled. Nevertheless, they had little recourse, other than budget cuts and angry letters, to show their displeasure. Since they supported mass transit, they had no desire to cut UMTA's budget. The only alternative, and not a very effective one, was to write angry letters.

Congressman Glenn Anderson of the oversight committee responded to the UMTA reorganization with one such letter:

> My primary concerns center around your assertion that the reorganization became necessary at least in part, because the "organization structure did not relate to new program directions." I do not recall, frankly, providing UMTA or any agency of the Administrative branch, with "new directions." I do suspect that this may refer to administrative *proposals*, thus far not authorized or approved by the Congress of the United States, to eliminate operating assistance for the nation's transit properties, and refuse to provide a federal share of the amounts necessary to fund new transit systems.

By reorganizing in a manner that anticipates proposed, but thus far unapproved program changes, I am concerned that UMTA may be usurping, or at least subverting, the authority of the legislative branch to act at a later date.[25]

Despite the congressional irritation with the manner in which it was accomplished, the reorganization was approved by the secretary and became effective in March of 1982.

When the reorganization study began, it was not clear how many people, if any, would have to be separated. The reorganization was initially designed independent of the need to reduce staff but with the expectation that more staff and more resources could not be allocated to solve UMTA's problems.[26] Yet the reorganization was accompanied by a reduction in force, even though employees believed the reorganization itself was not an adequate reason for the reduction. It was discretionary, not imposed by Congress, and could have been carried out without a RIF, since it had initially been designed without one.

One possible reason that the reorganization became linked with reductions in force is that some employees did not seem to fit in the new structure. However, it seems equally likely that the reduction and the reorganization had little to do with each other. The reorganization may simply have offered a convenient opportunity to carry out a reduction in force that had been decided on for entirely other reasons.

The RIF apparently occurred because the president had announced a policy of reducing the federal work force, and Secretary Lewis was conforming to that policy. The conclusion that there was a political reason for the reduction, is based in part on statements from informants and in part on elimination of the other possible causes.

There are many possible reasons for a reduction in force besides a reorganization. The most dramatic and acceptable of them are budget cuts recommended by the administration and supported by Congress. Then the number of positions may have to be reduced to save money, especially if there has been a reduction in salaries and expenses. Alternatively, positions may have to be reduced to accommodate to congressionally reduced emphasis on some program areas, which reduces workloads. In the UMTA case, personnel reductions were made before Congress acted on reauthorization, and it was difficult to find a clear budgetary mandate (endorsed by Congress) that would result in reduced personnel ceilings.

In the beginning it did not appear as if the administration was supporting a reduction in force at all. When the Reagan administration formulated its budget proposals for fiscal year 1982, it reduced the UMTA budget by 20 percent compared with the Carter budget proposal, but it recognized that many of the agency's reported managerial difficulties stemmed from under- rather than overstaffing. Consequently, the administration did not recommend a proportionate reduction in staffing levels. Proposed personnel ceilings were reduced by only 15 percent from President Carter's proposal. Given the current staffing levels, this request would not result in any necessary reduction in force.

Judith Connor, then assistant secretary of transportation for policy and international affairs, testified in budget hearings in March 1981 concerning the disproportionate support for personnel in the budget proposal. The line-item request for administration was nearly $29 million.

> This level will support staffing requirements which will bring total personnel to 574. Management audits have shown the necessity for a critical minimum number of staff necessary for proper program management. Coupled with proposed program reductions, the request will support the manpower resources needed to competently manage the program.[27]

The administration succeeded in getting congressional approval for program reductions almost exactly as in the president's original budget request, but Congress reduced the administrative portion of the budget below the level of president's request in March. Instead of $28,952,000, it granted only $26,888,000.

Given the reduction of nearly $2 million in the administrative budget, and an average GS salary at UMTA at about $30,000, the cuts translated into about fifty to fifty-five positions. That was very nearly the number recommended for reduction in force by the secretary of the department of transportation. At that point it looked as if Congress, not the administration, was responsible for the personnel reductions at UMTA.

However, Art Teele, the UMTA administrator, testified on Capitol Hill in October 1981 that even if Congress did not cut UMTA's budget by an additional 12 percent, the agency would have to cut seventy positions, given its current salaries and expense budget.[28] Informants reported that the extra fifteen positions were not budget related but were intended to give the administrator some additional flexibility.[29] Thus the size of the reduction in force seemed to have been determined primarily by a congressionally mandated reduction in the administrative budget and secondarily by the administrator of the agency.

This interpretation assumes, however, that there were not other savings possible in the administrative budget, and it also ignores the ability given by Congress to transfer program funds from other accounts to cover administrative costs of that program.[30] Congress clearly intended the transferred funds to prevent the necessity of reductions in force. During the 1983 budget hearings, Congressman Benjamin sharply questioned the financial rationale for personnel cuts:

> Originally, the administrative expense category was cut by action of both appropriations committees. However, it was our understanding that by approving the use of $1.6 million of section 6 funds to pay salaries, that no RIFs would have to occur. Isn't it true that with the additional 1.6 million, the amount available for personnel compensation in fiscal year 1982 exceeds

that available in fiscal year 1981? Eighteen and a half million versus almost 19.5 million in 1982. If this is true, then money was not a reason for the RIF. What was the reason?[31]

UMTA submitted a written answer stating that the RIF had resulted from reorganization, not from financial shortfall.

According to informants, independent of these budgetary concerns, the secretary began to reduce personnel ceilings throughout the department almost as soon as he took office. In February of 1981, he reduced the UMTA ceilings from 630 to 543, effective at the end of the year. UMTA succeeded in delaying a reduction in force by raising the ceiling for 1981 to a level above current staffing levels, using the argument that the study group had not yet reported and that reductions should be compatible with the redesign of the organization. The ceiling was lowered only to 573, and a RIF was averted for 1981, but it hung over the agency for 1982.[32]

At the beginning of June 1981, before the Omnibus Reconciliation Act and hence before the administrative budget was reduced by Congress, UMTA administrator Arthur Teele sent a memo to all staff warning them of the possibility of a reduction in force.[33] Though he may simply have been anticipating what Congress was going to do, the timing suggests that a policy decision had been made somewhere in the White House to carry out a reduction in force. The decision was timed with the one at HUD to carry out a reduction, and the HUD RIF was similarly difficult to justify on budgetary grounds. The secretary of transportation did not announce formal ceiling reductions until August, just after the omnibus reconciliation.

In August, the agency was asked to get down to 516 full-time permanent staff by the end of fiscal 1982.[34] Given the current staffing levels at the end of 1981 (547 full-time permanent staff), it was reasonable to assume attrition could bring the staffing levels down to 516. Though attrition was running lower than normal in many federal agencies because there were no jobs to go to, once a reduction in force was announced, the attrition rate usually increased markedly. Moreover, many UMTA employees were engineers, traffic planners, and other technically skilled professionals who were able to find jobs in local transportation agencies. By the time of the reduction in force, staffing levels were in fact below the secretary's target for UMTA. *Had it not been for the additional fifteen positions required by the UMTA administrator, there would have been no need to carry out a reduction because of position ceilings.*

Why then did the agency choose the disruptive process of reduction in force if there was no obvious need? The agency had decentralized functions to the field without reducing the staffing levels at the central office. Thus, although the agency as a whole was under the secretary's ceiling, the headquarters office was over ceiling, a situation analogous to that at HUD.

Vacancies in the field could have been filled through voluntary transfers from headquarters, reducing the size of the RIF, but few employees responded to the invitation to voluntarily move their households. An alternative would have been to force people to take the field positions. In such an action, no one need be separated from the organization. This measure is expensive, however, because the agency has to pay moving expenses and there are no salary savings from laying off employees. Thus the agency chose to restrict the reduction in force to headquarters, which meant that a larger number of people would have to be separated than current agency-wide staffing levels suggested.

The confusion about the source of the reduction in force was exacerbated by the reorganization, which created some new positions that were excluded from the RIF. Administrators argued that these could not be easily filled by existing staff; thus there were vacancies at headquarters at the same time that people were laid off, a fact that created a great deal of bitterness.

For whatever combination of reasons, by the time the reorganization went into effect, it had been determined that UMTA would have a reduction in force. Combining the reduction with the reorganization made it possible to select positions to eliminate that did not appear on the new organization chart.

Because there was a reorganization plan, choosing the positions to eliminate could have been done without regard to current incumbent. However, there is considerable evidence that the selection of positions was influenced by the incumbent as well as the existence or nonexistence of the position in the new organization. Reportedly the choice of the number of office director positions to be eliminated and the actual selection of the positions to eliminate were determined after discussions of the characteristics of incumbents.

Calculating from the raw data provided by the agency, there were sixty-six positions eliminated; the incumbents of sixty-one of those positions were initially sent separation notices. That meant that sixty-one out of sixty-six employees had no one to bump and no where to retreat. Their skills and experience were usable no place else in the organization. It is unlikely that this outcome occurred by chance. It reflected the narrow definition of what other work employees were capable of doing and was an example of the use of trial runs. The limited number of bumps meant that the selection of a position to eliminate was nearly equivalent to the selection of a person to fire.

Not only did the manner in which the reduction in force was carried out encourage the interpretation that individuals had been targeted for the reduction, but there is also evidence that the new organization was designed around certain staff members, who were told they would have a place in the new organization. This was often, though not always, the case.

For example, the answer desk was created before the rest of the reorganization took place. Staffers were detailed to the new positions and reportedly told that because of their experience they would have a good chance of being placed in those positions during the reduction in force. Other managers who lost their jobs were told they did not qualify for answer desk positions. Given the centrality of the answer desk in the agency's plans to increase its responsiveness and the increased role of this body in stating and issuing policy, it is easy to see why it would have to be staffed by people who were loyal to the administration.

MANAGEMENT: RECOVERY AND PROTEST

Although sixty-six positions had been eliminated from the old organization, there was not a net decline of sixty-six positions at UMTA because a number of new positions were created in the new organization that had been held out of the reduction in force; that is, employees were not allowed to bump into them.[35] Immediately after the RIF, there began a scramble to see who would fill the new positions. Some of the employees who had been separated or bumped were offered positions in the new structure, and some were not, thus engendering further charges of favoritism.

After the reduction in force, some of the affected employees were encouraged to speak to the administrator of the agency. If they asked for a position in the new organization, the request was often granted. Vacancies in the field offices also created a little more flexibility; in at least one case, a new regional position was created to absorb an employee who had been separated from employment. Whatever impersonality clung to the formal procedures for reductions in force issued by the Office of Personnel Management appeared to be nullified during the recovery period.

The administrator was able to pick and choose among affected employees, keeping some and rejecting others. It appeared that UMTA laid off more staff than it needed to and selectively hired back some employees, perhaps as a way of changing program direction or getting rid of deadwood.[36] The rehires were typically not permanent full-time staff, but they did add to the staffing levels. After the reduction in force, the number of full-time permanent staff was reduced, but the number of total full-time equivalent staff was increased. (The full-time equivalent figure included temporary staff and part time employees counting two half time people as 1 full time equivalent.) These figures suggest that the workload was not reduced and that there was some rehiring.

Despite the appearance of favoritism with which the reduction in force was run, opposition was slow to form inside UMTA. The union at UMTA was never particularly strong or active, which is not surprising given the overwhelmingly professional cast of the employees. Moreover, a professional personnel director experienced in RIF procedures was brought in to carry out the reduction and presumably to minimize mistakes that could be actionable. In addition, a firm was hired to write up and modernize all position descriptions. Unlike HUD, where poor position descriptions led to a technically poor reduction in force, UMTA had professionally updated position descriptions to start with. Although there were later to be many complaints concerning the targeting of individuals, there were no complaints about the position descriptions.

Agency administrators skillfully prevented congressional protest. The documents concerning the reduction in force were delivered to the oversight committee within days of the effective date of the reorganization. Individual congresspersons did oppose the reorganization, and there were many questions on the reduction in force and reorganization during the agency's 1983 budget hearings. Congressional interest appeared to be limited to asking difficult questions, however, and Administrator Teele kept responding that the personnel appeals would be settled by the appropriate channels, namely, the Merit Systems Protection Board.[37]

The only suggestion of successful congressional intervention came from one of the discharged employees, who reported that the employees were beginning to make contacts or use their contacts on Capitol Hill. The former employee reported that when one of the offices was virtually eliminated by transferring staff out, in a function that Congress had not eliminated, Adam Benjamin, chairman of the appropriations committee's Subcommittee on Transportation, was informed, and Administrator Teele rehired some employees (though not the same ones who had been transferred).

Interest groups followed program funding carefully and lobbied Congress skillfully on programs, but they had little interest in administrative costs and staffing levels. In one lobby group's records, program funds, presidential cuts, congressional approvals were listed, but the salaries and expense budget lines (which pay for personnel) were omitted. The interest groups played no role whatsoever in protesting reductions in force and reorganizations.

The most likely source of opposition then, was from the affected employees themselves, but without an active union, there was no way for them to compare information and discover a pattern of events. However, organized opposition was roused by several circumstances.

First, the personnel officer who had been hired to run the reduction in force was reportedly a crusty curmudgeon. As one of the employees put it, "The agency hired a RIF master. He is sharp. A venerable foe. He takes everything personally. He turned blue when anyone objected [to his actions] in the testimony." He knew no one in the agency, had no warm ties, and radiated no sympathy. When people came to talk to him after the reduction in force, he tended to annoy rather than calm them.

Second, the agency did not focus heavily on outplacement activities, with only three days of counseling provided by an outside firm. Compared with other agencies, UMTA created an image of not caring what happened to the employees who were laid off.

Even more important in forcing an opposition group to coalesce, an agency official urged employees who had just received their separation notices to act professionally and not to stir up emotions and sympathy from other employees. The request seemed callous to the group, given their recent notification of job loss. In the wave of anger that followed, the affected employees decided to form a group and fight the reduction in force together. They retained a single attorney and appealed to the Merit Systems Protection Board both jointly and individually. The agency's responses to their requests for information and the testimony of the agency before the Merit Systems Protection Board brought to light many of the practices mentioned above.

The protesting group of former employees questioned the restricted definition of what other jobs they could perform—that is, the narrow "competitive levels". They also questioned promotions and detailing (a formal loan of personnel from one office to another) to protect particular individuals, selective rehiring, and the good faith of the agency in running a reduction in force at all.

After a wait of several months, the Merit Systems Protection Board ruled in favor of the agency, thus ending the protest. The RIF at UMTA was determined to be legal.

OUTCOMES

Not all the impacts on the agency of the reorganization, the reduction in force, and the reauthorization are clear. On the one hand, there was a high level of uncertainty and a lowering of morale and productivity. On the other hand, the president was able to increase the policy responsiveness of the agency, which was an important goal. Some participants thought the organization came out better managed, at least in the short term, while some thought it was worse.

Uncertainty

Even those most sympathetic to the administration and most positive about the internal changes admitted that the continued uncertainty was enormous. For example, one official described the organization's capacity to function after the reorganization and reduction in force but before the reauthorization act:

> The organization is not frozen in its tracks. The future is unclear, but because of the block grant and new federalism proposals, not because of the reorganization. That is uncertain. It's not that we cannot manage and that the work

force doesn't pull together. Those issues have changed. The issue is new federalism or block grants. The changes could be dramatic.

Some agency officials were unable to estimate the effectiveness of the reorganization at the time of the interviews, because the chaos accompanying the reduction and the reorganization had been nearly continuous. Rumors of a RIF preceded the actual reduction by many months, increasing the attrition rates among those who felt vulnerable and increasing the anxiety level among many employees. The reorganization itself caused a certain amount of chaos as people shifted to take positions in the new organization.

Moreover, the long time delay after employees challenged the good faith of the agency in appeals to the Merit Systems Protection Board kept the whole reduction in force tentative until that judgment was rendered. Employees who were not affected by the reduction reportedly questioned what would happen to them if it were ruled illegal and the separated employees were all reinstated.

To add to the continuing confusion, the agency administrator was given to sudden reorganizations of his own apart from the larger, well-prepared, and documented reorganization. These were reportedly done as rewards and punishments for people who had pleased or irritated him. They had the effect in this case of prolonging the chaos, preventing people from settling down, and exaggerating the notion that favoritism ran through the whole restructuring period.

The continuing level of attrition contributed its share to the uncertainty. As one employee put it, "There has been an exorbitant attrition rate; it continued at the same rate as in December, January, and February. [After the reduction in force, attrition continued at the same rate as prior to the reduction]. About one to one and a half people per week. It was hard to make phone calls; people kept moving."

Lowered Morale

As the high rate of attrition suggested, and as management generally agreed, morale in the agency was terrible, even among those not directly affected by the reduction. One top-level official responsible for running the reduction observed, "Everyone at UMTA was affected, whether RIFfed or not. If you chose fifteen employees at random, and asked them questions on the impact of the RIF, few of them would be even moderately positive. It scarred and seared them all."

One of the people affected by the reduction described morale in the following terms:

We were zero. Now we are minus ten. Morale was bad; now it's terrible. People who were friends aren't talking. It's so depressing. We used to play baseball. No one plays anymore. Now people talk only about prospective RIFs, how the lawsuit is going, and who will be released [from employment] if the appellants win.

One informant put it briefly: "There is a hell of a morale problem." Another was more specific:

People are burned out, tired. There is a lack of enthusiasm for making deadlines. It's bad because the administration [of the agency] is so irrational in its demands for loyalty. How can you respect someone who reshapes an office for his own needs, and has a GS-15 doing clerical work? It became so difficult to get out of bed in the morning that you didn't.

It's a poisonous atmosphere, all over the feds. The middle manager's role was to protect his staff. This RIF was demoralizing because people's supervisors threw them to the wolves to protect their own asses. There was so much wheeling and dealing. One day you would hear that your job was abolished, and the next day you'd hear that it wasn't.

Lowered Productivity

Though it is sometimes difficult to link morale to productivity, in the case of UMTA the linkage was fairly direct, and employees were willing to talk about it. One employee described the situation in terms of enthusiasm to meet deadlines:

UMTA has had a reputation of being slow to deliver, not making deadlines, not responding to congressional requests, and so on. It has deteriorated even more now, in spite of Teele's efforts to control timeliness. It hasn't succeeded. Grant packages are still lost, deadlines are still [not?] met. Few people are concerned about deadlines. Most people want to do a good job. People are young, professional, progressive, bright, hard workers; they care, they believe in the program. But if you don't make a deadline, no big deal. Even in the chief counsel's office—they used to be on top of things, but there is less concern now. And they were not RIFfed or downgraded.

Another employee described productivity in terms of absenteeism and increases in illness:

There is an increase of "mental health" days. People stay home. People are less discreet about it.... You don't need a doctor's slip until three days, so people take two days. People have used a lot of annual leave. Some people are even borrowing it against the future....

People call in sick when they interview for jobs. It means they are scared. And more people are legitimately sick, with migraines and other stress symptoms. Productivity is nonexistent, even when people are there. They would like to care, but it's difficult to exhibit concern to grantees when you have your own battles to fight. It is difficult to keep your perspective that the rest of the world doesn't care. It plays in Peoria. The faceless bureaucrat is a convenient scapegoat.

One employee linked some of the causes of deteriorating morale directly with the difficulty of motivating employees to get work done:

> They [the political levels of the agency's administration] keep going through new carpets and desks, they use overtime for chauffeuring, they probably spent $80,000 in redecorating. Yet people were downgraded. You can't get loyalty, people won't do overtime. A furlough, no raises, then the executive director tells people that money and slots were there in the congressional actions and attrition would put us below anybody's cuts. That the RIF was done as an experiment "to see if we could do it with fewer personnel." Those statements compounded the difficulties. It was hard to get the organization to function.

Effects on Management

The effects of the reorganization and reduction in force on internal management were quite different at UMTA than they were at HUD. At HUD, many of the worst effects were based on inexperience in dealing with RIF procedures and on the negative impacts of the RIF rules themselves. At UMTA, the reduction in force was run by a professional hired because of his experience, and very few technical mistakes were made. There was a well-thought-out reorganization at UMTA, part of the purpose of which was to improve management; there was no reorganization accompanying the reduction in force at HUD. Given these major differences, one would expect the effect of the cutback procedures on management to be both different and more benign at UMTA.

Of those who evaluated the early impacts of the restructuring, the opinions varied. Most informants interviewed in August of 1982, some six months after the reduction in force and the reorganization, felt that it was too early to fully evaluate the effects of the changes. As one said, "It's too soon to tell. This year is still a disaster. Some of it is due to the RIF, some of it to the reorganization. It will be the second quarter of next year before it smooths out."

The administrator in charge of the reorganization felt that the reduction in the number of middle-level office directors was a definite plus, because the remaining ones had a broader span of control and more work to do. There would be less demoralization from having too little to do. Fewer problems of a minor nature were reportedly being referred up the bureaucracy, which was considered a sign that the reorganization had been successful. Since clearer guidelines for action had reportedly reduced the fear of making mistakes, lower-level managers felt less need to pass up all small matters.

Despite this analysis by upper-level management as to the impact of reorganization on lower-level managers, the reduction in force reportedly had the opposite effect. The chaos introduced by the changes also worked against the expected beneficial effects. The following excerpts from an interview illustrate these countertrends and employees responses.

Informant: People are afraid of looking bad in Teele's eyes. There is no logical way to anticipate what he wants. Internal people don't know to whom to go. Planning was reorganized two weeks ago. Nothing fits any more. People are afraid to make mistakes. "Who did that?" "T—did that." "I told her not to do that."

Interviewer: Doesn't that predate the RIF?

Informant: Some of it does [but the RIF made it worse].

In the UMTA case, then, the administrator was a man whom employees found hard to read and anticipate and who inspired a fear of making mistakes. The reorganization may have alleviated the fear of accidentally making a policy mistake, but it did not alleviate the personal fear of accidentally crossing the administrator. The reduction in force, with its appearance of favoritism, exacerbated this latter fear.

Another informant stated this idea succinctly. "The organization lost effectiveness because of the particular people RIFfed. People are afraid to make decisions. Before, people were making decisions. Now they are afraid to."

Opponents of the reorganization argued that the new structure did not solve the managerial problems of the agency. It had simply changed a professional, decentralized bureaucracy into a more formalized and centralized bureaucracy in which the fear of stepping out of line or out of hierarchy slowed work down and reduced the amount of informal consulting with experts. Decisions reportedly took as long as or longer than before and were based on less information.

One informant emphasized that real managerial issues were often ignored when the reorganization was being designed.

> There was no accepted work flow plan. What happens to the grant from time one? That was relegated to "We'll take care of that later." It was haphazard. We should have worked on a process flow of products. So now people get a piece of paper and say, "What is this?" "It's not my job."

Another informant underlined the cost of reorganization in a different manner. She argued that although there were many problems in the structure prior to reorganization, an informal organization had grown up to adjust to them and was generally successful. The change in structure destroyed the informal organization, and there was no way to get around the difficulties it caused.

> At one time UMTA was characterized by camaraderie. Everyone knew everyone, and could ask for help, and knew where to go for it. We had an organization chart, but we were disorganized. But things got accomplished because of overlapping structure. It worked because of the interaction between the offices. That has disappeared.... The structure is in place, but the infrastructure is not. It is not there informally any more.

Another managerial issue raised by the reorganization and reduction in force was that they were based on questionable assumptions. Both the reorganization and the reduction were intended to implement the president's policies in the expectation that Congress would go along, but it did not. The reduction was based on the premise that the agency could do the same amount of work with fewer employees, which also turned out not to be true. Because the agency had laid off too many employees, it had to transfer people into the offices that had been decimated and hire additional employees.

> UMTA is hiring. They are discovering that they overRIFfed. They severely weakened several programs and are now trying to repair the damage. The headquarters staff is now close to what it was. But the status of the employees is different. Many are now temporary, not to exceed one year. People have come back under such arrangements, or as "sole source contractors." [A sole source contractor supplies goods or services without having to go through competitive bidding.]

Expanding an agency's work force with temporary employees and sole source contractors is usually a less cost-effective way to carry out work. It reinforces the idea that the agency could afford to maintain prior levels of staffing and had no reduction in work load to justify a reduction in force, and it raises the question of what the agency will do in following year.

SUMMARY AND CONCLUSIONS

The administration had some explicit budgetary and program goals for the Urban Mass Transit Administration. After making some initial budget cuts with the consent of Congress, the president ended up compromising some of those goals in the reauthorization legislation. Particular congressional supporters of mass transit engineered a coalition of interest groups that protected mass transit revenue and programs. The president's proposed decentralization, which was to be part of the new federalism proposals, failed dramatically.

The portions of his program that the agency could undertake without congressional approval, or with minimal congressional oversight, proceeded independently, however, and with somewhat greater success. The administration attacked a number of regulatory issues with some success, especially where there was no interest-group involvement or interest group support for deregulation. The procedures for regulatory review were tightened up and adhered to, and the agency reorganized itself in accordance with the president's proposed changes, more or less bypassing its congressional oversight committees.

In line with proposed program changes, and in an effort to make the agency more responsive to the president's policy initiatives, the agency management also carried out a reduction in force. It is not clear whether it intentionally cut too many personnel and then hired back in order to rid itself of particular staff, or whether it believed it could operate the agency with fewer personnel and then found out that it could not. Members of Congress may have pressured the agency to restaff offices whose programs had not been eliminated by Congress. Possibly all these things were going on.

The purpose of the reorganization was to enhance the agency's responsiveness, especially to the president. In line with that goal, centralization was increased. The reorganization conformed to a pattern observed in several other agencies. There was a centralization at the top with a broadening of the politically responsive, decision-making group. Policy making was placed only in politically trusted hands. The number of offices at the middle level was reduced. This shift not only reversed the decentralization of the Carter years but also illustrates the trend noted elsewhere in the Reagan administration of separating political from administrative functions.[38]

One observer at UMTA, relying on earlier discussions at OMB, labeled the change "from program to policy management orientation."[39] When the program orientation was uppermost, the program officers (at the middle level of the organization) were the dominant portion of the organization. They made policy as they handled technical problems and tried to make the programs run. Policy was sometimes inconsistent as different managers in different programs responded to problems.

When policy concerns were uppermost, the answer desk was created, and new SESers were requested for the top of the organization while the program officers lost control. The people on the answer desk were carefully selected. Their job was to respond to requests from Congress, from the secretary of the department, and from the field, and to implement policies consistently. Presumably the source of those policies was the newly expanded secretariat, not the program managers trying to solve day-to-day problems.

As a result, the agency was restructured not simply to answer many of the criticisms of poor management that had been laid against it but to make it more politically responsive to the administration's broader policy objectives. To the extent that there really has been a shift from program to policy, there has been a major change at UMTA. Moreover, this change is illustrative of what is happening in a number of agencies since the Reagan administration took office.

The cost of the reorganization, the reduction in force, and then the reauthorization has been continuing uncertainty in the organization, poor morale, and, at least for a time, poor productivity. The informal organization has been disrupted, and employees often do not know to whom to go for assistance and fear stepping out of line. At least for the short run, and despite the clarification of policy directions, the increase in fear has prevented employees both in the field and at headquarters from making decisions.

Nevertheless, there may have been some managerial improvements at UMTA as a result of presidential policy. The shift from discretionary grants to formula grants may reduce interest-group and congressional interest in UMTA's day-to-day activities, which may make the agency easier to manage. It will almost inevitably make the decentralization to the field easier, since there will be less need to clear grant allocations with headquarters. The simplification of grant application procedures has certainly reduced regulation.

On the other hand, the increased emphasis on policy responsiveness and the centralization of policy making in the hands of a few decision makers at the top of headquarters are bound to have a centralizing effect on decision making and to encourage managers to seek policy guidance on many issues before acting. This may create a bottleneck as requests for guidance exceed the capacity to make reasonable decisions, even with a slight expansion in the size of the policy-making group.

NOTES

1. For example, the handicapped have pressed to have all buses equipped to handle their needs, while local governments have pleaded for modification of the rules to allow other ways of serving the handicapped.

2. Congress had criticized agency management, and there was much criticism within the Department of Transportation. Some of the critical studies include U.S. Department of Transportation, Office of the Assistant Secretary for Administration, *UMTA Management Alternatives: History, Problems and Organization* (unpublished, August 1979); Booz Allen and Hamilton, *Preliminary Diagnostic, Analysis of the Programs, Procedures and Structure of the Urban Mass Transportation Administration*, Phase one, final report (Washington: Booz Allen and Hamilton, 1979); and General Accounting Office, *Soaring Transit Subsidies Must Be Controlled: Report to the Congress by the Controller General of the U.S.* (CED-81-28) (Washington: Government Printing Office, 26 February 1981).

3. In a self-study preparatory to the reorganization, program management was criticized as follows: "Program management lacks clear delineation of responsibilities among headquarters offices and between headquarters offices and the field; fails to deliver program guidance to assure consistency among regions; fails to look beyond day to day events; lacks goals and criteria to guide decisions; does a poor job of project oversight; and overvalues 'getting out the bucks,' while under-

valuing 'selling ideas and innovations.'" UMTA Working Group, *Final Report*, April 1981, p. 31.

4. For example, Carl Richardson, regional administrator for region 4, wrote UMTA administrator Art Teele, 3 February 1981, "At present a new policy question seems to require an inordinate amount of time. For example, a policy question on spending grant funds on art in transit stations required over one year for an answer."

5. An exchange between Congressman Adam Benjamin and Carole Foryst, associate administrator for policy, budget and program development, illustrates these congressional concerns with agency management [I have abbreviated the discussion slightly]:

Mr. Benjamin: What criteria will you be employing to measure the effectiveness of your agency during the next four years?

Ms. Foryst: That was actually an excellent question because we have really been struggling with it in a way....

Mr. Benjamin: You have indicated that your goals are twofold. One is to improve the transportation system. If you have any quantifiable goals, would you supply them for the record? ...

Ms. Foryst: Yes, we would be glad to do that. But I just would like to add at this point that we may not have the data base available for a while....

Mr. Benjamin: Even the use of ballpark figures would be acceptable to us. We don't know where you feel you are and where you think you are going. We are going to see you at least a year from now, if not before. We would like to be able to talk to you in terms of what you have achieved or failed to achieve.

House Committee on Appropriations, *Department of Transportation and Related Agencies Appropriations 1982: Hearings*, Part 4, 97th Cong., 1st sess., 1 May 1981, pp. 572–73.

6. "With a staff of fewer than 600 persons, UMTA has been hardpressed to keep track of the flow of capital grants, operating assistance projects and the score of outlays made annually for research and development, demonstrations, and training. In 1980, the agency processed 498 operating assistance grants, and 223 capital grants, with some of the individual grants representing dozens of projects. In one regional office, two individuals were responsible for overseeing 136 projects, involving 31 properties. An official in another regional office candidly admitted to subcommittee investigators that the regional office had to treat the federal assistance program as a block grant program because of the limited number of persons available for project oversight."

The source for this quotation is House Subcommittee on Investigations and Oversight of the Committee on Public Works and Transportation, *Oversight of the Federal Public Transportation Assistance Program, the State of Public Transportation in the Nation, and a Recommended New Block Grant Concept: Report*, 97th Cong., 2d sess., May 1982, p.

7. Some of these arguments are summarized in Administrator Teele's opening statement to the House subcommittee on the *Department of Transportation and Related Agencies Appropriations*, to justify the 1982 budget request. See *Hearings*, 1 May 1981, pp. 528–29.

8. Eugene McCallister, ed., *Agenda for Progress* (Washington, D.C.: Heritage Foundation, 1981), p. 167.

9. There was an exchange on this issue during the House subcommittee hearings on UMTA's 1983 budget. Congressman Adam Benjamin asked Administrator Teele when the administration intended to resume new rail starts now that inflation was declining, since the starts had supposedly been delayed because of

inflation. Administrator Teele replied, "If you look at our proposed legislation, we are proposing to eliminate the new starts as an eligible category under our section 9 capital formula program, and therefore submit to you that the new starts category would never be eligible under the new section 9 program." House Committee on Appropriations, *Department of Transportation and Related Agencies Appropriations for 1983: Hearings*, 97th Cong., 2d sess., 1982, pp. 653–54.

10. Administrator Teele referred to the cost of new starts in the outyears in his testimony before the House Appropriations Subcommittee on Transportation and Related Agencies, concerning the 1983 budget request. He argued that the huge amounts involved created "a certain imprecision in the appropriation process that this administration would rather defer" until the budget was balanced. *Hearings*, 1982, pp. 651–52.

11. See House Subcommittee on Surface Transportation of the Committee on Public Works and Transportation, *Review of the Administration's Fiscal Year 1984 Budget Proposals for the Urban Mass Transportation Administration; the National Highway Traffic Safety Administration; and the Federal Highway Administration: Hearing*, 98th Cong., 1st sess., 23 February 1983, p. 46.

12. Administrator Teele, in trying to answer why the administration submitted a request for deferral of 1983 funds immediately after the passage of the 1982 reauthorization act, answered, "That is a decision that was made by the administration officials. . . . It is a device the administration has chosen to use." He later admitted to not being privy to administration decisions in some areas. Overall he gave the impression that decisions were being made elsewhere in the administration. *Review of the Administration's Fiscal Year 1984 Budget Proposals for the Urban Mass Transportation Administration, Hearing*, 23 February 1983, pp. 45, 47.

13. George Smerk, "Federal Mass Transit Policy—1981–1982: A Fall From Grace?" *Transportation Journal* 23, no. 1 (Fall 1983): 57.

14. *Oversight of the Federal Public Transportation Assistance Program, the State of Public Transportation in the Nation, and a Recommended New Block Grant Concept: Report*, May 1982.

15. Smerk, "A Fall From Grace?", p. 46.

16. These figures are calculated from the comparative data in the 1983 budget justification presented to Congress. *Department of Transportation and Related Agencies Appropriations for 1983: Hearings*, 1982, p. 589.

17. This information is derived from a comparison of section 5 program requests in the 1983 budget justification and the section 5 program actuals for 1983 reported in the 1984 budget justification. Not all section 5 funds can be spent on operating subsidies, but the tables in the budget justification break out separately the lines which may and may not be spent on operating funds. See p. 634 of the 1983 budget justification for the Department of Transportation and Related Agencies, and p. 583 of the 1984 budget justification. The budget justification is the department's detailed budget request, reprinted in the Appropriations hearings each year.

18. *Review of the Administration's Fiscal 1984 Budget Proposals for Urban Mass Transportation Administration: Hearing*, 23 February 1983, p. 21.

19. The administration's determination to veto any legislation which contained federal operating subsidies is described in the 1983 budget hearings. *Department of Transportation and Related Agencies Appropriations for 1983: Hearings*, 1982, pp. 676–77.

20. Smerk, "A Fall From Grace?" p. 55, and "Implementation of the Federal Public Transportation Act of 1982," *48 Federal Register* 3300–3302 (1983).

21. Reagan Plan: Transit May Go to States." *Passenger Transport*, 16 July 1982, p. 1. The article reported, "Mass transit construction and operating funds could be part of the latest new federalism proposals announced by President

Ronald Reagan in a July 13 speech before members of the National Association of Counties." p. 1. The Department of Transportation and OMB were reportedly at work on the amount of the turnback in funding; that is, they were trying to decide how much federal money would go to the states along with the program.

22. Members of the American Public Transit Association testified before Congress concerning the effects of past and proposed budget cuts by the administration. This testimony summarizes the position taken by APTA for several years—namely, that the state and local governments were themselves too hard pressed to fund local transit. *Review of the Administration's Fiscal Year 1984 Budget Proposals for the Urban Mass Transportation Administration: Hearing*, 23 February 1983. See especially pp. 85–86.

23. This quote is from a letter from Congressman Glenn Anderson to Administrator Teele, dated 19 April 1982, concerning the reorganization.

24. The reorganization is described in documents submitted as exhibits to the Merit Systems Protection Board when affected employees appealed the reduction in force. It is also described in documents submitted to UMTA's authorizing committee and in budget hearings.

25. Glenn Anderson's letter to Administrator Teele, 19 April 1982.

26. See the affidavit of Raymond Sander, Executive Director of UMTA, before the Merit Systems Protection Board, *Betty Bennet, et al v. Department of Transportation*, (Washington Regional Office, 23 April 1982). The introductory statement outlines the logic of the reorganization as it evolved and refers to the assumption that more staff would not be added. It does not, however, assume a reduction in force.

27. From the opening statement of Judith Connor, Senate Committee on Appropriations, *Department of Transportation and Related Agencies Appropriations, Fiscal Year 1982: Hearings*, 97th Cong., 1st sess., 1981, p. 632.

28. Reported in Raymond Sander's affidavit to the Merit Systems Protection Board.

29. That the administrator lowered the personnel ceiling below that given by the secretary is documented in a memo from Arthur Teele to his executive staff. The memo is dated 13 August 1981 and concerns "FY 1982 Employee Reductions —UMTA." In the memo Teele stated, "Additionally, please note that I am establishing the UMTA ceiling at 501 rather than the OST [Office of the Secretary of Transportation] imposed ceiling of 516. *Therefore for planning purposes, UMTA will be working on a FY 1982 ceiling of 501.*" (Italics in the original.)

30. Congress granted the agency permission to use de-obligated section 6 resources to offset the administrative costs of the section 6 program, which were normally covered by the salaries and expense budget. Administrator Teele thanked the House Subcommittee on Department of Transportation and Related Agencies during the 1983 budget hearings. *Department of Transportation and Related Agencies Appropriations for 1983: Hearings*, 1982, p. 627.

31. *Ibid.*, p. 934.

32. From the affidavit of Raymond Sander before the MSPB, *Bennet v. Department of Transportation.*

33. *Ibid.*

34. *Ibid.*

35. From the affidavit of Alton Ressler before the MSPB, *Lim v. Department of Transportation*, Washington Regional Office, 22 April 1982, p. 6.

36. Secretary of Transportation Lewis argued that in a perfect world, he would choose who would be kept and who would be fired, but since he couldn't do that, he recommended eliminating programs, overcutting, and then rebuilding, being careful to observe the law. He was quoted in the *Washington Post*, 9 March 1982, and the quotation was used in the 1983 budget hearings in the House, *Depart-*

ment of Transportation and Related Agencies Appropriations for 1983: Hearings, 1982, p. 811.

37. See, for example, *Department of Transportation and Related Agencies Appropriations for 1983: Hearings*, 1982, pp. 881–12.

38. See, for example, Chet Newland, "A Midterm Appraisal—The Reagan Presidency: Limited Government and Political Administration," *Public Administration Review* 43 (January/February 1983): 1–21.

39. This theme was raised in the working papers that provided the background for the Working Group Report, the document that shaped the reorganization. However, the topic was not included in the final report.

7

The Office of Personnel Management

Cutting Back the Federal Work Force and Cutting Back OPM

This chapter deals with the effects of the president's cutback policies on the Office of Personnel Management (OPM) and the effect of cuts and policy changes in OPM on the management of the federal work force. The chapter indirectly deals with the broader issue of whether the president was able to improve management while cutting back the nonmilitary portions of the federal government.

The Office of Personnel Management experienced deep budget cuts in 1982 and milder ones in 1983. The agency ran a huge reduction in force and a furlough and reorganized three times during this study. OPM had no major interest-group support to buffer it against cuts, and its own leadership did not fight for its budget levels. Almost everything that can happen to an agency during cutback happened to OPM. Its case is thus an excellent one to illustrate the impact of cuts on agencies.

Cutbacks at OPM also had potential impact on the management of the federal work force. This potential impact raises several questions that are addressed in this chapter. Did OPM's cutbacks, reorganizations, and internal policy changes affect its role in the management of the federal work force? Was OPM able to implement the conservative philosophy of making the federal government cheaper and more like a business? Did the agency enhance managerial discretion over federal employees and hence improve the quality of management, or did it politicize both itself and personnel policy in an effort to carry out the president's goals?

The OPM case illustrates better than the other cases how much autonomy the president had to cut back agencies. The president tends to have more autonomy over personnel decisions than over program design or budget decisions; thus if he controlled the agency that set personnel policy, he would have enormous control over the policy itself. How effective was the president's control in this area? How significant were the changes that were made? What were the constraints, if any, on the president's autonomy?

Finally, the OPM case raises the curious issue of how an agency whose role is to cut back the federal work force cuts itself back. The agency was running reductions in force government-wide at the same time that it was running a reduction inside OPM. Everything it did inside OPM was thus held up to scrutiny. Policies OPM drew up for other agencies were applied to OPM; the agency's internal management experiences were used to inform its policies for the rest of the government. The close connection between OPM's internal management and its external activity raises the question of what impact this connection might have had on OPM's policies and operations.

BACKGROUND

Responsibilities of OPM

The Office of Personnel Management is responsible for implementing the civil service laws and regulations. In addition, it performs routine personnel functions such as keeping records on federal personnel, administering benefit programs, and handling routine recruitment for the federal government.

One of the main functions of the Office of Personnel Management is to carry out the Civil Service Reform Act of 1978 (PL 94-454). The purposes of this act were to give federal managers greater flexibility in managing human resources, to supply new tools to motivate supervisors and employees, to offer a comprehensive personnel system for executives, and to provide support to agencies to help achieve good management of government programs. OPM's responsibilities under the act also include safeguarding the career civil service system from political abuses.[1]

OPM's role in implementing the Civil Service Reform Act was to design and implement performance evaluation and merit pay systems and to improve the productivity of federal employees. OPM was required to evaluate at periodic intervals its successes and failures in implementing the reforms.

The act authorized some decentralization of personnel functions from OPM to other federal agencies but was somewhat ambiguous about exactly what OPM was to do for the agencies and how it was to do those tasks. OPM concentrated on training federal agencies' personnel officers to carry out the reforms. It left control over personnel decisions with the agencies but then set up systems to advise and oversee the new decentralized personnel functions.

Level of Political Support

Because OPM was primarily a housekeeping agency, it had little or no interest-group support. However, since the function of OPM was to protect the civil service against political pressures and to enforce the civil service laws, it is possible that it could be viewed positively by federal employees, who would rise up to protect it if it were threatened. However, federal employees did not rally around OPM. It was clear that through the first three years of the Reagan administration they did not see OPM as an advocate of their rights or as a promoter of their welfare. In fact, many increasingly saw OPM as a threat.

Nor did OPM have strong congressional support. The General Accounting Office (GAO) had been persistently critical of OPM's attempts to implement the Civil Service Reform Act.[2] Congressional committees used information provided by the GAO and often took a critical stance toward the agency.

Congress kept a close watch on OPM through detailed oversight hearings, requests to the agency for information, and GAO investigations. Moreover, the 1978 Civil Service Reform Act set up OPM's sister agency, the Merit Systems Protection Board (MSPB), as a monitor on OPM's actions, and the MSPB submitted an annual study on OPM's progress and problems. All this oversight and criticism created an atmosphere inside OPM of being under the microscope of a somewhat hostile scientist.

The Senate Committee on Operations and Civil Service and the House Committee on Post Office and Civil Service, the authorizing committees for OPM, were both generally hostile to the agency, especially after Dr. Donald Devine was appointed director. They held extremely thorough and occasionally unpleasant hearings on OPM's activities. The Manpower and Housing Subcommittee of the House Committee on Government Operations held hearings that were somewhat critical of OPM's attempts to place separated employees in new jobs, and the Committee on the District of Columbia had hearings on the impacts of federal cutbacks on Washington, D.C.

The Federal Government Service Task Force, composed mostly of members of Congress from in and around Washington D.C., took a particular interest in the reductions in force, monitoring them in the agencies and looking for impacts on women and minorities. The members of the task force fed information to congressional committees and testified at their hearings. They also proposed their own version of RIF regulations that was more protective of federal employees than were existing regulations.[3] In short, the representatives of federal employees in Congress went to bat for them, on the authorizing committees, on task forces, and on the District of Columbia Committee. Ironically, protecting the federal employees put them on a collision course with OPM.

The President's Control of OPM

Not only did the agency lack strong congressional support, in one sense it lacked the support of its own leadership. The president appointed as the director Dr. Donald Devine, a person who was politically conservative and agreed with the president in many major respects. Dr. Devine cut back the agency's budget and staffing levels, reorganized, and defended the cuts in Congress. He never hinted, as Art Teele of UMTA did, that there might be unmet needs requiring additional funding. He argued that the agency was doing better with fewer people. They had streamlined processes and were more cost effective.

The president had excellent control over the top levels of OPM. However, Dr. Devine initially displayed so little loyalty to the agency that when he tried to implement the president's program, he created a deep rift between the political leadership and the career bureaucrats.

THE PRESIDENT'S GOALS AND THEIR IMPACT ON OPM

The president gave OPM two broad tasks to carry out as its part in his cutback program: to manage personnel reductions and to reduce the cost of the work force.

Managing Personnel Reductions

Setting Up a Task Force

OPM geared up to manage reductions in force across federal agencies beginning in April of 1981, when it became clear that the president wanted to reduce the size of government. Director Devine set up a RIF task force. Every unit in OPM that had any connection with reductions in force was represented on the task force—for example, advisory services, public relations, and training. The task force had a small full-time staff. As a group they designed work plans that would be carried out by the operating units. The group achieved internal coordination of policy so that only one set of advice went out to the agencies.

A member of that task force described its functions and operations:

A big charter established the assignment. Survey everything that had been done, everything that should be done, and devise an action plan. Plan every phase of the reduction in force.... We turned out work plans, which were carried out through the operating units. We wrote a new chapter in the personnel manual. We designed training materials, put out *Fed Facts*, up to date and accurate. We worked under the tight time table. The director wanted OPM to supply agencies with consistent, up-to-date information, not a training course six months out of date.

The functions of the task force gradually expanded to include policies on furloughs and "outplacement" ("outplacement" is jargon for finding new jobs for employees who were affected by reductions in force). Formed in April 1981, by August of 1981 the task force took on the question of placement of "surplus employees," determining what level of service to provide for them, preparing bibliographies on outplacement, and designing audiovisual guides for outplacement directors.

The task force also came to play a monitoring role for Director Devine on how well the procedures were working:

> There was a continuing monitoring effort; we were the eyes and ears of the agency in the RIF, outplacement, and furlough. We were to keep our antennae up for problems in regulations and in carrying them out. We had to decide if there were problems, should we send the compliance people in? Are they serious enough about outplacement? When he [Devine] has to testify, he has the freshest and best information and is attuned to new possibilities for improvement. How the real world feels, not how the policy analysts feel. We talk to people in the trenches. He [Devine] can combine policy concerns with down-to-earth concerns. He can say, "It happens this way," or "We don't regulate in that area."

Implementing Humanitarian Policy

OPM did an admirable job in putting together RIF materials quickly and getting the information out to the agencies in a timely manner. But there were aspects of the personnel reduction policy that were problematic, particularly those that were considered "humanitarian." The president had specified that the reduction in staffing levels be done in the most humanitarian manner possible, and that meant both avoiding reductions in force when possible and emphasizing job placement for people forced out of jobs.

OPM staff took this statement of policy seriously. It informed agencies of the alternatives to reductions in force and urged them to exhaust all other alternatives before considering RIFs. OPM also sought to improve existing placement activities and tried to persuade other agencies to become more active in both job placement and rehiring laid-off employees. Unfortunately, both these attempts at humanitarian personnel reduction turned out to be controversial and half-hearted.

First, OPM backed down from its stated policy of avoiding reductions in force if at all possible. OPM had its own reduction in March 1982, and its employees tried to use the advice they had given to other agencies to stop the reduction. Dr. Devine went ahead with the RIF, despite the opposition based on OPM's guidance to other agencies.

In hearings on 3 March 1982, just as OPM's reduction in force was beginning, Director Devine expressed his new thoughts on the matter. He argued:

> I do not think it is possible and we have given a lot of thought to this, and I have had discussions around the executive branch on this question. I do not believe you can come up with one set of instructions that says when you have to use RIF, when you have to use furloughs, and when you use attrition. It is very much a hands-on decision process in which you have to look at the resources in the agency, at the mission of the agency....."[4]

OPM's support of various plans to reemploy those laid off during reductions in force was only lukewarm. Dr. Devine endorsed the existing Voluntary Interagency Placement Program (VIPP), which was only voluntary, as the name implies. OPM did revise its program for displaced employees (DEP), requiring agencies to operate programs for rehiring their own displaced employees. Dr. Devine reported in hearings that together the Voluntary Interagency Placement Program and the Displaced Employee Program placed 2340 federal employees in 1981. The agencies reported placing 5236 employees who had been affected by reductions in force.[5]

These figures met with considerable skepticism. Many employees questioned the effectiveness of agency placements, arguing that agencies' outplacement officers took credit for all new jobs found by employees whether they had been helpful in that placement or not. OPM estimated that they placed about 25 percent of those who registered for the Voluntary Interagency Placement Program. OPM claimed that was an excellent record, even while acknowledging that not all those eligible for the program had signed up for it; thus 25 percent was high as an estimate of the proportion of those needing help who got it.[6]

Some employees were very critical of the program. They argued that it seemed to be a bottomless hole into which they tossed their résumés. They handed in an application with their name and skills and then had to wait with no activity, no communication, and no leads they could follow. They felt they could not take action on their own behalf to examine possibilities or call attention to themselves to prospective employers. Most of them never heard from the program again.

As OPM learned more about how the reductions in force were working, it seemed to become more sensitive to the need for good job placement as part of the preparation for the reductions. However, its advice to agencies concerning job placement sounded less humanitarian than it did managerial and financial. OPM advised agencies to consider placement activities before the reduction in force rather than after, because such efforts would not only improve morale but would also reduce the costs of severance pay and unemployment benefits and minimize the amount of time that employees spent writing résumés.[7]

In short, OPM did a good job of managing the government-wide reductions in force but did not seem to follow through on the president's guidance concerning the way in which the reductions should take place. The agency backed away from a policy of discouraging reductions in force by forcing agencies to exhaust all other alternatives first, and it only put half-hearted effort into its job placement activities. To the extent that OPM did encourage agencies to engage in early job placement activities, the motivation appeared to be minimizing the cost and damage to agencies resulting from RIFs rather than concern for the employees. The policy was a credit to OPM in the management area but negative in the employee relations area.

Revising the Reduction-in-Force Regulations

Consonant with the view that OPM's encouragement of job placement activities was an exercise in limiting damage to agencies' management, OPM set itself the task of revising the existing regulations for reductions in force so that they would cause less agency disruption. In the spring of 1983, OPM proposed regulations to revise the RIF procedures. These reduced the possible depth of demotions and the length of bumping chains. That meant that one person could not be demoted from management to a position in the mail room, and it also meant that one person could not replace someone else, who would replace someone else, and so on, in a long chain.

The revisions also reversed the order in which factors would be considered when deciding on an employee's retention status, putting performance evaluations before rather than after seniority. The change would have the effect of making the evaluations slightly more important in calculating retention rights and making seniority slightly less important. The new regulations made no change in the importance of veterans' benefits, which was the only part of the regulations mandated by Congress. (For details of the new regulations, the reader is referred to Chapter 2.)

The new regulations should certainly cause less damage within an agency and make it easier to identify and get rid of nonproducers during a reduction in force. On the other hand, the proposed new regulations give federal employees considerably less security in their jobs. They make it easier for a manager to target an individual for layoff for other reasons than merit, and they make demotions more serious because they not only take away status but also reduce pay. Faced with the prospect of reduced salary, many employees who have retention rights and would not actually be forced to leave would have to resign.

Reducing the Cost of the Work Force

The second part of the president's personnel policy was to reduce the cost of the federal work force. After taking office, the administration quickly submitted a legislative proposal to change the way federal salary and benefit levels were determined (Federal Pay Comparability Reform Act of 1981, H.R. 3140 and S. 838).

Under existing law, federal compensation is based on comparability with the private sector. A survey is done each year by OPM to determine wages in a number of occupations. The Advisory Committee on Federal Pay looks at the evidence and makes recommendations to the president on salary levels. Historically, benefits have been handled separately.

The president's comparability reform proposal put wages and benefits in a single package and recommended that instead of being comparable to pay in the private sector, federal pay should be set at 94 percent of private-sector pay. OPM argued that there are unmeasured benefits of working for the federal government, such as job security, which attract people to federal jobs. If such benefits were estimated, they could be subtracted from salary, and the total compensation package, including wages and benefits, would still be comparable. This argument assumed not only that the unmeasured benefits equaled six percent, an undocumented amount, but also that salaries and benefits could be looked at as part of one package.[8]

The president's proposal threw a measurement burden onto OPM, which reacted to the proposal by commissioning a study of private-sector salaries, with information on benefits. In July of 1981, OPM released its report based on this data.[9] It decided that federal benefits were, as a package, more generous than those of the private sector, even though only one benefit, retirement, was more generous, and the other benefits were less generous. This initial work done by OPM as a backup to the proposed legislation was later used as an argument to reduce employee benefits, but the president's bill itself died in Congress.

The Pay Comparability Act, which was the law in effect, contained a provision allowing the president to ignore comparability issues in case of national need, such as periods of high inflation or other economic emergencies. In recent years the comparability requirement has generally been ignored, and presidents, including President Reagan, have set federal pay below levels required for comparability. Using the OPM survey of private-sector wages to assess comparability, the Congressional Budget Office (an arm of Congress) estimated that public employees had fallen about 20 percent behind the private sector by 1983.[10]

OPM continued to battle to reduce compensation. Director Devine made some reductions to existing benefits and planned to change others. According to Congressman Steny Hoyer, OPM underestimated the cost of health insurance by $440 million, and then instead of asking OMB and Congress for a supplemental appropriation, argued that the program was underfunded and gave employees a choice of increasing their contributions to the system or choosing less expensive insurance with reduced coverage.

These changes in the insurance package were challenged in court, "forcing OPM to postpone in 1981 'open seasons' awaiting final judicial rulings. In February 1982, the courts recognized the Director's authority to remedy the shortfall, minimize premium increases and return the program to financial stability."[11]

Dr. Devine continued to try to find ways to control the costs of insurance. In 1983 he proposed a voucher system. A voucher for a specific dollar amount would be given to each employee, who could spend it for insurance with any recognized carrier. The employee could buy less expensive insurance and get a refund from the government for the difference, or more expensive insurance and pay the difference himself.

With respect to pension system underfunding, Dr. Devine proposed to raise the employee and employer contribution to the system and reduce the benefits. The proposed changes included an increase from age fifty-five to sixty-five for normal retirement, increases in the payroll tax (the employee contribution) from 7 percent to 9 percent to 11 percent, and severe decreases in benefits for early retirement.[12]

The administration's attacks on salary and benefit levels assumed that federal employees were overpaid, while the Congressional Budget Office estimated, *on the basis of the OPM comparability survey*, that federal employees were paid less on the average than their private-sector counterparts. This contradiction placed OPM and Director Devine in the awkward position of having to deny the validity of the OPM private-sector wage survey.

Dr. Devine responded to the problem by arguing that the survey was not measuring salaries correctly because it sampled too few small- and medium-sized businesses and ignored the salaries of local and state governments in setting comparability. He proposed a different type of survey. To open the whole issue up for examination, OPM did a study, dated December 1982, on different approaches to the measurement of federal pay.[13]

Director Devine eventually gave up on cutting pay by redefining the way comparability was calculated, disbanding the research program inside OPM that had been generating proposals. The administration and Congress were reportedly too far apart on the issue to make legislative action likely. In the meantime, however, the president continued to set pay at levels below comparability, and in 1983 it was rumored that he was considering a pay freeze for 1984.

To summarize, the administration's approach to reducing pay levels was to begin with the assumption that federal officials were overpaid and that either salary or benefits should be reduced. If federal officials were overpaid in benefits, then their salaries could be reduced. That initiative was blocked by the General Accounting Office and Congress. The administration then shifted to cutting back directly on benefits. OPM cut insurance levels and proposed major changes in pensions, which had to be approved by Congress. In the meantime, despite the lack of success in formally changing the pay comparability calculations, the president continued to determine wage increases way below what would be required for comparability to the public sector.

IMPLEMENTATION OF THE PRESIDENT'S PROGRAM INSIDE OPM

The president's program had continuing impacts inside OPM. These included not only trying implement policy directives for the federal personnel system but also absorbing budget cutbacks, reducing staffing levels, and reorganizing OPM's structure.

Budget Cutbacks

The budget cutbacks occurred in stages, with continuing unknowns throughout most of fiscal year 1982. OPM's budget was cut 4 percent in the omnibus reconciliation of July 1981, and then in September the president called for an additional 12 percent cut, which passed Congress in December 1981. These cuts were from a base of approximately $120 million. As the associate director for administration put it:

> In October, we knew we would have a problem. We were on notice to take a 4 percent cut. And there was the potential of an additional 12 percent. By January we had already reduced our spending rate by $4½ million, through a [hiring] freeze and other object spending ["other object" spending is the expenses portion of salaries and expenses]. Come January, we had to make up $12 million.

According to the associate director, the budget office at OPM came up with a strategy for savings in November and December 1981, and that proposal was sent on to management to explore its feasibility. The plan included $3½ million savings from a furlough (mandatory leave without pay) of ten days. A $2 million savings was estimated from lending employees to other agencies, but this was basically a figure controlled by other agencies, not OPM. An additional $2 million was expected to be saved from attrition (this estimate was low; there was almost $4 million in savings from attrition), and management planned to save another $3 million by controlling "other object" spending. In addition, the agency estimated $2 million savings from a reduction in force.

Since 85 percent of OPM's budget was in salaries and expenses and only 15 percent was in other areas, a 16 percent cut necessarily affected salaries and expenses. In addition, they agency had already cut deeply into the expense lines. "That was why our strategy was for reductions in force, furloughs and detailing. We couldn't absorb more in 'other object' budget lines. Only $6 million of the 'other' category is discretionary. We proposed to cut $3 million, or 50 percent of the discretionary money. We also proposed some cuts to the nondiscretionary area."

OPM set up a group of three people to monitor the actual cost savings on operating costs, attrition, and detailing. The agency did manage some extra savings in mail costs because of reduced activity and reduced personnel, which amounted to $1 million and saved three furlough days.

In short, OPM's budget cuts were deep, they were congressionally mandated, and they automatically translated into personnel cuts because most of OPM's budget is tied up in personnel lines. However, many employees did not really believe that a reduction in force was inevitable or that it was done for purely financial reasons. There was a sense that the agency was shooting itself in the foot.

For example, the 12 percent cut (after the 4 percent cut) appeared to be just the implementation of the president's request for an additional across-the-board 12 percent cut. In fact, however, by November, when the Congress acted on this proposal, it had become reluctant to follow the president's lead, and most agencies were cut not 12 percent but about 4 percent. That comparison makes OPM's cuts seem extremely high. OPM's leaders did not fight the cut but presumably could have reduced it if they had fought.[14]

The belief that OPM was voluntarily cutting itself back seemed to be confirmed when some employees took seriously the advice that OPM was giving other agencies.[15] Some staffers, using the guidelines stressing that all other sources of savings should be depleted before a resorting to a reduction in force, drew up a plan that would save OPM enough money to prevent a reduction during fiscal year 1982. That memo was circulated anonymously inside OPM and did a great deal to destroy the notion that the RIF was financially inevitable.

Many officials at OPM, including both career officials and political appointees, were frankly embarrassed by the comparison between what OPM said and what it did. A strongly worded memo was written and circulated by the assistant director for planning and evaluation in response to Director Devine's proposals for a reduction in force. The memo argued, among other points, that enough savings could be achieved by reducing 117 positions by attrition, but that if RIF were chosen, because of its greater costs, 277 people would have to be fired to achieve the same dollar savings. "Does it make sense to fire more than twice as many people as we need to in order to make dollar savings?"

Even more pointedly, the memo argued, "To date, OPM has not followed its own guidance to other agencies in the FPM bulletin, entitled, *Personnel Actions during Budget Reductions. . . .* The budget resolution was passed a month ago. To date, we are not aware of any major management actions which will allow OPM to better cope with the budget situation. It is almost as if we were deliberately denying ourselves cost savings opportunities other than RIF and furlough." The memo went on to describe some of the cost-saving strategies that could close the budget gap.[16]

Presumably as a result of the widespread circulation of this memo, the director of OPM gradually changed from "cost savings" to "skills imbalance and reorganization" as the stated cause of the reduction in force, but he did not withdraw the RIF. According to an informant in the personnel office, the reduction in force became necessary because the previous year there had been a reorganization without a RIF. Staff without positions were gradually placed elsewhere in the organization, as vacancies appeared. However, the new positions they took were still considered low priority. There were reportedly too many psychologists in the organization, considering both the deemphasis on testing and the director's disapproval of group satisfaction measures as a means to improve morale and productivity.

The Reduction in Force

The Reasons for the RIF

The change from RIFs necessitated by budget cuts to those caused by "skills imbalance" seemed to confirm the emerging suspicion that the RIF was discretionary with the agency leadership and not actually necessary. When employees found the director immovable on the issue, they moved their protest to Capitol Hill. On 24 February 1982, Pat Schroeder, chairman of the House Committee on Post Office and Civil Service, Subcommittee on Civil Service, wrote to Don Devine asking for "assurances that OPM is conducting its personnel reductions in accordance with the OPM bulletin entitled *Personnel Actions During Budget Reductions.*[17] The agency responded to the congressional inquiry, but it did not budge from the planned reduction in force.

Several explanations emerged for the director's apparent determination to run a reduction in force. The first was that Dr. Devine wanted to set an example. This impression was reinforced by Director Devine's formal presentation on Capitol Hill in hearings for the fiscal year 1982 budget:

> Our 1982 budget reflects the goal of streamlining the federal government. We are eliminating some programs, cutting back on others, and strengthening programs critical to our primary mission. In fact we are taking the lead in economizing: OPM has taken program cuts substantially above the governmental average. (For example, *OPM's amended budget request includes an 8 percent reduction in full-time equivalent employment, whereas the government-wide reduction, excluding D.O.D., is only 4.6 percent.* Of the twenty-four largest executive branch departments and independent agencies,

OPM had the fourth largest percentage reduction in full-time equivalent employment.[18]

Further support for the idea that the reduction in force was being used as an example was found in a public statement made by the deputy director of OPM, Loretta Cornelius, indicating that OPM could serve as a "model" for other agencies in the way to conduct a RIF. She was also quoted as saying that "OPM can be a model" for both other federal agencies and the private sector in several areas. These areas included handling budget cuts, reallocation of resources, and conducting RIFs and outplacement programs.[19]

The second explanation that emerged was that Dr. Devine wanted to show how poorly the reduction in force procedures worked in order to gain support for changing either the RIF regulations or laws. There is little evidence on this point one way or another. Dr. Devine had expressed discontent about the reduction-in-force regulations considerably before he changed them, though he stated that he did not want to change them the first time they were being used and add to the general chaos. This seemed to indicate that he was waiting for a better opportunity. The fact that his later revision of the regulations was based on the experience of agencies in running the reductions in force confirmed the impression in some people's minds that he had run OPM's RIF for the purpose of providing information. The proposed changes in the RIF regulations gave less protection to civil servants, which caused some employees to accuse Dr. Devine of having planned out the whole issue of revising the regulations many months in advance, using the employees at the agency as pawns in that strategy.

A much simpler and less Machiavellian explanation for the timing of the reduction in force is that Dr. Devine felt the agency should do its share of reducing staffing levels to achieve the president's goals of personnel reduction. The budget problems, whether self-imposed or not, were real, and Dr. Devine viewed the agency as overstaffed. In addition, since agency leadership anticipated continuing reductions in budgets, short-term actions to reduce the budget would be inadequate.

The RIF Process

If there had to be a reduction in force, OPM was going to run it perfectly as an example to other agencies and was going to learn as much from the experience as it could in order to prepare revisions in the regulations.

The personnel office and a small internal task force on RIFs began preparing for the reduction in force in December 1981. The reduction was to be large—215 jobs were to be eliminated and many individuals were to be transferred or demoted.[20]

The first task in implementing the RIF was to "purify" the data base— that is, verify and update all personnel information concerning staff in the central office. The target date for the RIF was 20 March 1982. In the personnel office, there was a team of seven people to work on the reduction in force, with all the personnel office employees as staff to those seven people. This group worked more than full time for about three months to prepare letters informing people what their current options were, to determine severance benefits, and to calculate all the other information in a letter announcing a reduction in force.

The team was overwhelmed with the sheer mechanics of implementing the reduction. To handle policy issues and to oversee the process, a smaller RIF task force (like the one set up to work on the RIFs government-wide, and with the same director) was designated to work on the internal reductions. This group did for OPM what the larger group did across agencies. It tried to anticipate problems and lay out solutions, and it periodically sent out employee bulletins on various phases of the RIF process.

Initial letters of general warning of impending reductions in force went out in January, and on 3 March 1982 the first set of notices to individuals was sent out. The RIF process had to be repeated six or seven times before the reduction was finally completed, because some employees were offered alternative jobs which they chose to decline, while others either retired or found transfers to other agencies. Some of the assignments were incorrect. Each time an offer was declined or a mistake discovered, all those below the person in question on a bumping chain were also affected. Revised letters and offers were calculated and sent out.

Although there were some complaints about competitive levels being too narrow and about mistakes in the retention registers, the reduction in force was carried out with great expertise. When a GAO team was called in to examine the procedures at OPM, it found no major irregularities.[21]

For example, the competitive levels were relatively broad in most job classifications, and those drawn up by the personnel office were based on good position descriptions. If this procedure is well done, it means that when employees are shifted around, they should have enough experience to be able to do their new jobs with reasonable competence. If it is badly done, people will be shifted into positions they cannot handle.

Managers indicated that the reduction in force was run impersonally, that they did not know who would finally be affected by the reorganization and the RIF, and, though there may have been some dry runs (as charged by the unions), there is considerable evidence that the reduction in force was run impersonally. Since the RIF regulations then in effect were designed to be impersonal in order to protect individuals against politically motivated firings, a well-run reduction in force was necessarily impersonal.

Recovery and Furlough

Since a reduction in force scatters work groups and puts people in new jobs and under new bosses, the chaos following it can be very extensive. One of the first techniques for recovery is usually a series of more or less formal swaps to get people back to their old jobs, on a temporary or permanent basis.

OPM, in an effort to make the system of placements work, forbade most formal transfers back to old positions for a period of ninety days, which was the limit of how long it was supposed to take for people to learn their new jobs. Since people were to be well matched to their new jobs on a skill basis, OPM was asking office directors to be patient and allow employees who bumped into their offices to learn their new roles. As one informant in the personnel office put it, "We did not do all this matching of skills for nothing." This formal control on transfers probably lengthened the period of recovery and increased the amount of disrupted work, although the logic of it is clear.

Since whether or not a person in traded is at the discretion of the managers of various offices, the union claimed that reassignment back to old positions was based on favoritism. Reportedly, those who were not favorites, especially women and minorities, were left in the new positions.[22]

The second most important mechanism for recovery after a reduction in force is the repromotion system for those who have been demoted. If a vacancy occurs at a level above where the demoted person now is located but below the original position from which the person was demoted, the person has a weak priority for that position and a stronger priority for positions opening at the original rank. Employees who have been demoted are referred to all such openings (for which they are qualified) from a repromotion list.

If referred employees are not selected for repromotion, however, there is not much burden of justification on the part of the manager doing the selecting, since repromotion rights last indefinitely. That means that managers get to pick freely among candidates for repromotion. The factors governing retention are generally not so important during repromotion. *Employees may be demoted impersonally, through RIF, and then selectively repromoted.*

At OPM, because the competitive levels were broadly drawn, there was bumping between offices. For example, a person in the computer section of compensation could be bumped into the computer section in pensions. Bumping from office to office opened up the possibility of career repromotions. In a career repromotion there is no competition. If an employee has been bumped from a position in one office to a lower position in another office which is still on the same career ladder, his new supervisor may choose to repromote him back up to his old level.

For OPM as a whole, it is estimatd that of those demoted during the RIF to GS-5, GS-7, or GS-9, on a career ladder going up to GS-12, about half were repromoted. By 1 September 1982, about five months after the reduction in force, 100 of the 257 employees who were demoted had been repromoted an average of 2.8 grades; 89 of these had been repromoted to their old grades or higher.[23] Since the average grade reduction for the demoted employees had been 2.74 grades, the repromotion action probably brought about 40 percent of those demoted to near their old ranks in five months.

In addition to this discretion in repromotions, there was a great deal of discretion in rehiring those who had actually been laid off. Rehiring would take place if new vacancies occurred, or to finish a project. Thirty-one of the 184 laid-off employees were hired back after five months.[24]

In addition to all the recovery activity, there was also a furlough. The reduction in force was intended to save money, but the amount of money to be saved depends on how early in the year the RIF takes place; OPM could not run its RIF early enough to save enough money to prevent a furlough.

The furlough was originally designed to last twenty-two days, with an initial period of ten days and then an assessment of how many more days would be required; in the end, there were six days. The furlough aggravated the chaos because personnel did not know how any days they would work and hence how much salary they would have.

In response to union pressures, the agency administration allowed employees some discretion as to when they would take their furlough days. Thus when the furlough was canceled, some had taken more furlough days than others, creating an equity problem requiring innovative record keeping and remedial measures. The union also appealed the furloughs, adding another managerial headache.

Reorganization

During the period of this study OPM was reorganized three times. These reorganizations reflected budgetary pressures—the need to drop some functions and consolidate others—as well as the policies of Director Devine.

A GAO report on changes at OPM from March 1981 to December 1982 noted that OPM began to reorganize *before* the budget cuts occurred. OPM decided to offer less advisory management assistance to federal agencies than it had provided in prior years, to terminate some programs, and to concentrate on what Dr. Devine considered basic personnel functions. These included activities such as recruitment and staffing, managing pension funds, overseeing civil service laws and regulations, and assisting agencies and affected personnel dealing with reductions in force. Dr. Devine also regarded as basic functions improving productivity by consolidating productivity and performance appraisal systems, and making performance appraisal, merit pay, and executive bonus programs work.

Informants at OPM argued that not only did the redirections occur before congressional action on the budget, but they occurred before the president presented his budget proposal to Congress in March 1981. Dr. Devine was involved in designing the budget proposal:

> When the director came in, he [Dr. Devine] was on the transition team. [The Carter?] proposals were returned to him by OMB; he recommended changes, which were ratified by OMB. Such as eliminating the Intergovernmental Personnel grants, cutting consulting services staff [consulting services provided managerial assistance to federal agencies]—those were targeted cuts. He had OMB authority and knocked it off. Without RIFs. He counted on attrition [at that point].

Dr. Devine's explanation for the redirection was, first, that agencies were responsible for their own personnel functions and that OPM was thus responsible primarily for oversight of civil service laws and regulations; second, that since basic Civil Service Reform Act reforms were already in place in the agencies, OPM could cut back in the area of teaching agencies how to implement them; and third, that previous administrations had not paid enough attention to the management of benefits such as health insurance and pension systems.[25]

OPM went through three reorganizations, in November 1981, January 1982, and November 1982. The overall impact of these reorganizations was, first, to deemphasize agency relations and supervision; second, to recentralize control and reduce the number of units reporting to the director; and third, to create a top-level policy unit and centralize policy making in that unit.

The third reorganization, in November 1982, was the one that created the policy unit, by combining Planning and Evaluation, Labor Management Relations, Public Affairs, and what was left of Interagency Relations. This policy unit at the top of the organization is analogous to the unit created at UMTA to carry out the same function. The merging of policy making and public affairs assures that one (correct) policy will be announced to the agency and its publics.

To complete this policy-control link, Dr. Devine simultaneously created five new regional representatives, between the regions and the central office. Each was to be responsible for activities in two regions, to help organize and direct activities of the Federal Executives Board, to help manage the Combined Federal Campaign, and to perform "other responsibilities for the Director, OPM."[26] Dr. Devine indicated that part of their function would be "public affairs."

Given the recent reductions in force, the furloughs, and the high level of internal opposition, Dr. Devine needed a stronger rationale for the creation of these new positions than he gave. The new positions and the new appointees aroused suspicion on the House oversight committee. Members of the House Post Office and Civil Service Committee, Subcommittee on Civil Service, questioned the appointments, suggesting that they had been recommended by the White House. Director Devine did not respond to questions concerning the qualifications of the appointees for the positions; he simply indicated that the committee had copies of their résumés.[27]

Whether the new appointees were recommended by the White House or not, they were political appointees with policy and public affairs responsibilities between OPM and its field offices. Thus while at the level of the career officials the number of employees was being cut back, the top policy levels were being expanded.

The way the reorganizations were carried out is suggestive of the extent of the split between the political policy levels and the career levels of the agency. As one high-level career official put it:

> I had nothing to do with the reorganization. The director and the senior staff —the personal staff of the director, the special assistants, certain of the political appointees—they designed the new organizational structure. We [career officials] were the recipients of the reorganization, but we had nothing to do with it. It was just announced. Next week, the chart changed as they sorted it out. They decided some parts could be improved.

This same informant described how the new structure worked to centralize control over policy: "There are a small number of people close to the boss, who act as a coordinating mechanism. The director says, clear the paper through Planning and Evaluation, then I'll look at it. Those who had easy access no longer do."

OPM'S GOALS: CSRA AND PRODUCTIVITY IMPROVEMENT

The president's goals affected both work assignments and cutback management at OPM. These two effects alone would seem to absorb an agency, given the three reorganizations, the reduction in force, the furlough, the 16 percent budget cuts, the pay comparability studies, the battles over benefits, and the new RIF regulations. But OPM also had its legislatively mandated Civil Service Reform Act legislation to carry out, which fit well with the president's program to improve management and which the agency director had included in his goals for 1981 and 1982.

When Dr. Devine was appointed director of OPM, and before the cutbacks began, a considerable contingent of OPM's work force was involved in oversight and investigation of federal agencies. These employees were helping to implement the new features of the reform act, including performance evaluation; they were investigating personnel procedures to ensure conformity with civil service laws and regulations; and they were trying to improve agency management.

Between March 1981 and December 1982, according to the GAO, OPM reduced its oversight of other federal agencies. "Agencies are now more on their own and cannot count on, and do not receive, as much OPM advice and assistance as they did in prior years."[28] "OPM officers told us that the central and field offices now are conducting fewer reviews and special studies of the application of civil service rules and regulations, and that the scope of some evaluations has been reduced."[29] This reduction in oversight must be viewed in light of Director Devine's stated priority, as well as the mandate of the law itself, for reviewing agencies' compliance with civil service rules, regulations, and merit system principles.

Part of OPM's responsibilities included an evaluation of the implementation and impact of the Civil Service Reform Act reforms. The CSRA evaluation function inside OPM lost several staff members with expertise as a result of the reduction in force and an internal reorganization of its parent unit, the Office of Planning and Evaluation.[30] Part of the monitoring effort of OPM requires a survey of federal employees concerning their reactions to the implementation of the CSRA. This survey has not been done very frequently and appears to have been cut back in scope.

The units inside OPM that corresponded to different parts of the reform, such as a merit-pay unit and a performance-evaluation unit, were abolished, and their remaining functions merged with program offices. The argument given was that "since nearly all agencies had already implemented reform act initiatives, OPM no longer needed to maintain a separate staff for that purpose."[31]

The productivity program was abolished in early 1982, and then a new productivity unit was created late in 1982 to develop a system of combining pay with performance evaluation. All the units formerly working on merit pay and performance evaluation were included in the new unit. The director has thus pinned all his hopes for improving productivity on this one program, but there have been some major obstacles and setbacks to the accomplishment of this goal.

One problem is that employees approve of the idea of performance evaluations but do not believe the evaluations are or will be fairly administered in their agencies. Further, some employees believe that the addition of salary increments to the evaluations will corrupt them. If the performance evaluation scheme is not yet accepted as fair, then the connection of pay to that system will not improve productivity.

The second problem that OPM encountered had to do with the actual implementation of a merit-pay plan. The Civil Service Reform Act links pay to performance for officials in supervisory and management positions in pay grades 13–15. Agencies were given three years to prepare for full implementation the deadline for which was October 1981.

Dr. Devine's plan was to change automatic step increases to merit pay which would be awarded only to those with a performance rating of outstanding. The implementation of the new plan reportedly got bogged down in the transition from the old to the new system. Under the old system, step increases for individual employees became effective on the anniversary of employment. Dr. Devine wanted to implement the new system at the beginning of fiscal year 1982 so that everyone who received an increment would get it at the same time.

According to the version put together by the Merit Systems Protection Board, at the last moment, just before the new system was to be put into effect, the General Accounting Office stepped in and blocked implementation, arguing that the use of the beginning of the fiscal year as the starting date would mean that the new system would cause millions of dollars in overpayments. It argued that OPM did not have the authority to spend more money than the law provided. The GAO also objected to the way the merit increase pool was calculated for individuals whose pay had reached pay-cap levels.[32]

As a result of the GAO actions, Director Devine decided to

> grant the 1981 comparability adjustment to all merit-pay employees regardless of their performance. (Within-grade increases or quality-step increases, however, would not be available to this population; only a greatly diminished pool to be distributed on the basis of merit.) These GAO and OPM decisions reduced merit pay—the portion of the payroll distributed on the basis of performance—80 percent from originally planned funding levels.[33]

In other words, for fiscal year 1982, the merit pay plan was aborted.

The issue of how to merge merit pay and performance evaluation remained alive at OPM, despite initial failures. In 1983, OPM proposed a change in regulations that would extend merit pay to all federal white-collar employees, not only to managers and supervisors at the GS-13–15 levels. Since many agencies were already evaluating the performance of nonmanagerial staff, the proposed extension is not likely to provoke much opposition.

To summarize, although Dr, Devine promised a return to basic personnel functions, dropping nonessential functions and focusing on implementation of the Civil Service Reform Act and oversight of civil service regulations, the agency did cut back on supervision and investigation, as well as on the evaluation of its own implementation of the Civil Service Reform Act. Although OPM did give some attention to issues of productivity, it came up with no quick or easy ways to implement performance evaluations and merit pay. Early attempts to combine the two floundered.

AGENCY OUTCOMES

Disruption

The first outcome for OPM was of nearly continuous disruption. First there was a reorganization in March of 1981, then a second and more extensive reorganization in January 1982. In March 1982, the organization experienced a major reduction in force. Almost every office was affected.

After the RIF, informal trades and reassignments combined with career repromotions, created turmoil for the first sixty to ninety days after the reduction; then detailing increased between offices, followed by reassignments and repromotions.

All of this was then handled simultaneously with a massive furlough, which meant that staff were periodically not present on days of their choosing. To this picture must be added the OPM policy of encouraging transfers and details to agencies outside OPM as a way of reducing costs. Some of the people on assignment elsewhere would come back to OPM and some would not.

There was also chaos introduced by a long-term hiring freeze, which began with Reagan's government-wide freeze and continued until well after the reduction in force. There was also a pre-RIF freeze on promotions and a higher-than-expected post-RIF attrition rate.

Taken together, these shufflings, freezes, details, reorganizations, program terminations, layoffs, and furloughs created internal chaos for close to two years.

Time Expenditure

The most obvious impact of the reduction in force and surrounding activities was the sheer amount of time involved in preparing for them and carrying them out. Over seventy people in the personnel office worked fifty-hour weeks for three months to prepare the reductions. The political leadership prepared the reorganization almost simultaneously. Meanwhile, the union negotiated over the RIF procedures and outplacement programs.

Agency leadership was in a constant battle with the union over information requests and later fought the same battles with Congress and the GAO. The union filed a group grievance against the reduction in force. OPM did not accept most of the grievance, but the personnel office feared that the MSPB might accept the case and give it a hearing. As a result, the office had to prepare defenses even though it did not allow the cases. There were also grievances against the furloughs. Pursuing these actions took the time not just of union members and personnel officials but also of legal counsel.

Lowered Morale and Productivity

The effects on morale of the continuing chaos and of the reduction in force in particular were predictably great. The agency experienced a much higher rate of attrition than expected, which continued after the reduction; when possible, many employees left the agency voluntarily, suggesting a potentially serious morale problem.

The following excerpts from field notes illustrate the view of one OPM manager on the impacts of the RIF on morale and productivity.

Q: Do you have any estimates of the damage to the organization in terms of bumping, morale, unfamiliar jobs, and so on?

A: All RIFs stink. RIF, any reduction in personnel, is disruptive. Ours is a comparatively mechanical system. The neutrality of it helps a little. They [separated employees] are out through no fault of their own. But it leads to great unhappiness with the institution. There is a real and imagined belief that the system works to their disadvantage. People look out for number one and stop work. You don't owe anyone anything except to get out. Work doesn't get carried out. Supervisors lose leverage.

But people are generally civilized. Everyone is upset and your supervisor is getting knocked out too. It's turbulent, and it leaves a residue. The residue is people in the wrong type of jobs.

I think of it [separations] on the order of the death of neighbors, loved ones. The shock is great, but it's short-lived. Some [personnel actions] are like crippling diseases. You keep seeing them [those who have been bumped or demoted]; they peddle the mail around, they are GS-13s [upper-level managers]. Each time I see them, I ask, how long will this last? It takes time to undo.

An OPM employee volunteered a similar assessment, noting some of the causes of employee disaffection, such as continuing rumors, scapegoating of bureaucrats, and unnecessary and highly symbolic expenditures on political-level officials while the career officials were being furloughed to save money.

As of last week, we learned through rumors that we will be reorganized again. It has prevented much productivity since last September [1981]. The way it has been handled, it made people disinvest emotionally. There is a lot of job-hunting activity, and we spend a lot of time saying goodbye to people. It's like working in a morgue, except you don't bury the bodies. Nothing goes on here now.

It's Kafkaesque here. For a long time, fully a year, he [Devine] kept denying that there would be RIFs. But the rumor mill kept saying he was waiting. He lost credibility.... Another rumor, there will be a shakeup among SESers, especially in the regions, there will be transfers from one city to another....

There were rumors, then actual RIFs.... It took so long to do, no one could do any work.

There is a general negative feeling against federal employees. We have joined the Jews in that respect, as a scapegoat. Even in Washington....

We were put on a furlough, while the political appointees wanted a private bathroom and moved us to create the space. It took the work crews overtime pay to build the bathroom, while we were on furlough....

There are rumors of a RIF in the fall.

A former employee, who had been fired during the RIF, drew a picture of the agency that underscored the effect on morale of the chaos, the lack of direction, and the reduction in work.

The Office of Program Evaluation lost a whole bunch of people. They are supposed to administer the opinion survey [of federal employees concerning implementation of the Civil Service Reform Act]. Now we aren't doing that.

[We? They?] have money, and hired back staff in evaluation, but now there are staff but there is still no work for them. . . . Our office is not challenged, projects have no reality, and people have nothing to do. Supervisors try not to notice.

We read in the newspapers what Devine is thinking and wants, managers have no direction from him. He refuses to tell what he is thinking and wanting. . . . A joint task force was appointed to write position papers. Everyone sits around and attempts to pretend this is a serious project which can succeed. We can come up with what Devine wants. For those who have no option to get out of government, it's hard for them to admit they have nothing to do. . . .

What is the mandate of the office? What are you doing? They can't answer. They are spinning wheels. Some will just try to survive Reagan, and ride through these times of chaos.

[This situation of not having enough work] applies beyond the Workforce Effectiveness and Development Group [which was severely cut back]. The Office of Training, that was a core function; now federal agencies cannot afford it; the training function is slipping. No part of the agency is busy and humming. There is no emphasis on civil service exams now; they are letting that slide by.

It is clear from these evaluations that morale and productivity were adversely affected by the reductions in force and the demotions, by the continuing rumors, and by the lack of direction and clear mission as the agency reorganized. But these accounts suggest that employees either left the agency or passively waited for the next administration. In fact, a number stayed on and became angry. The degree of internal polarization between career and political officials markedly increased.

Polarization

The increased degree of polarization inside OPM was so marked that it was observed even by OPM's clients, the personnel and management officials in other federal agencies. When interviewed by a team from the General Accounting Office, some of these officials argued that OPM was not operating as a team because of a basic mistrust between its career employees and its noncareer management people. One personnel official attributed OPM's staff morale problem to staff's uncertainty about and noninvolvement in OPM policy making. One department's director of personnel charged that

OPM's staffers were uncooperative and refused to adapt to and accept some of the changes instituted by the director, attempting instead to stonewall and undermine these changes.[34] It was not possible to prove (or disprove) this charge, but it is clear that the agency was polarized.

Structurally, the organization was much more polarized after the reorganization and the reduction in force. There was a deep schism between labor and management and a rift between the political leadership and the career officials. This rift involved a lack of communication downward of policies and approaches, as well as a distortion of information upward, especially concerning the effects of the reductions. Political-level officials were generally informed that employees were responding to the RIFs "professionally" regardless of the extent of loss of morale and willingness to work, and regardless of the level of bitterness.

There was doubt about the necessity of the reduction in force, which generated much internal opposition, both from career officials and from the union. Dr. Devine's public statements to the effect that RIFs were not as serious as the Washington press claimed, and that the RIF procedures should be made simpler and less damaging to use, alienated bureaucrats inside and outside of OPM, adding an anti-Devine flavor to some of the opposition.[35] The union at OPM printed up T-shirts reading "Devine's Guinea Pigs," which it sold to employees. Outside the union some employees referred to Dr. Devine angrily as "Machiavellian" and "a destroyer."

The apparent inequity involved in furloughing employees while managers moved walls around for their own comfort and privacy infuriated some employees. Upper-level managers explained that the construction had been approved and funded from a previous year's budget but that the GSA had not gotten around to doing the project until 1982. The result was unfortunate but unintended.

Relations between the union and management at OPM both reflected and contributed to the bitterness. Issues which should have been resolved amicably became grounds for appeals. The union fought a constant battle to be kept informed of pending personnel actions. Most important, the union maintained good contacts on the Hill and instigated congressional inquiries when it was unable to get information from managers.

In short, bitterness over the reduction in force combined with changes in the organizational structure to create a highly polarized environment, at least in the short term. This polarization decreased communication and eroded trust, making management more difficult.

BROADER IMPLICATIONS OF THE CHANGES AT OPM

The OPM case has implications beyond the impacts of the budget cuts and program redirections on the agency itself. Because OPM plays a major role in management of the federal personnel system, the changes in the agency have an effect on the management of the federal work force. Further, the OPM case illustrates the ability of the president to both cut back an agency and redirect personnel policy independent of other institutional actors, such as Congress and the GAO. Finally, it raises the question of what role the personnel office will or can play in maintaining a neutral and competent civil service.

Management of the Federal Work Force

OPM had an impact in changing policy in three areas of personnel policy. First, the administration with help from OPM managed to redefine the issue of how compensation for federal employees would be determined. Second, OPM did a major revision of the regulations on handling reductions in force. Third, OPM redefined the program for improving productivity and in the process contributed to a more negative incentive system for federal employees. Overall, OPM backed away from the notion of the federal government as a model employer.

Redetermining Compensation

As discussed earlier in this chapter, OPM redefined the issue of how compensation would be set, even though the administration did not succeed with its original proposal to formally set the federal wages at 94 percent of private-sector wages. OPM started with the assumption that federal employees were overpaid and looked around for various formulations that would document that overpayment and allow OPM to cut back wages and salaries.

The argument was made that because the total compensation package of wages and benefits was high, wages could be reduced to compensate; President Reagan continued the practice of previous presidents of reducing federal employees' salaries below the comparability level. Then the argument was made that the compensation package was high because benefits were too high, and benefits were cut more directly. Though some of these benefit reductions required congressional approval, some were done by OPM independently.

Throughout the argument the administration pointed out that since there were still many applications for vacancies in the federal government, government positions must be attractive, and reductions in those attractions would not cause any harm. There was no attempt to measure the quality of applicants or the cost of turnover, and no implicit marker concerning how many or how few applicants would be an acceptable number.

There are several possible long-term implications of the compensation issue. First, if the changes in the retirement system are adopted, then early retirement will be discouraged and senior managers are likely to stay on a decade longer. If those managers are highly skilled and experienced, keeping them on will be a marked improvement; if they are "burned out" or simply marking time, keeping them on longer will be harmful, particularly because the reductions in force weeded out younger people with less seniority, and hiring freezes have prevented agencies from bringing in new blood.

Second, because the arguments used by the administration to reduce compensation have no logical stopping point, it seems likely that compensation will be continually eroded, making federal employment less desirable. The eventual effects on the quality of applicants for federal jobs is unknowable but likely to be in the direction of deterioration of quality. To the extent that this occurs, it will not help make government more productive or better managed, even with easier procedures for the elimination of unproductive people from the work force.

Third, OPM's changes in the benefits packages ought to make them more financially solvent; the improvements are not just reductions for employees but attempts to bring costs into line with contributions. If OPM succeeds in introducing a voucher system for insurance, it will have found a way to control costs over time. OPM will give employees a certain dollar allowance for insurance. Then any changes in benefits levels or costs of insurance will be borne directly by employees. Presumably the free market will keep costs down, although this part of the model remains to be demonstrated. Even if the market does not bring costs down, OPM and the federal government will be out of the business of trying to respond to increasing health care costs in personnel benefits programs.

Revising the RIF Regulations

Partly because of the experiences of federal agencies in using reductions in force, OPM proposed new regulations that would limit the damage done to agencies during the RIF process. The new regulations increase the role of performance evaluations, relative to seniority, and reduce the allowable depth of demotions.

The implications of the new regulations are complex. They make reductions in force easier and hence more tempting, to use. They make it easier to determine who will be laid off, they increase the cost savings to agencies, and they reduce the protections of employees. Whether this increased managerial discretion is a good thing depends on whether it is used to remove people from employment who are not working hard or contributing much to the organization, or whether it is used to fire people bosses don't like, feel threatened by, or disagree with on policy matters.

One important implication of the new regulations is that employees feel less protected. The reductions in force that occurred under the old regulations made some employees more fearful of expressing contrary opinions lest they lose their jobs. The new regulations will reinforce those fears, at least in the short run. If the rules are not abused and RIFs are seldom used (and only for clear financial reasons), then the fear should fade.

Redefining Productivity: Creation of a Negative Incentive System

The Civil Service Reform Act emphasized the evaluation of individual performance and linking that performance with salary, to improve the motivation of senior-level managers. Dr. Devine took the linkage between performance and financial rewards very seriously as an incentive to perform, and perhaps as a punishment for poor performance. He proposed to take away automatic step increases based on longevity and replace them with merit pay, and to extend the system to all white-collar employees.

The combination of performance evaluation and merit pay was the only productivity improvement plan approved by OPM. Issues of worker satisfaction, quality of working life, and group morale were downplayed in favor of individualized incentives. The fact that the administration relied so completely on this one incentive system meant that when it went awry, so did the productivity system.

The merit-pay plan went awry in several ways. First, the system was woefully underfunded. It is not clear whose fault this was, but it is clear that what was supposed to be an incentive system turned into a discouragement system. People who were on merit pay earned smaller increases than those not covered by merit pay, creating bitterness and frustration. The number of people likely to get pay increases based on merit was very small, because people could receive bonuses only if they had received a rating of "outstanding." A particular problem with the system is that those whose salaries were already at the ceiling for the top pay category were not eligible for merit-pay increases regardless of the level of their performance. If employees cannot hope to realistically get any salary increases from a merit-pay plan, it cannot work as an incentive system.

The merit-pay plan was also unsuccessful as a productivity improvement because employees questioned the fairness of their performance evaluations. If people do not believe that their performance is being fairly measured, they are not going to try to work harder to get better evaluations, whether or not money is attached to the ratings.

A variety of events, some intentional and some unintentional, combined to make the actual incentive system negative rather than positive. Part of the problem was that some employees would be losing step increases, while very few would get new merit bonuses. Another part was that the reduction in force not only introduced a new level of job insecurity but also posed the possibility of separation from employment for poor work or for disagreement with the boss. Moreover, the system of agency-wide notice of an impending reduction in force made people who were not going to be affected by the RIF fear for their jobs.

Merit pay was intended to give managers increased flexibility and one more tool to encourage increased productivity, but it was not intended to, and cannot, provide incentives for increased productivity to the entire work force. It is too small a program and rests on too shaky a base. When that problem was combined with the philosophy that government is riddled with lazy employees who need to be removed and that their removal will automatically improve productivity, the result was a more punishment-oriented incentive system.

If the negative aspect of the incentive system persists, then employees are likely to become more afraid of expressing dissent, indicating when a policy is unlikely to work, or otherwise catching errors. They are likely to become more passive and not put out their best efforts. They will seek to avoid being noticed. Some of this was observed in agencies after the reductions in force, but the key (and unanswered) question is how long it will continue.

The President's Autonomy to Manage Cutback

The president controlled the Office of Personnel Management because his appointee, Dr. Devine, agreed with his policies and tried to implement them. The degree to which the president controlled the cutback process, then, depended to some extent on the degree to which OPM was able to take action on its own to carry out those policies.

Much of what OPM accomplished of the president's policy objectives it did on its own. It carried out some actions by fiat and handled many others by issuing new regulations based on existing laws. It avoided asking for new legislation, to the extent that was possible. Other institutional actors sometimes questioned OPM's rights to act on its own to the extent that it did. Sometimes OPM won these arguments; sometimes the other actors did. But even when OPM seemed most independent, it was usuaully taking stock of potential opposition. It backed off from some issues, and it phrased others in terms that would be more acceptable.

OPM made two important changes entirely on its own. The first was the change in the insurance package, which gave employees a choice of higher contributions or lower benefits. This change was challenged in court, and OPM won, on the grounds that the director did have authority to make the changes. The second independent change was a redefinition of OPM's oversight role of federal agencies' personnel and management functions.

The change in the RIF regulations was done in spite of congressional oversight but was hampered by union activity. In August 1983, Congress passed a two-month restriction on issuing the regulations, which OPM observed. Then Congress ordered the OPM not to spend any money on implementation of the new regulations until Congress reconvened in January 1984. OPM dodged the intent of the congressional restraint, issuing the regulations but excepting OPM employees, because the only cost of implementation would be inside OPM. At this point the unions took OPM to court and managed to get a temporary restraining order. The final outcome of the court action was not known at the end of 1983, but it seemed likely that OPM would get some revised RIF regulations implemented.[36]

One area where OPM failed in taking independent action concerned the implementation of the merit-pay plan. OPM failed to implement the plan by the mandated deadline because the plan was blocked by the General Accounting Office. Significantly, the issue was not simply one of how to make a transfer from one system to the next, but whether OPM had the authority to control the size of the merit-increase pools and change the total funding mandated by Congress. The GAO decided that OPM did not have that authority.

A second area in which OPM could not take unilateral action was in formally redefining the basis for compensating federal employees. OPM eventually backed off from formally changing the pay comparability standards when it became clear that Congress was not going to pass the administration's proposal. This did not stop consideration of the issues but forced a repackaging so that they would not require congressional approval or would be presented to Congress in another and less threatening manner. Thus OPM retreated from formal legislated changes in salary compensation to reductions in benefits. Some of these changes OPM did on its own; others required congressional approval. OPM asked for congressional action on pensions, where the issues of overgenerosity and underfunding were relatively clear.

OPM also adapted to perceived congressional intransigence when it revised its reduction-in-force legislation. It weakened the seniority principle and strengthened the merit portion slightly, so that the reductions in force would not be eliminating the best workers, but it did not try to change the veterans' preference portion of the regulations. This was the only part based on law; any change would have required legislation, and it was well known on Capitol Hill that benefits for veterans could not be reduced.

In short, OPM had considerable latitude for taking action, as long as that action did not require explicit congressional approval. Where congressional approval was required, it was often not successfully obtained. Therefore, OPM tended to skirt Congress where possible and to rely heavily on administrative discretion and new regulations based on existing laws. Although individual members of Congress were upset with actions taken, they seemed to have little recourse other than to embarrass the director in hearings and request information from the agency. Where OPM exceeded its authority and transgressed on congressional authority, the General Accounting Office was effective in curtailing action.

The Role of the Personnel Office

The role of OPM changed in two important ways. First, it continued to decentralize personnel functions to the agencies and reduced its oversight of civil service regulations. It also reduced all sorts of assistance of the agencies, such as help in carrying out the requirements of the Civil Service Reform Act and in improving management practices. Second, the Director of OPM carried out his policy goals with such flamboyance and sense of combat that he politicized himself and OPM.

The decentralization of personnel functions and the reduction in oversight assumes that all the reforms were in place and agencies could carry them out more or less on their own. In fact, not all the difficulties involved in performance evaluations or merit pay had been worked out, and some continuing effort on the part of OPM is undoubtedly still necessary.

The decentralization carries out the spirit of the reform act, giving greater autonomy over personnel matters to managers. As such, it may be a good thing. But it also opens the way to possible abuses of civil service laws and regulations, because investigations and special studies have also been reduced.

Dr. Devine described the change in OPM's role as a return to bedrock personnel functions, but that description is misleading. Several basic functions, such as recruitment and overseeing the civil service regulations, were cut back. The changes are better described as increased decentralization of personnel functions to the agencies, decreased oversight of them, and an increased role in carrying out presidential policy. It was in the latter area that most of OPM's energy seemed to be funneled.

Director Devine pictured himself as a member of the president's cabinet and hence as a political advisor to the president. He was outspoken to the press about his policies and flamboyant in his press releases. He seldom consulted with unions, with Congress, or with the GAO before he took action or made policy statements. This way of doing business, by drawing up public battle lines before issues were discussed, annoyed some members of Congress and confused OPM's employees, who scrutinized the director's public statements for policy guidance.

The combination of Dr. Devine's style and the policies he was endorsing set him against much of the federal work force. Instead of a promoter of the welfare of the work force, or a protector of its neutral competence, OPM was becoming an opponent, arguing that federal workers were overpaid, implying that many were lazy, mocking their benefits as welfare, and making light of the reductions in force.

Dr. Devine was chided both by members of Congress and by OPM's sister agency, the Merit Systems Protection Board, for being insensitive to the effects of his flamboyance on the morale of the federal work force. He seemed to take this advice to heart. He toned down his antibureaucrat rhetoric. He began to blame poor systems of administration rather than poor workers. However, since so many of the changes in policy he has introduced reduce the security and pay of federal employees, federal workers are unlikely to be reassured by the more civil tone of the director's communications.

The personality of the director is an issue only because he represents the class of appointees the president installed as directors and secretaries of the agencies and departments. The appointees were to take over their agencies and concentrate policy making in the hands of those who agreed with the president's policies, and Dr. Devine has done that. The question arises whether that is an appropriate role for the director of the Office of Personnel and Management. It may be that OPM in particular should be headed by someone more politically neutral, in line with the agency's role in maintaining the political neutrality of the work force.

There is no evidence to date that the changing role of OPM has substantially altered the political neutrality of the work force. However, the agencies have been made more sensitive to presidential policy, it has been made easier to conduct a reduction in force and to single out individuals to fire in a RIF, and OPM has reduced its surveillance of the agencies so that any abuses that occur are likely to go unnoticed. These changes therefore suggest the need for careful observation in the future.

NOTES

1. General Accounting Office, *Retrenchment and Redirection at the Office of Personnel Management* (GAO/GGD-83-95) (Washington: Government Printing Office, 22 August 1983), p. 1.

2. The following are some of the GAO reports on OPM's implementation efforts: *Federal Merit Pay: Important Concerns Need Attention* (FPCD-81-9) (3 March 1981); *Serious Problems Need to Be Corrected Before Federal Merit Pay Goes into Effect* (FPCD-81-73) (11 September 1981); *Actions Needed to Enhance the Credibility of Senior Executive Service Performance Award Program* (FPCD-81-65) (30 September 1981); *Obstacles Hamper the Office of Personnel's Evaluation of the Implementation of the 1978 Civil Service Reform Act* (FPCD-81-69) (14 September 1981); *Civil Service Reform After 2 Years: Some Initial Problems Resolved, but Serious Concerns Remain* (FPCD-82-1) (10 November 1981); *Better Guidance Is Needed for Determining When Examining Authority Should Be Delegated to Federal Agencies* (FPCD-82-41) (1 July 1982); *Delegated Personnel Management Authority: Better Monitoring and Oversight Needed* (FPCD-82-43) (2 August 1982).
The GAO also did a number of studies critical of other phases of OPM's work.

3. Congressman Barnes drew up a proposed bill called "Fair Reductions in Force Practices of 1982," which would have made it mandatory for all agencies contemplating a reduction in force to carefully consider all the alternatives and to

estimate carefully the costs to be incurred and to be saved by the RIF over the current year and the following two years. A reduction in force would have to be certified as the most cost-effective technique before the agency would be allowed to carry it out. Discussion Draft, dated 3 June 1982, 97th Cong., 2d sess.

4. House Subcommittee on the Treasury, Postal Service and General Government Appropriations of the Committee on Appropriations, *Treasury, Postal Service and General Government Appropriations, for FY 1983: Hearings*, 97th Cong., 2d sess., 1982, Part 4, p. 95.

5. House Subcommittee of the Committee on Government Operations, *Exploring Job Help for RIF'd Federal Workers: Hearing*, 97th Cong., 2d sess., 1982, pp. 172–73.

6. *Exploring Job Help: Hearings*, 1982, p. 178.

7. House Subcommittee on Civil Service of the Committee on Post Office and Civil Service, *Civil Service Oversight Hearings*, 98th Cong., 1st sess., 1983. The report, *A Report on Reductions in Force in Selected Federal Agencies, June 1982*, was reprinted in the hearings, p. 172.

8. The history of the pay comparability program and its weaknesses is discussed in the GAO report, *Proposal to Lower the Federal Compensation Comparability Standard Has Not Been Substantiated*, Report by the Controller General (FPCD-82-4) (6 January 1982).

9. *Total Compensation Comparability: Background, Method and Preliminary Results*. Reprinted in *Treasury, Postal Service and General Government Appropriations for FY 1983: Hearings*, 1982, p. 17.

10. The compensation comparability issue and the 20 percent lag figure are discussed in the 1984 budget hearings. David Rosow, of the Advisory Commission on Federal Pay gave a good synopsis of the issues on pp. 509–11 of House Subcommittee on the Treasury, Postal Service and General Government Appropriations of the Committee on Appropriations, *Treasury, Postal Service and General Government Appropriations for FY 1984: Hearings*, 98th Cong., 1st sess., 26 April 1983, Part 4.

11. Office of Personnel Management, *OPM: The Year in Review, 1982* (Washington: Government Printing Office, November 1983), p. 14.

12. *Treasury, Postal Service and General Government Appropriations for 1984: Hearings*, 1983, p. 516.

13. Office of Personal Management, *A Study of Approaches to Federal Pay*, December 1982, reprinted in the *Civil Service Oversight: Hearings*, 1983, pp. 25–44.

14. A political official at OPM confirmed in an interview that the agency did not try to fight the additional 12 percent cut.

15. See the Federal Personnel Manual *FPM Bulletin*, no. 351-32, dated 4 December 1981. Subject: *Personnel Actions during Budget Reductions*.

16. Memo from Michael Senera, assistant director for planning and evaluation to Donald Devine, director, 5 January 1982. Subject: *Strategy for OPM Budget Reduction*.

17. Letter from Pat Schroeder to Donald Devine, 24 February 1982.

18. From the statement by Donald J. Devine, Director, OPM, in his FY 1982 budget request. House Subcommittee on the Treasury Postal Service and General Government Appropriations of the Committee on Appropriations, *Treasury, Postal Service, and General Government Appropriations for Fiscal Year 1982: Hearings*, 97th Cong., 1st sess., 1 April 1981, pp. 1–2. (Italics added for emphasis.)

19. *Government Employee Relations Report*, 23 November 1981, p. 939:7.

20. The raw data on the RIF came from the report prepared by OPM for the GAO. It is entitled, *To GAO, 4/29/82*. Notably, many of the demotions were among the GS-13s, -14s, and -15s. The GS-13s in particular were often deeply

demoted. Seven of them were demoted to GS-3s, and another five were demoted to GS-7s. The GS-14s and -15s tended to bump into the positions vacated by the GS-13's. The result was to systematically lower the rank and responsibility of many of the upper-level career officials.

21. General Accounting Office, *Retrenchment and Redirection at OPM* (GAO/GGD 83-95) (Washington: Government Printing Office, 22 August 1983), p. 11.

22. See *The Employee Advocate: A Newsletter of the Employees at OPM* 3, no. 12 (May 1982), p. 1.

23. General Accounting Office, *Retrenchment and Redirection*, p. 14.

24. *Ibid.*

25. *Ibid.*, p. 20.

26. *Ibid.*, p. 22.

27. *Civil Service Oversight Hearings*, 1983, p. 97.

28. General Accounting Office, *Retrenchment and Redirection*, p. 24.

29. *Ibid.*, p. 29.

30. *Ibid.*, p. 27.

31. *Ibid.*, p. 27.

32. Merit Systems Protection Board, *Significant Actions of the Office of Personnel Management 1981*, reprinted in *Civil Service Oversight Hearings*, 1983, pp. 86–451.

33. Merit Systems Protection Board, *Significant Actions*, p. 410.

34. General Accounting Office, *Retrenchment and Redirection*, p. 33.

35. Devine's argument that the RIFs were not significant and had been blown up by the press was probably not tactful. For those going through the RIF, the effects seemed devastating, and Devine seemed to be making light of their suffering. In fact, however, the newspaper article which seemed to be the basis of this story does not refer to the suffering of individuals, lightly or otherwise. It refers only to the number of people RIFfed, arguing that not many people were actually separated in that fashion. See Keith Richburg, "OPM Chief Says RIFs No Problem," *Washington Post*, 24 May 1982.

36. Nancy Lewis, "Judge Blocks OPM on Fed Jobs Rule," *Washington Post*, 24 November 1983.

8

What Have We Learned?

In Chapter 2, four key questions were posed: Can the president successfully order agencies to terminate their own programs? Does the president
have enough power to force Congress to cut the budget, or can he cut back
programs, budgets, and personnel without congressional consent? Do
organized interest groups determine which programs will be cut back and
which ones will not? Is it possible to simultaneously shrink the federal
government (or shrink particular agencies) and improve the quality of
management?

These four questions were discussed with reference to the federal
government in general, as background for the case studies. In this chapter,
the answers to the same questions will be presented with reference
primarily to the case studies. The chapter serves as both a summary of the
common themes in the case studies and a statement of the conclusions of
the study.

THE PRESIDENT'S CONTROL OVER THE AGENCIES

President Reagan's use of the Nixon strategy to take over the agencies was
very successful. For example, the president appointed people loyal to his
program as departmental secretaries and agency directors. These appointees
gathered around them others who agreed with their positions and concentrated policy making in that group. Through reorganizations and reductions in force, agencies were centralized, reducing the number of upper-

level career administrators and reducing contact between the policy-making group and career officials.

This pattern of political control and centralization of policy making was marked in the ETA, at UMTA, and at OPM. It was not noticeable at the Bureau of Health Planning because the bureau was only a small unit, and political control did not initially reach down that far in the Department of Health and Human Services. It was less marked at HUD because of the congressional constraint on reorganizations, but the proposed reorganization for the HUD field offices was consistent with the general pattern of centralization of political control.

Career officials found it very difficult, and in several cases impossible, to win over or co-opt the president's appointees. The political leadership of the agencies accepted the administration's proposed budgets and even drew up their own budget reductions. Dr. Devine of OPM, for example, was on the transition team and reportedly was given a free hand in what to cut. The Bureau of Health Planning was not given much autonomy over cutback decisions, but the leadership of the other agencies in the study drew up plans for reductions in force, reorganizations, and furloughs.

There were several exceptions, however, in which the secretaries argued successfully with the president over programs and funding levels. Secretary Pierce of HUD was convinced by career staff to fight for the Urban Development Action Grants, and Secretary Lewis successfully fought for a trust fund from gas tax revenues to fund capital projects for mass transit. Overall, however, there was very little effort on the part of presidential appointees to resist the president's proposals or fight for larger budgets.

Even the Bureau of Health Planning, where the director was extremely loyal to programs (not a Reagan appointee), did not resist the president's program with much energy. The agency director basically accepted the president's goal for the program and sought ways to keep the program alive without federal funding.

The political appointees of the Department of Health and Human Services adhered closely to the president's policies and kept close control over the bureau. The leadership of HHS issued a ruling to the bureau indicating that none of its current programs would be considered for future funding. The bureau responded by proposing some new programs. When funding for these was denied, the bureau appealed the decision inside HHS, but when the appeal was denied, the agency dropped the effort. The failure of the administration to successfully terminate the program was due to congressional reluctance to act on the issue; agency intransigence was not a factor.

The ETA, whose career officials were also loyal to programs, tried to protect programs from targeted cuts by using some traditional budget tactics. That is, they offered up programs to cut that they knew would be unacceptable to Congress. Congress did indeed reject the cuts, but the tactic was not successful. The Office of Management and Budget restored the positions which had been cut, but not the budget, essentially forcing the agency to take the budget cuts elsewhere. In short, the administration was on top of the situation and controlled the agency.

There was little, if any, footdragging by career officials in the implementation of policy. The new policies were sometimes protested within the channels of the administration, as the policy to terminate the Urban Development Action Grant was opposed at HUD. Career officials who did not like the new turn of events often left the organization, causing high rates of attrition, as at OPM. The union at HUD tried to stop a department-wide reduction in force, and employees in OPM tried to argue that means other than RIFs should have been used to save money. But there was no evidence that new policies, such as turning programs over to the states or deregulation, were purposely delayed or ignored. The agencies' employees did what they were supposed to do, including terminating their own programs.

The only evidence of any effort to sabotage the administration came from reports at HUD. Employees who resented new policy directions and reductions in force anonymously called or wrote to the inspector general to report on wrongdoing by the political leadership of the agency. These reports included charges such as unwarranted travel and use of public resources for private gain. They embarrassed the administration and in one case forced a resignation, but there was no widespread organized effort to make such complaints.

In short, the agencies were much more controllable when it came to cutback and new policy initiatives than one might have imagined. The president's strategy for taking control of the agencies was generally successful. His appointees were generally not co-opted by the career officials, and the appointees successfully took control over policy making in their agencies. Though there was some internal protest, especially against reductions in force, employees generally carried out the new policies as best they could.

THE PRESIDENT AND CONGRESS

Congressional opposition to the president's program was effective in some areas but not in others, and opposition was stronger in some committees than in others. In general, authorizing committees were more active in opposing the administration than appropriations committees, although the appropriations committees did sometimes rebel against the president too. The Barnes Task Force on Federal Government Service, although just a task force rather than a standing committee, was the most active of all, because its members represented the federal employees in Maryland and Virginia.

Congress was effective mainly in its traditional areas of control, over budget levels and reauthorizing legislation. It blocked or delayed the administration's proposal to terminate the health planning program, not reauthorizing it but keeping it alive with continuing resolutions and funding the program considerably above the level of the president's request. Congress defied the president's all-out determination to eliminate operating subsidies for mass transit. It became balky in granting his requests for rescissions and deferrals. For example, the House rejected the president's request for a deferral of mass transit trust fund revenues.

Part of the reason for the success of Congress in areas such as re-authorization of legislation was a skillful orchestration of interest groups. One often thinks of interest groups influencing members of Congress but seldom considers that congressional committees themselves line up interest groups and help to form coalitions among them that will be strong enough to overcome presidential opposition. This tactic was used extensively by the House Committee on Public Works and Transportation. For example, the reauthorization act for UMTA was combined with the reauthorization for the Federal Highway Administration in order to form a coalition between the highway and mass transit lobbies.

When the administration and the agencies steered clear of budget and reauthorizations, Congress had less control and was often defied. Thus UMTA reorganized and cut back personnel levels in such a way that congressional committees had little say. Congress delayed reduction in force at HUD, but courts eventually ruled that it did not have the right to exercise a legislative veto over administrative decisions. Congress was unable to take any action on OPM's change in insurance benefits for federal employees and only delayed the implementation of new regulations on reductions in force.

Congressional committees held hearings, made inquiries, and harassed agencies with GAO investigative teams looking for violations of the law. Congress had a hard time proving anything illegal had been done or demonstrating that the agencies were incapable of carrying out their missions. For example, Dr. Devine of OPM testified before Congress that OPM was carrying out all its mandated activities, many better and more cheaply than before. The GAO questioned how well the agency was implementing some of the civil service reforms but could find nothing illegal.

Generally, members of Congress had little leverage over the agencies, since the traditional threat—of cutting the agencies' funding—was meaningless in a situation in which the administration, including the agencies' leadership, was seeking to cut back the agencies' budgets. Denied real leverage, Congress had to resort to legislative vetoes of administrative actions (which were usually declared illegal) and other forms of oversight. Congress could have challenged some of the new regulations by passing new laws, but it did not do so during this study.

To summarize, effective congressional opposition when it occurred was in the area of funding levels and reauthorization; Congress had less authority (if any) over internal reorganizations and staffing levels, even when these changes implied extensive policy changes. Congress had a hard time proving anything illegal had occurred. Individual members of Congress fumed and wrote angry letters but were generally unable to take more effective action.

CUTBACK AND THE INTEREST GROUPS

Looking back at the cases, it is clear that agencies which had strong interest-group support had different experiences than those with weak interest-group support. Those in the former category were able to reverse termination decisions, get programs reauthorized, and reverse cuts in funding levels.

HUD's Community Development Block Grant and Urban Development Action Grant were threatened with termination, as was the little Bureau of Health Planning in the Department of Health and Human Services. The Community Planning and Development program, with the help of interest groups, managed to stabilize funding levels for CDBG and UDAG and remove the threat of termination. The Bureau of Health Planning, without major interest-group support, has not yet been terminated (as of June 1984), but its budget has been severely cut back, and the threat of termination has been continuous for more than three years.

For the Urban Mass Transportation program, with strong interest-group support, cuts in funding levels were reversed, and the administration proposal to eliminate operating subsidies was successfully opposed. The Office of Personnel Management, with virtually no interest-group support, experienced deep and continuing cuts. The Employment and Training Agency, which had alienated much of its clientele, suffered deep program cuts and terminations.

The cases thus confirm the traditional understanding that interest groups and clientele will fight for their programs when the programs are threatened and will often defend them successfully. One can also draw some less obvious inferences about the impact of interest groups on cutback.

For example, one can infer that while some programs are protected by interest groups, not all of them are. Some have weak support or none or have positive opposition, and these are more likely to be cut. It is not the case that federal agencies cannot be cut back, only that the actual cuts are likely to follow the levels of interest-group support. What is the implication of selecting agencies to cut back on these grounds?

Regulatory agencies which have done a moderately good job will have made many enemies and hence be more likely to be cut or terminated. For example, the American Medical Society intensely disliked the health planning program. If it had been less effective or more accommodating, the program would not have roused such bitter opposition. On the other hand, agencies which have been effectively taken over by their interest groups, such as UMTA, are less likely to be cut back than agencies which have kept interest groups at a proper distance. Agencies involved in housekeeping, and hence in improving management of the federal government, are the most vulnerable to cutbacks because they have almost no clientele or interest-group support.

The ironic effect of a cutback program may be to cut back moderately effective agencies (and in the process undermine effective management) and leave the badly run agencies alone. In addition, those agencies involved in helping the government to be better managed are themselves most likely to be cut back.

A second observation about interest groups is that the model of a threatened agency appealing to its interest groups or clientele to rescue it has been the exception, not the rule. The interest groups discussed in the case studies were alert and looking for situations in which their interests needed to be protected and hence did not usually need to be alerted by the agencies concerning upcoming threats. More important, the agency heads often wanted to cut back their budgets and so found no reason to bring in interest groups. Under these circumstances, interest groups might be organized by congressional committees, or they might act independently.

Only two of the five agencies actively tried to protect themselves by (subtly) using interest groups, the Bureau of Health Planning and Community Planning and Development. The Bureau of Health Planning's efforts failed, while CPD's efforts were more successful. In the final analysis, then, only one agency, CPD, followed the path of being threatened, helping to inform its interest groups to fight for it, and reversing the administration's decisions.

The third observation about how interest groups behaved in the case studies is that they formed some odd and effective coalitions. The highway lobby and the mass transit lobby joined together to fight for an increase in the gas tax, which they would both share. They also fought for mass transit reauthorization together because it was wrapped up with the highway and safety reauthorizations. Business groups fought side by side with representatives of neighborhood groups and representatives of the poor to keep Urban Development Action Grants and Community Development Block Grants alive.

These coalitions not only affirm that politics makes strange bedfellows but also suggest that the packaging of legislation affects the ability of the administration to cut back or terminate programs. Congress can put legislation in relatively tamper-proof packages, or it can break out individual pieces of legislation to stand on their own.

When the Bureau of Health Planning was in one unit with the popular Hill-Burton hospital construction program, it was relatively untouchable.

When new legislation broke the two apart, the bureau became much more vulnerable. As long as mass transit was packaged with highways, it was relatively safe. The grouping of UDAG (which served primarily business) with the CDBG (which served primarily people of low and moderate income) saved both programs.

The observation that Congress packages legislation to maximize political support is not new or startling. For example, the tendency to water down demonstration programs by increasing the number of sites involved, in order to maximize the number of supporters of the legislation, is well known. The case studies simply extend that logic to the cutback situation, illustrating that Congress may package reauthorization legislation in such a way that a range of powerful interest groups are attracted to support the legislation.

Since one of the president's most successful tools in cutting back the budget was to package cuts in the omnibus reconciliation in such a way that Congress could not break out particular programs to protect, and since Congress used packaging to prevent the president from cutting programs, the politics of packaging became an important part of the politics of cutback. Packaging became a key way of either keeping interest groups out of the process or forcing them to fight each other over limited resources, or it became a tool to create coalitions of interest groups to defend programs and funding levels.

To summarize, interest-group support was extremely important in determining which programs would be terminated and cut back. Ironically, the selection of agencies without strong interest-group support for cutback and termination probably had the effect of making management worse, because effective regulatory agencies and housekeeping agencies were more likely to be cut. Interest groups did not tend to be closely allied to the agencies; with one exception, they were not invoked by the leadership of agencies to rescue programs. The groups often acted independently, but their activities were sometimes manipulated or orchestrated by the office of the president and by Congress.

CUTBACK AND THE QUALITY OF MANAGEMENT

There were some improvements in management during this study, but the overall impact of cutback on federal agencies was a deterioration of management and productivity. Many of the negative effects were short-term results of changing directions and short-term impacts of reductions in force, but some of the negative consequences of cuts and the way they were implemented will last a long time.

If the management of cutback had been better, some of these consequences would have been reduced or eliminated, but it is likely that there would still have been a deterioration in the quality of management and the level of productivity. Some of the problems caused by cutback simply cannot be easily eliminated.

The Impacts of Cuts and Policy Redirections on Federal Agencies

Uncertainty

One of the impacts of cutbacks and policy redirections was a marked increase in uncertainty, which affected the quality of decision making. Budget battles, in which agency cutbacks or program termination were proposed, were long drawn-out affairs. Between rescissions, deferrals, continuing resolutions, appropriations, supplement appropriations, and re-authorizations, the agencies were sometimes involved in fighting for their funding levels three, four, or five times a year.

Each time there was a budget struggle, there were a number of different actors and several sets of interactions to watch. Thus in a single budget decision there was an OMB recommendation as well as sub-committee recommendations in each house, votes in each house, and then compromises between each house worked out in conference. Then the president could veto the bill. At each stage in the process the amount of money involved could change. The expected levels of funding and staffing went up and down on a weekly or even daily basis.

HUD tended to get its appropriation early in the year and hence avoid some of this uncertainty, but the Bureau of Health Planning was badly affected by these fluctuations. The ETA found it difficult to figure out how many people to fire in a reduction in force because it did not know how much money it would get in supplemental appropriations late in the year.

To add to the uncertainty, next year's budget process was often begun before this year's budget was complete. Especially when the administration zeroed out a program in the following year's budget proposal, the agency could be fighting several battles for survival simultaneously. This source of uncertainty affected HUD's Community Planning and Development Program.

There was no annual, year-long budget. In one case money that the agency thought it had saved for the purpose of reallocation was taken away. At the Bureau of Health Planning, at Community Planning and Development, and at the Urban Mass Transit Administration, Congress approved the programs' funding, while the administration, planning to terminate or cut back the programs, reduced the number of personnel. Planning was impossible in this environment.

The uncertainty also affected the quality of decision making. As funding went up and down and the rumors of impending reduction in force came and went, morale went up and down. When morale was low, not only was there no planning but there was no motivation to make hard decisions.

Only the most routine of activities were undertaken. This pattern was most visible in the Bureau of Health Planning and in the ETA.

In addition to the uncertainty introduced by the budget process, several of the agencies in the study had to face reauthorization. The legislation for health planning, for urban mass transit, and for employment and training all expired during the study. These agencies often did not know whether or when they would get new legislation or what its characteristics might be. It might be radically different from the old legislation. To the extent that the new laws required less supervision or administration from Washington, even successful reauthorization could mean continuing staff and budget reductions.

Disruption

The tools of cutback left a trail of chaos throughout the agencies *at least* six months long. At OPM, after two years, the chaos was still continuing, although it seemed to be slowing down. Salary, hiring, training and travel freezes, reductions in force, furloughs, reorganizations, and space contractions left employees in the wrong places at the wrong times with the wrong skills and often unable to carry out their supervisory tasks.

The president's programs to review proposed regulations before they were issued and to control information collection slowed down both processes, adding considerably to uncertainty about what could be done and when it could be done. The weakening or eliminating of regulations often made routine processes highly problematic. It was no longer clear what set of rules, if any, covered a situation or for how long. OMB's restrictions on information-gathering processes by the agencies often made it difficult, if not impossible, for agencies to monitor their programs and judge their progress toward legislatively mandated goals.

Lowered Morale and Productivity

The uncertainty, combined with the expectation and occurrence of RIFs, helped to produce a fearful atmosphere. Many employees believed the reductions in force were targeted, that managers chose to fire employees they did not like, and that opposition would not be brooked. Fear of reductions came to substitute for the expectation of rewards for good work well done.

Satisfaction derived from working toward social goals was undermined by funding and staffing cuts and by weakened regulations. Many bureaucrats felt that the president blamed them personally for whatever was wrong with government. The loss of positive incentives and the increase of fear and insults intimidated many officials. Many reported wanting to leave the bureaucracy; others just withdrew their efforts. Lack of motivation was widespread.

Productivity was affected by the amount of time absorbed in preparation, execution, and defense of the reductions in force and in recovering from its worst effects. Reorganizations also cut into productive time, as employees were shifted around. Transfers to new jobs and demotions undoubtedly affected productivity. In the case of transfers, there was a new job to learn; in the case of demotions, an employee was paid at a higher rate for doing lesser work. Most of these effects were temporary, except that they kept occurring in sequence; no sooner had one passed than the next came along.

Some of the impacts on management were long-term, however. Among these were the reopening of social cleavages inside the agencies, the greater possibilities for abuse of grants, the reduction in the attractiveness of federal employment, the aging of the federal work force, and the opening up of the civil service to the possibility of political influence.

Polarization

As the reorganizations and reductions in force took place, the agencies tended to become more polarized. The career officials became cut off from the political levels, and the union management relationship became more hostile. The RIF regulations, with their bias against women and minorities, tended to refresh old conflicts between males and females, whites and blacks. Informal communications between groups became more difficult.

Increased Waste, Fraud, and Abuse

An increased possibility of abuse in grants stemmed from the continued reduction in headquarters personnel and from the decentralization of programs to the states with a minimum of oversight. Reductions in travel funds and information collection budgets further reduced the ability of Washington offices to know how money was being spent.

Both ETA and UMTA were understaffed at the time their staffing levels were cut back. At the bureau of health planning, staff contemplated the possibility of having only six staff members to oversee millions of dollars in grants. They envisioned writing checks and trusting grant recipients to do what they were supposed to do. If there were abuses, they would not be caught.

Reduced Quality of Work Life

The reduction in the appeal of federal employment is likely to be a long-term effect of the cutback period. Federal employment is less attractive because salaries have been reduced, pay ceilings have been maintained for top-level executives, bonuses have been underfunded, benefits have been reduced, and job security has been lessened by the fear of reductions in force. Attacks on federal bureaucrats and federal programs have also reduced the appeal of federal jobs. Over the long run, the bureaucracy will probably attract less able people, especially as federal compensation falls further and further behind that of comparable private-sector jobs.

Aging of the Work Force

Continuing hiring freezes have combined with reductions in force to age the work force. That means that because of retention status granted on the basis of seniority, younger people are much more likely to be laid off during reductions, and hiring freezes make it difficult if not impossible to replace them. This problem was most marked at the ETA, where personnel reductions had been going on for years, and continued hiring freezes had prevented the agency from hiring any new employees.

Not only is the work force going to age, or at least to miss an age cohort if it resumes hiring later on, but it is going to become more homogeneous. Because the RIF rules protect veterans and those with more seniority, they are biased against women and minorities. The work force may thus became increasingly composed of older white males.

The result will undoubtedly be a reduction in the number of ideas being presented, in the challenges to the status quo, and in creative energy. The increasing homogeneity of the work force may also reduce its representativeness. The importance of this factor is not clear, however, since the policy-making role of bureaucrats has largely been removed from them to political appointees.

Increased Vulnerability to Political Influence

The OPM case made it clear that the administration has increased the *possibility* of increased political influence over the bureaucracy. The reduction of OPM's oversight of the agencies combined with increased managerial discretion in the agencies over who may be fired leaves much more discretion in the hands of agency managers. This could be used to hire political appointees into civil service positions and fire those not in agreement with the administration.

The Impact of Cuts and Policy Redirections on Employees

To summarize the impact of cutback on employees, three quotations from the field notes are useful. In the first quote, a manager describes his employees as "knowing it's not going to end." In the second quote, a bureaucrat fired during a reduction in force observed (quoting the comic strip character, Pogo), "We have seen the enemy and he is us." In the third quote, an informant described the atmosphere in Washington as "Kafkaesque."

"Knowing it's not going to end" refers to the president's plans for the agency, which were passed by the Congress. Those plans included a slow devolution of functions to the states. Deregulation, too, will reduce workloads, making it possible to shrink the number of employees. Thus, regardless of the level of particular budgets, employees continued to anticipate future reductions in force. There was no possibility of recovery, only some more time in which to look for other work. Morale for many employees remained poor and motivational energy low. There seemed to be no way to reverse the situation and hence no motivation to innovate or to improve management.

The second quotation, "We have met the enemy and he is us," refers to the role of the career bureaucrat in implementing the president's cutback scheme. Personnel offices were absorbed in firing people and defending their procedures. Managers were involved in deciding how to dismantle programs. The overriding belief that the bureaucrat's job is to carry out the president's policy clashed with pride in program accomplishments. Few managers protested the reductions in force. Only the unions and some employees who had been fired openly criticized what was happening. The "enemy is us" thus refers to career bureaucrats terminating the employment of fellow bureaucrats.

But the phrase probably also refers to the fact that many agencies cut themselves without congressional mandates. Many of the reductions in force were determined by personnel ceilings that were allocated by the secretary; an internal reallocation of personnel ceilings would have avoided a RIF, but such a reallocation did not occur. Sometimes when personnel ceilings were not given as the reason for the reduction in force, reorganization was used as the reason. Reorganizations are run at the discretion of the agency and the secretary. "The enemy is us" in the sense that the agencies shot themselves in the foot.

The third quotation, "Washington is Kafkaesque," summarizes the personal reaction to much of what happened. The reductions in force, the reorganizations, and the space reductions created situations in which colleagues and office mates were there one day and gone the next. Telephone numbers changed constantly, but directories could not keep up. With fewer secretaries, many phones went unanswered. It was often unclear who was still employed or what work they were doing. People who were demoted were referred to as the "walking wounded," a visual reminder of status reduction without apparent cause.

There was a sense of being punished, of being targeted for punishment, but of not knowing what one had done wrong or might do wrong. Reductions in force were often taken very personally. The number of mistakes in running the reductions meant that some people thought they would be affected and were not, while others who had been assured they would not be affected were bumped by disabled veterans. There is a kind of absurdity in this process, in the Kafkaesque sense.

The absurdity was probably magnified by the separation of staffing levels from budget levels as those two allocation processes came to run on separate tracks. A sense of the absurd was probably also introduced by the slow-motion quality caused by travel freezes, freezes on regulations, reductions in information collection budgets, and mandated slowdowns in the rate of disbursements.

To summarize, whether one looks at the personal level or at the institutional level, the short term or the long term, the overall effect of cutback and policy changes was to make management worse and to open the civil service to possible political abuses.

Ways in Which the Management of Cutback and Policy Redirection Could Have Been Improved

The cutbacks could certainly have been managed better. The reductions in force could have been implemented in a way that would have reduced damage to agencies and morale. The president could have merged budget reduction and personnel reduction targets, he and Congress could have taken action more quickly and more definitively, and the administration could have paid more attention to productivity improvement.

Improving the Operation of Reductions in Force

The reductions in force could have been run more efficiently. Work histories of employees should have been kept up to date. A computerized personnel system which records promotions and position descriptions and calculates length of employment on a continuing basis should have been available to each agency. The agencies should have had good-quality position descriptions up to date before the reduction in force, since these would have helped prevent employees from being bumped into positions they could not perform.

A less mechanical change would have been improving the quality of the personnel office. That office is important in minimizing errors and in educating managers and employees to their rights and obligations under RIF regulations. The personality of the personnel director, and his or her ability to communicate sympathy as well as provide aid to affected employees, makes a big difference in whether or not employees protest their fate, appealing to the Merit Systems Protection Board and taking their complaints to Capitol Hill and the press. Agencies should have given more attention to both the quality of the personnel office and the personality of the personnel chief.

The impression of targeting individuals for dismissal, which alienates the work force and creates an atmosphere of punishment for unknown crimes, should have been avoided by not shortening the bumping chains. It would have been all right if more people had been involved in a reduction in force, provided that each person so involved was not badly hurt. When there is no bumping, or almost no bumping, the impression of manipulation is conveyed. A narrow construction of what kind of work people can do also tends to foster a belief that there was targeting.

From the perspective of maintaining the morale and motivation of the work force, one of the most important factors was the apparent necessity of the reduction in force. If the RIF was for the purpose of saving money because Congress had cut the agencies' salaries and expenses budget and no other savings could possibly be made, then the personnel cuts were considered inevitable. Other reasons for reductions in force did not work so well.

In the future, care should be taken that reorganization is not used as a reason for reduction in force; it gives the impression that the management of the agency has chosen to carry out a RIF for its own political or personal purposes. Similarly, using personnel ceilings as the reason for a reduction in force gives the impression that the agency, or the agency in concert with OMB, cut the agency staffing independent of congressional action on funding.

Attention should also be given to the timing of reductions in force. The timing sends an important signal about its real purposes—unless it occurs in the first quarter of the fiscal year (or in response to a late appropriation), it is probably not for the purpose of saving money.

Given the RIF regulations, it seems better to reduce by attrition if at all possible. Reductions in staffing levels by attrition save more money in the current fiscal year because they do not require severance pay or unemployment compensation. A smaller reduction by attrition is equivalent financially during the fiscal year to a somewhat larger reduction in force. Reduction by attrition also avoids demotions and bumping, which reduce productivity.

Outplacement programs in particular should be encouraged; they are not only humanitarian but also cost effective if successful in placing people. They are more cost effective than encouraging early retirement, which draws down the retirement funds and throws off actuarial estimates of costs. In the future, employees are more likely to believe that a reduction in force is coming and take advantage of outplacement before they are fired.

Merging Budget and Personnel Allocations

There were other things besides the running of reductions in force which could have been managed in such a way as to reduce the amount of damage to agency operations and morale. For example, the setting of targets for personnel reduction independent of budget levels was good politics but poor administration.

The president could have achieved personnel reductions entirely through reductions in the salaries and expenses lines of agency budgets, but such reductions would have had to have passed Congress. From the president's perspective that would have been a disadvantage. However, personnel levels and actual budget and program levels ought to be co-ordinated. There is no administrative logic to picking a number of staff out of the air and saying that is the number of positions that will be reduced. Staffing ought to fall out of decisions on budget and program levels. The separation of the allocation of budget from the allocation of personnel raised the possibility of severe disjunctions between staffing levels and workloads.

Another advantage of allowing budgets to determine staffing levels is that it would have been better for morale. Bureaucrats would have felt less personally attacked by the administration if the president had not singled them out for cuts.

Taking Quick and Definitive Action

Managerial damage could also have been reduced if the administration had been quicker to recognize when the opposition to its plans was over-whelming. The president and OMB often held tenaciously to cutback and termination plans after it became obvious that interest groups were organized and unwilling to let the administration have its way. The result was long drawn-out battles.

The administration proposed no funding of some programs year after year, and each year Congress restored funding or the administration was forced to withdraw its proposal. The outcome was to maximize the uncertainty in the agency and convey the message to employees that the president disapproved of the program and nothing they could do would affect his determination to end it. This blanket disapproval was a negative incentive to performance, and it hung over the agency for a long time.

The anticipation of termination, especially if the termination is delayed or opposed by Congress, undermines the leadership inside an agency because there is no incentive to make difficult decisions. The agency has to try to stay alive (in case Congress finally rescues it) and also to terminate itself (because the president has requested it). If the agency lingers on, expecting termination, it may become moribund, absorbing public funds but producing little.

Improving Productivity

Finally, the damage to agencies could have been minimized if more attention had been paid to improving the productivity of agencies that had been cut back. A clearer demarcation of when the cutbacks were over would have been helpful in allowing agencies to recover, but for many not only did the threat of further cutbacks hang over their heads but continuing reorganizations prevented stabilization. OPM experienced three reorganizations in less than two years, and UMTA experienced two in several months. A single well-thought-out reorganization would have done much less damage.

Cutting back the budget is not sufficient to improve productivity. A productivity program also needs to address and reduce the alienation of the work force. Full funding of the merit-pay plan, especially for members of the Senior Executive Service, would have helped achieve this goal.

To summarize, the experience of the agencies in the case studies suggests a number of ways that the administration could have reduced the damage done by the cutbacks, but it does not indicate that anything like "turnaround management" is likely or even possible in the federal government.

Likelihood of Turnaround Management in the Federal Government

The Reagan administration has adopted much of the conservative ideology about running the government like a private firm. Part of that ideology indicates that when a private firm is "fat," it makes poor decisions, wastes resources, and becomes unprofitable. If the process is allowed to continue, competition will bring the organization to bankruptcy. This process can be stopped and reversed by a good manager who comes in to solve problems, cut costs, eliminate unprofitable product lines, and restore competitiveness. This process is called "turnaround management."

The idea has been transferred to the public sector. Some of the agency officials in the study argued that they were engaged not in cutback but in turnaround management. The logic that was used is that government is fat and needs to be cut; if it is cut, it will run better and turn out a better product for less money. The Civil Service Reform Act, with its emphasis on giving managers more discretion to eliminate deadwood, is consistent with this philosophy.

However, it is unlikely that turnaround management can be applied to federal agencies. Many of the improvements mentioned in the previous section are unlikely to be implemented, and there are some other reasons why turnaround management is unlikely to occur.

The first set of reasons has to do with lack of incentives. There is a lack of connection between agency funding levels and the quality of management. Poor management is not punished and good management is not rewarded. In addition, there are few incentives for bureaucrats to improve their productivity.

The administration did not pick agencies to cut based on their inefficiency or poor management. It picked programs partly for ideological reasons and partly for budgetary reasons. Its success in cutting back programs was based on the level of interest-group support. There was no sense that better-managed agencies would be rewarded by increased funding. If a budget is cut no matter how well managed the agency is, there is little motivation to try to do better.

Agencies that experienced a turnaround in funding levels did so because interest groups and Congress restored funding. The interest groups are almost exclusively interested in getting money out to their clients or constituents and pay little attention to managerial problems. Members of Congress pay more attention to management, but those who are in favor of the program do not want to punish the agency with budget cuts if improvements are not made, and those who oppose the agency want to cut its budget regardless of managerial improvements. If the agency's budget has been recovered without managerial improvement, there is no particular incentive to improve management.

Moreover, Congress lost its incentives to try to persuade agencies to improve management. Congress can threaten to withhold funds to agencies that are badly managed or add funds to those that improve. But if the agencies' leadership wants to cut back the budget, these threats and promises have no force.

Though Congress had no leverage in the cutback situation to impose punishment for poor management or rewards for increased productivity, in theory the administration could have put some such incentives in place. However, the administration was too focused on saving money to concentrate on how to improve productivity.

The administration's focus on productivity was only in those areas that were consonant with dollar savings. For example, a 2 percent reduction in the budget of an agency without a commensurate drop in workload was called a productivity cut. Since no attention was paid to levels of output, it is not clear that a budget reduction will have any positive effect on productivity. In fact, it might have negative impacts.

Individual motivation was to be supplied by the merit-pay plan, but the plan was so seriously underfunded that it could not possibly have served as an incentive to the work force. Moreover, the administration was intent on wiping out automatic step increases and continually reduced salaries below the levels required for comparability with the private sector. The effort to save money by reducing compensation worked against an incentive plan.

A third approach to productivity improvement was to eliminate from the work force those who did not work hard and did not carry their share of the load. Those remaining would then by definition be more productive, since the same amount of work would be done by fewer people. In addition, presumably people would work harder because they would fear being fired.

The logic seems fair, but it ignores the impact of reductions in force on the work force, especially when separations seemed to be focused on individuals. For the administration's system to work, bureaucrats would have to trust that the system would be used only to eliminate nonproducers, and that basis of trust was certainly not there after three years of the Reagan administration. In some of the case study agencies it seemed that managers could not resist firing a few people they did not get along with. Problems of rater subjectivity in performance evaluation had not yet been worked out, and employees generally did not trust the evaluation system to measure their performance adequately.

If the reductions in force are used extensively, they are not likely to improve productivity, even if they are targeted on nonproducers. Even the new RIF regulations are likely to increase chaos and lower morale. Fear of job loss is likely to make employees more reluctant to call attention to themselves and less likely to express an opposing opinion; it is unlikely to produce better-quality work.

The second set of reasons that turnaround management is unlikely to occur in federal agencies has to do with the president's relationship with Congress. It was clear during the study that Congress had control over budget and reauthorizations and increasingly used that power to block the president's cutback program. Such opposition between the president and Congress would seem to be inevitable unless the president's party overwhelmingly controlled both houses. The result of this built-in antagonism, however, was to contribute long-term causes of poor management during cutback.

The opposition between the congress and the president over what should be cut and by how much prevented quick and definitive action on many proposals. Threats of termination hung over some agencies year after year. The president proposed and Congress avoided or reversed the proposals. This long-term threat was devastating to morale and contributed to poor decision making and low productivity.

Congressional battles with the president over funding levels resulted in the fragmentation of the fiscal year into repeated continuing resolutions, followed later in the year by appropriations. The battle also involved rescissions, deferrals, and supplemental appropriations, which together kept the level of funding in the air most of the fiscal year. This uncertainty made it difficult to estimate how many employees the agency could afford and also made program management more difficult, since the agencies often did not know how much money they had.

The third impact of congressional opposition to the president over budgets and reauthorizations was to encourage him to carry out his goals by other means, which did not require congressional approval or required only tacit congressional consent or inaction. Thus the president relied on reduced personnel ceilings, reductions in force, reorganizations, furloughs, deregulation, and new and revised regulations. He also used rescissions and deferrals.

The president's more independent actions had a number of effects that prevented turnaround management. In some situations, the administrative tools were used to dismantle agencies and render them ineffective without congressional approval. In others, the president's independent actions put agencies in a bind between the president, who wanted to terminate them, and Congress, which wanted to keep them going. The reliance on these administrative tools gave the impression that the agencies were dismantling themselves voluntarily, which had a negative impact on the cooperation of employees. And the continuing reliance on these tools prevented agencies from recovering from the effects of staff and/or budget reductions.

To summarize, there were five factors preventing turnaround management:

First, the administration could not select inefficient or badly managed programs to cut back, even if that had been its goal, because the final determination of what would be cut was determined by Congress and interest groups.

Second, congressional opposition slowed down administrative action, and caught some agencies between the president and Congress. The slowness of the action had a negative effect on management and decision making. It is difficult to see how this could have been avoided.

Third, in an attempt to get around congressional delays and rejections, the administration resorted to administrative tools that were often highly damaging to agency management and morale, especially when they occurred without congressional action on budgets and programs.

Fourth, the effort to cut back budgets led to underfunding of reward systems, the substitution of a negative rather than a positive incentive system, and very little emphasis on productivity improvement. As long as the primary emphasis is on dollar savings, as is typical during a period of cutback, this outcome is likely.

Fifth, congressional incentives to agencies to improve their management are based on the threat of withholding funds if the agencies do not comply and providing funds if the agencies demonstrate improvements. This incentive system dissolves during a period of cutback. The president has to choose secretaries and directors who agree that cutback is desirable; that is a crucial part of the cutback implementation. When that occurs, the agencies do not try to get additional funds. Reduction in funds is no threat, and increase in funds is no incentive.

This analysis suggests that if budgetary cutbacks and policy reorientation are the primary goals, improved management and healthier, better-run agencies are not likely to be the outcomes. There is now ample evidence that federal agencies can be cut back, and it seems likely that their management can be improved. However, it does not seem likely that both goals can be achieved simultaneously.

SUMMARY AND CONCLUSIONS

Although the major themes of the case studies have been summarized in this chapter, it may prove useful to the reader to have a summary of the book showing the relationship between the political process of cutback and the impacts of cutback on the agencies.

1. The president can control the bureaucracy through his appointments to top agency positions. His appointees can take effective control of their agencies through reorganizations and reductions in force, without being co-opted by career officials.

2. Federal bureaucrats are not the self-directed and uncontrollable folk they have sometimes been presented as in the literature. They follow the president's directions, even to the point of cutting their own agencies and refusing to provide documents to Congress. If they strongly oppose the president's directives, they resign, appeal, or withdraw their energies, but they do not generally obstruct policy objectives.

3. There is such a thing as a self-destroying agency, one which will not fight for its existence or its funding levels. It will not describe to Congress the harm done by the cutbacks, and it will not try to rouse interest groups to fight on its behalf. If necessary, the leaders of such an agency will terminate it.

4. The president was able to achieve a temporary suspension of interest-group politics because of his enormous popularity at the polls. As this popularity returned to more normal levels, interest-group politics (and congressional opposition) resumed.

5. Interest-group politics, when it did reappear, did not take the shape of "iron triangles." That is, there is little evidence of a coalition among agencies, interest groups, and congressional committees. In some cases, interest groups and agencies combined to fight the OMB proposals without any congressional involvement; in other cases, interest groups tried to influence Congress without agency approval or backing. In still other situations, congressional committees forged coalitions of interest groups to support legislation and funding levels.

6. Interest-group and congressional opposition and congressional slowness made it difficult for the administration to orchestrate budget cuts at will. As a result, the administration relied heavily on internal reorganizations and personnel cuts, over which it had more control, and it emphasized deregulation. The result of its use of these tools was to make management worse and to reduce productivity.

7. The short-term impacts of budget cuts, reductions in force, fur-

loughs, and reorganizations on agencies included poor morale, reduced productivity, unwillingness to make hard decisions, and a tendency to make the same decisions over and over as the environment changed. Also there was considerable disruption as people were shifted all over the organization.

8. The long-term effects of budget cuts and policy redirections on the bureaucracy include increasing polarization between management and labor, political appointees and career officials, veterans and nonveterans, and blacks and whites. Other long-term effects include the aging of the work force and its increased homogeneity and decreased representativeness.

9. Federal employment is becoming less desirable and is likely to attract fewer able managers and technicians; it also seems probable that the continuing salary declines in comparison with the private sector will ensure that the best and brightest go elsewhere for employment. Those who remain are more likely to keep a low profile and not recommend contrary ideas or criticize administration proposals. In addition, the civil service has become more vulnerable to political influence; hence, in the future it may be both less neutral and less competent.

10. Although it does appear possible to cut back the federal government (or at least some agencies), it does not seem possible to do so without reducing productivity and making management worse.

Glossary

A 95 Review Process A regional planning function to coordinate the impacts of federal grants on neighboring local governments.

Administrative Presidency President Nixon's plan to control the federal government by appointing people loyal to his ideas as secretaries and undersecretaries; this concept was later elaborated by President Reagan.

Appropriation Legislative permission to spend a particular amount on a program in a specified period of time.

Authorization Legislative design of a program including a ceiling amount for funding.

Block Grant The consolidation of specific federal grants/programs into a larger grant, providing some autonomy to states and localities to allocate the grant according to their priorities.

Bumping Forcing someone out of his/her position so that someone with a higher retention status may occupy the position. (*See Retention Status.*)

Categorical Grant Grant for a single specific purpose.

Competitive Level A group of positions requiring similar skills set up by evaluating position descriptions.

Continuing Resolution The legislation enacted by Congress to provide budget authority for specific ongoing activities if the regular appropriation has not been enacted at the beginning of the fiscal year.

Davis-Bacon Requirement A regulation mandating that projects paid for with federal funds pay prevailing wages. This has often meant union wages and has raised the cost of public projects.

Decentralization   The assignment of duties, responsibilities, power, authority, and so on from a central unit to peripheral units, such as from headquarters in Washington to an agency in Illinois, or from the federal government to local governments.

Deferral   (*See Impoundment.*)

Deregulation   The process of eliminating/altering rules and regulations that caused inflexibility for the private sector in order to increase productivity. This process includes the termination of regulatory agencies and reduction in enforcement of existing laws.

Detail   A formal loan of personnel from one office to another.

Federal Register   The government publication in which new rules are announced.

Fiscal Substitution   Substituting grant money for regular revenue.

Fiscal Year   The year for accounting purposes, often different from a calendar year. In the federal government, the fiscal year begins on 1 October.

Furlough   Unpaid, mandatory vacation.

Grace Survey   A survey on cost control, to make government function better and more efficiently (named after Peter Grace, who headed the commission making the survey).

Gramm-Latta Amendment   A proposal introduced in the House of Representatives during the 1981 omnibus reconciliation. It substituted the president's proposal for the congressional committees' proposal.

Hiring Freeze   Control over and limits on hiring new personnel.

Impoundment   The decision of the president not to spend all the money that Congress has approved for the fiscal year. Since 1974, the president has had to ask congressional approval for impoundments. These requests may take two forms: 1) *rescission*—the permanent legislative withdrawal of the appropriation; 2) *deferral*—the temporary delays in committing funds or in actual outlays.

Management by Objectives (MBO)   The managerial technique which requires employees to negotiate with their boss regarding their workloads and targets. These targets become a standard or yardstick for evaluating performances.

Omnibus Reconciliation   A process of agreement between congressional committees to limit themselves to certain specified spending levels, which will determine the spending levels in the appropriations bills.

Outplacement   Finding new jobs for people affected by reduction in force.

Performance Evaluation   A systematic assessment of employees' performance in terms of quantity and quality of work.

Pork Barrel Programs   Programs that congresspersons use to allocate projects, dollars, and jobs to their districts or states. These programs are difficult to cut.

Position Ceiling   The number of personnel allocated by the Office of Management and Budget to each agency. These ceilings are supposed to act as upper limits on the number of personnel in each agency.

Position Description A written document indicating job duties, responsibilities, and workload of a certain position.

Reduction in Force (RIF) The procedures for laying off federal employees, embodied in regulations issued by the Office of Personnel Management.

Reform 88 A presidential initiative to improve government management over a several-year period. The content of the plan remained vague.

Regulation 1) rules derived by agencies to implement legislation; 2) government's role in telling state and local governments and private organizations how to carry out their business.

Reorganization An attempt to improve efficiency and effectiveness of a certain organization by restructuring it. Reorganization is also employed for purposes other than improving organizational effectiveness, such as for political reasons (i.e., to kill that organization or reshape its priorities).

Rescission (*See Impoundment.*)

Retention Status The order in which people will be let go from an organization during a reduction in force.

Retreat Right The right to return to one's former position, if his/her present position has been eliminated.

Supply-side Economics The policy of reducing taxes of businesses and restricting the growth of government. This policy is intended to provide capital to businesses to aid expansion and create new jobs.

S.E.S. Position A position in the Senior Executive Service, a corps of the most senior-level managers, including GS-16 and up. This corps is composed of both appointees and career officials who receive special training, separate incentive bonuses, and career development programs.

Skills Imbalance A situation in which an agency has too many employees with a particular set of skills. For example, an organization could have too many psychologists or too many neighborhood specialists. A skills imbalance is a possible justification for a reduction in force.

Sole-source Contract A contract granted without competitive bidding; one person or company supplies goods and services to a certain public agency because that person or company is the only qualified source.

Turnaround Management The process of bringing in a good manager to solve organizational problems, cut costs, eliminate unprofitable product lines, restore competitiveness, and so on.

Selected Bibliography

Abrams, Floyd. "The New Effort to Control Information." *The New York Times Magazine*, 25 September 1983.

Barker, Karlyn. "Judge Halts Demotion, Firing of HUD Workers." *The Washington Post*, 11 November 1982.

Behn, Robert. "Twelve Hints for the Would-be Policy Terminator." *Policy Analysis*, 1977, pp. 393–413.

Berman, Larry. *The Office of Management and Budget and the Presidency, 1921–1979*. Princeton: Princeton University Press, 1972.

Bozeman, Barry, and Straussman, Jeffrey. "Shrinking Budgets and the Shrinkage of Budget Theory." *Public Administration Review* 42, November/December 1982, pp. 509–15.

Broder, David S. "White House Opens Drive to Sell Governors and Mayors on Fund Cuts." *Washington Post*, 22 February 1981.

Clark, Terry, and Ferguson, Lorna. "Political Leadership and Urban Fiscal Policy." In *Urban Policy Analysis*, edited by Terry Clark. Urban Affairs Annual Reviews, Vol. 21, 1981, p. 91.

Cronin, Thomas. "Presidential Departmental Relations." In *Current Issues in Public Administration*, edited by Frederick S. Lane. New York: St. Martin's Press, 1982.

Delong, James V. "Repealing Regulation." *Regulation*, May/June 1983, pp. 26–30.

Demkovitch, Linda. "If the Health Planning Lid is Removed, Will a Hospital Boom Erupt?" *National Journal*, June 1981, p. 1110.

Derthick, Martha. *Uncontrollable Spending for Social Services*. Washington: Brookings Institution, 1975.

Eads, George and Michael Fix. *Relief or Reform: Reagan's Regulatory Dilemma*. Washington: The Urban Institute, 1984.

Ellwood, John W., ed. *Reductions in U.S. Domestic Spending: How They Affect*

State and Local Governments. New Brunswick, N.J., Transaction Books, 1982.

Fisher, Louis. *President and Congress.* New York: Free Press, 1982.

Fiske, Edward B. "Top Objectives Elude Reagan as Education Policy Evolves." *New York Times*, 27 December 1983.

Gottron, Martha, ed. *Budgeting for America.* Washington: Congressional Quarterly, 1982.

Heclo, Hugh. "OMB and the Presidency: The Problem of Neutral Competence" *Public Interest* 38, Winter 1975, pp. 80–88.

Hunter, Robert. "Labor." in *Mandate for Leadership*, edited by Charles L. Heatherly. Washington: Heritage Foundation, 1981.

Kaufman, Herbert. *The Administrative Behavior of Federal Bureau Chiefs.* Washington: Brookings Institution, 1981.

Kaufman, Herbert. *Are Government Organizations Immortal?* Washington: Brookings Institution, 1976.

King, Anthony, ed. *Both Ends of the Avenue: The Presidency, the Executive Branch and the Congress in the 1980s.* Washington: American Enterprise Institute, 1983.

Lane, Frederick, ed. *Current Issues in Public Administration.* 2d ed. New York: St. Martin's Press, 1982.

Levine, Charles, ed. *Managing Fiscal Stress.* Chatham, N.J.: Chatham House, 1980.

Levine, Charles, and Rubin, Irene S. *Fiscal Stress and Public Policy.* Beverly Hills: Sage Publications, 1980.

Lewis, Nancy. "Judge Blocks on Fed. Jobs Rules." *Washington Post*, November 1983.

Lovell, Catherine. "Federal Deregulation and State and Local Governments." In *Reduction in U.S. Domestic Spending: How They Affect State and Local Governments*, edited by John W. Ellwood. New Brunswick, N.J.: Transaction Books, 1982.

Marlow, Ruth. "Auditors Probe RIF Plan at HUD." *Federal Times* 18, November 1982, pp. 1.

McCallister, Eugene, ed. *Agenda for Progress.* Washington: Heritage Foundation, 1981.

Meier, Kenneth. "Executive Reorganization of Government: Impact on Employment and Expenditures." *American Journal of Political Science* 24, August 1980, pp. 396–412.

Nathan, Richard. *The Administrative Presidency.* New York: Wiley, 1983.

Nathan, Nathan and Fred Doolittle and Associates. *The Consequence of Cuts.* Princeton: Princeton Urban and Research Center, 1983.

Newland, Chester. "A Midterm Appraisal—The Reagan Presidency: Limited Government and Political Administration." *Public Administration Review*, January/February 1983, pp. 14.

Palmer, John and Sawhill Isabel, eds. *The Reagan Experiment.* Washington: Urban Institute, 1982.

Poole, Robert, Jr. "Community and Regional Development." In *Agenda for Progress*, edited by Eugene McAllister. Washington: Heritage Foundation, 1981.

Rourke, Francis. *Bureaucracy, Politics and Public Policy.* 3rd ed. Boston: Little, Brown, 1984.

Ritchter, Albert, and Colella, Cynthia. "The First 10 Months: Grant in Aid, Regulatory and Other Changes." *Intergovernmental Perspective*, Winter 1982, pp. 5–22.

Rosenbaum, Allan. "Federal Management: Pathological Problems and Simple Cures," *PS*, Spring 1982, pp. 189–91.

Rubin, Irene S. "Universities in Stress: Decisionmaking Under Conditions of Reduced Resources." *Social Science Quarterly*, September 1977, pp. 242–54.
Schick, Allen. *Congress and Money*. Washington: Urban Institute, 1980.
Schneider, W., and Schill, G. "The New Democrats." *Public Opinion*, November/December 1978, pp. 7–13.
Sears, David and Citrin Jack. *Tax Revolt: Something for Nothing in California*. Cambridge: Harvard University Press, 1982.
Seidman, Harold. *Politics, Position and Power: The Dynamics of Federal Organization* 3rd ed. New York: Oxford University Press, 1980.
Smerk, George. "Federal Mass Transit Policy—1981–1982: A Fall From Grace?" *Transportation Journal* 23 (Fall 1983): 57.
Sundquist, James. *The Decline and Resurgence of Congress*. Washington: Brookings Institution, 1981.
Wehr, Elizabeth. "Health Planning Lack Friends, but Its Enemies May Save It From Extinction." *Congressional Quarterly Weekly*, June 1982, p. 1335.
Wildavsky, Aaron, ed. *The Politics of Budgetary Process*. 4th ed. Boston: Little, Brown, 1984.
Young, John D. "Reflections on the Root Causes of Fraud Abuse and Waste in Federal Social Programs." *Public Administration Review* 43, Fall 1983, p. 57.

Index